NOTHING
WILL
BE
DIFFERENT

NOTHING
WILL
BE
DIFFERENT

a memoir

tara
mcgowan-ross

RARE
MACHINES

Publisher: Scott Fraser | Acquiring editor: Julie Mannell
Cover design and illustration: Laura Boyle
Printer: Marquis Book Printing Inc.

Library and Archives Canada Cataloguing in Publication

Title: Nothing will be different : a memoir / Tara McGowan-Ross.
Names: McGowan-Ross, Tara, 1992- author.
Description: Canadiana (print) 2021025811X | Canadiana (ebook) 20210259744 | ISBN 9781459748736 (softcover) | ISBN 9781459748743 (PDF) | ISBN 9781459748750 (EPUB)
Subjects: LCSH: McGowan-Ross, Tara, 1992- | LCSH: Indigenous women—Canada—Biography. | LCSH: Indigenous authors—Canada—Biography. | LCGFT: Autobiographies.
Classification: LCC PS8625.G695 Z46 2021 | DDC C811/.6—dc23

We acknowledge the support of the Canada Council for the Arts and the Ontario Arts Council for our publishing program. We also acknowledge the financial support of the Government of Ontario, through the Ontario Book Publishing Tax Credit and Ontario Creates, and the Government of Canada.

Care has been taken to trace the ownership of copyright material used in this book. The author and the publisher welcome any information enabling them to rectify any references or credits in subsequent editions.

The publisher is not responsible for websites or their content unless they are owned by the publisher.

Printed and bound in Canada.

Rare Machines, an imprint of Dundurn Press
1382 Queen Street East
Toronto, Ontario, Canada M4L 1C9
dundurn.com, @dundurnpress 🐦 f ⓞ

for Megan & Alaska

This time everyone has the best intentions. You have cancer. Let's say you have cancer. Let's say you've swallowed a bad thing and now it's got its hands inside you. This is the essence of love and failure.

— Richard Siken, *You Are Jeff*

I thought I had mono once for an entire year.
Turned out I was just really bored.

— Wayne Campbell, *Wayne's World*

"Them Changes"
by Thundercat.

Eve was explaining the way the Pap test works, in a lot of detail. I was loving it. I was wondering if Ben told her I was a nerd or if she did this for everyone.

Ben was my doctor. A thin, almost gremlinish man, he was not tall but was very *long* — long fingers, a long and perpetually craned neck. He had a bald spot, but also very pretty dark curls. He also had extremely large, kind eyes and a very impressive bedside manner, for a doctor.

I am not a doctor hater. I admire and respect doctors. I just think that in order to get through med school you either need to be a megalomaniac or a weird nerd, which is why visits with doctors are often so uncomfortable. Ben had never made me uncomfortable. One time, I asked him to prescribe me weed (before it was legal), and he said no, and I cried — but not because he was mean, just because I admire and respect doctors, and being told no by people I admire and respect makes me embarrassed. When I'm embarrassed I cry. So, that was really not his fault. Weed was also legalized quickly thereafter. You're not my dad, Ben.

I had recently asked Ben for a Pap test. He said that he thought it would be better if Eve did it. Eve was the nurse practitioner at his office, he explained. She was a woman and well-trained. While this would have made sense if I had ever indicated that I was uncomfortable, in any way, with a male doctor performing routine medical procedures on me, I had not — and this change of plans made me feel rejected. Why didn't Ben want to look at my cervix? I booked an appointment with Eve, feeling both the sting of the repudiation and extreme embarrassment about how affected I was by the whole thing. Were Ben and I not at *that point*? The *cervix* point? Why did I care? I made a mental note to talk to my therapist about it, while I changed the subject by showing Ben a new mole that had recently appeared on my knee.

So there I was, with my skirt up around my hips, squatting off the end of the table so that Eve could scrape my cervix. Eve had drawn the navy-blue curtains shut around the examination table, even though we were in a closed room, which was a classy touch. Everything in Eve's office was shades of dark blue, except for her triumphant diplomas, of which there were many. The diplomas were in big, beautiful mahogany frames. Eve's office was neater and better decorated than Ben's examination rooms. Eve's clothes were nicer than Ben's clothes. Eve was extremely helpful. Eve had an *even better* bedside manner than Ben.

I was less impressed by her good bedside manner, probably because she was a woman and because she's a nurse. As she cranked my vagina open with a plastic speculum, I thought, judgmentally, that nurses had to have better bedside manners because they dealt more directly with patients. As she inserted a long swab into my vaginal canal and started to scrape my cervix, I decided that wasn't fair, and who was I to undervalue this person's labour? She makes less money than a doctor, after all, and was she not at least as skilled? I applauded myself, silently, for catching my critical rhetorical error as Eve deposited my cervical mucus onto a piece of glass. My leg started to cramp from holding myself half-suspended off of an examination table. *As a society, we have a problem with systematically undervaluing the work of women*, I thought. *I have to work on my internalized misogyny.* I was genuinely proud of myself for thinking these things. *I miss Ben.*

"All done!" said Eve.

"Oh, really?" I said, pulling my skirt down and heaving my rear end back onto the table. "So fast."

When my underwear was back on, I asked her for a breast exam. I told her I felt myself up often, which was true, and that I had noticed a few small lumps in my left breast, and I wasn't sure what was normal to be there and what wasn't. I'd never had a breast exam before. She explained that my lack of breast exams were a normal result of my youth, and that most lumps were benign, and that she'd be happy to take a look. I took off my shirt and she very gently — maddeningly gently — pressed into the flesh of my breasts and lymph nodes in my armpits. I wasn't sure if she'd ever examined a *big person* before. *That's just skin and a bit of fat, girl,* I wanted to say, but I didn't. She was going to have to *really get in there* if she was going to feel anything.

I had to really get in there, to feel it. I'd found it first when I was lying on my back, on my mattress on the floor, probably watching television. I'd been working my fingertips into the plethora of tiny aches and pains all over my body — a mass of tight tissue in my left quadricep, the tension in the soft parts between my iliac crest and the pillowy expanse of my stomach. I had moved up to my head, and worked down again: my fingers on my sinuses, trying to push the liquid out — to somewhere, I didn't know where. My fingers making cold, shivering indentations when they found the tightness in my trapezius or the guitar string rigidity of my levator scapulae. On my chest, my hands moved the fat and breast tissue out of the way to uncover my constantly rigid pectoral muscles. That's when they found something. It was an accident. I was on my way to do something else. I only found one, at first: it was a little bit swollen, angry. Searching around more, I found another one in the corresponding armpit.

"Hm," I said, on the bed. I wasn't scared. There was no reason to be, yet. I made an appointment with Ben.

Now, Eve was doing the same thing, but while she had an embodied understanding of my breasts and the role they played in my life — unlike Ben, I guess, fine — she was exploring with altogether too much care: she didn't want to go looking, lest she burst a blood vessel or trip a nerve. We had just met. She didn't know how I would react.

"I don't feel anything abnormal," she told me, cheerfully. I told her that I usually couldn't, either, unless I was lying down with my arm up. I adjusted my arm position, and took her smaller hand in my bigger one. I guided her hand to where the lump was. Under my left nipple, just off to the left side.

She was very close to it, but she hadn't found it yet. I knew, from her examination pattern — one press directly in before cocking her hand to one side and then the other — that she would find it soon. Pinching a little, pressing up, assessing. "Nothing here," she said, but she was about to find it. I waited. Her hand touched it. "Yeah, a bit of firmness but no —" Her hand moved, but the lump did not. She got a different angle, tried again, and it was still there. She stopped moving. Her fingers had traced over the lump — found its edges, its borders. The lump was sliding around under her fingers. As the lump shifted, it turned my stomach. It didn't hurt, but the whole makeup of my breast moved as it did. There was a nervous, uneasy feeling that spread down the left side of my body. She ran her fingers over it a few times, confirming. She was thorough. "Okay," she said, finally. "Okay, yes."

"Them Changes" by Thundercat.

Emboldened by evidence, she made a perimeter sweep of the immediate area. She found more, hiding: smaller lumps. Multitudinous. Ones I did not find. I felt myself start to sweat — sour, vinegar sweat. She had found a small colony of firm, round things. One was cherry-sized, and the others peas. Like a planet and two soft moons.

"There are a few things here."

Dread arrives as sensation in your body and it is cold. Dread fills your stomach like a vase is filled with water. The coldness has a voice, and it's calm. It's certain. It has something to say to you from somewhere primordial, intuitive, and all-knowing. It says *something is wrong with you.*

"Okay." She stopped moving her hand, and then removed it completely. "You can get dressed."

Children who grow up in unstable environments are often better accustomed to chaos than they are to any kind of calm. There is a sick sort of pleasure I get from being approached with another person's serious problem; this pleasure, which is also relief, is multi-faceted. First, I no longer have to focus on whatever boring thing I was previously attempting to slog through in my own life. The misery of those I love is a perfectly good excuse to slack off. Furthermore, it actually leaves me with a situation in which I can argue that to not slack off would be morally wrong. Homework, housecleaning, whatever I actually have to do at work? All that trash be damned! Somebody needs me! This is part of what I have come to understand as a saviour complex.

Children take things for granted. Whatever is demonstrated as normal they will internalize as normal. This is why it actually doesn't matter if they have two moms, or a single dad, or a two-bedroom apartment, or a summer house, or whatever: If the adults in their life pass it off as normal, then it is. If the adults in their life pass off functional, communicative relationships as normal, a child will come to expect that as the norm. The same goes for martyrdom, overwork, charity, and hatred.

My parents tried very hard to provide me with a happy childhood so that I would internalize being happy as normal. Unfortunately for them, they were organic human animals and made of meat. When I was seven, my mother got the news that her meat was rotting. She was in the last year of her thirties. Being in your thirties seemed old when I was a child, because it was the age that my parents were. Now that my own thirties are very close, I understand what everyone was saying at the time. Too young. A baby. Too young to die.

My mother's prognosis was extremely poor from the moment her cancer was discovered. She did not die immediately. In a way, this is a kind of mercy. There is a qualitative difference, in my mind, between a death from a non-communicable, wasting disease and a sudden accidental death. It's not like my mother was perfectly healthy one second and then flattened by machinery the next. Perhaps most mercifully, her death was nobody's fault. I never had to do the work of negotiating whether I felt ready to forgive a drunk driver, a murderer, or an inattentive air traffic controller. There are some things you can do to cut the risk down: quit smoking, wear sunscreen. Do not vacation at the sites of recent nuclear meltdowns. None of these things are guaranteed. People get cancer and die. People have always gotten cancer and died.

When I was living in rural Ontario and going to high school, one of my best friends was Annie, who is an oncology nurse now. She says that miraculous recoveries are a part of life in the cancer ward, but they never happen to the people whose church groups come in and pray in a circle. They don't happen to the people who seem to deserve or expect it. They happen with a kind of absurd randomness that seems orchestrated: to the homeless man who only got off heroin for the experimental chemo treatment, who has no family and very little community, who genuinely did not expect to live and has no plans and very few prospects. Miraculous recoveries happen very rarely to the people who will leave the ward miraculously cured, stare up at the sky, and say, *Dude, what the fuck*, to the deaf ears of God.

Cancer isn't responsible: it doesn't care how morally pure or kind or hard-working or well-supported you are. It's just a thing that happens to people, and then those people die.

I begged God on my knees to get to keep my mother just a little while longer so much and so often and so loudly and with such a fervour that if anyone was listening, somebody would have answered. I was a good little girl and I deserved to get the few things I asked for. What I got instead was the understanding that God does not listen to little girls. Children normalize what is demonstrated as normal.

I had a child's naive hope that my mother would pull through the entire time, and in this way I understood the situation to be serious, and in this way I got to brace for her death, which is a kind of mercy. My father did a good job of making it clear that her survival was a very slim possibility. I held out hope, anyway. This remains my superpower: calculating the worst-case scenarios, accepting them, hoping for the best in spite of it all. Natalie Wynn, YouTube philosopher, highlights a cognitive distortion she calls *masochistic epistemology*: whatever hurts the most is true. It is a common affliction among the pseudo-intellectual: the assumption that the outcome that hurts your feelings the most must be the right one, not because of overwhelmingly convincing evidence in its favour or a lack of evidence against it, but simply because it hurts your feelings. The worst-case scenario is usually less likely than the whole range of other scenarios that are not as bad. That's just math.

As I left Eve's office, the forms for diagnostic imaging in my sweaty and shaky hands, I made a pretty profound realization. I'm good in a crisis, but I guess I'm only *really* good in the crises of others. In this one — not yet even confirmed crisis, requiring more evidence, not really *worth* panicking over, if you think about it — I was going to lose my fucking shit.

I reacted in a more collected way to the news my mother was dead than I did to the news that I had a very common breast abnormality that, in combination with my family history, made diagnostic imaging a good idea. I do not know if that means I was more emotionally mature at twenty-seven than I was when I was nine, or less so. I had two and a half years to brace for my mother's death, which was a mercy. When I met my current boyfriend, Sandy, he was still grieving: his friend Rosemary had died suddenly a few years earlier from a brain aneurysm. Nobody's fault. Nothing anyone could have done. She didn't hit her head, she didn't have any symptoms before. It was just one of those Judas-body, random malfunction things. She was twenty-seven.

I never met Rosemary, but I think about her all the time. My mother died and it was very sad, and it changed me forever. But was it a tragedy, necessarily? The way a Greek tale of hubris or betrayal is a tragedy? Is Rosemary's death a tragedy, or was it just horrible? Is there a lesson to be learned? Any kind of takeaway, other than some platitude about the fundamental impermanence and ultimate fragility of life on earth? Usually, when I think about Rosemary, the only conclusion that I reach is that a brain aneurysm is a crazy, scary, stupid way to die.

I walked to the bus stop from Eve's office with panic brewing in my stomach in a way it never had before: like a headache. Like a fever. I was sweating, looking for the bus. The humid early autumn in Côte Saint-Luc made me perspire and then go immediately cold. People had lots of different reactions when we told them Mom was gone. Shocked silence, sputtering out questions. Sudden tears. In a few cases, screaming. My dad took me out into the sunshine to tell me my mom was dead, the way you take a dog to the soft grass behind the shed to shoot it. I just crossed my hands in my lap and nodded. The feeling in my stomach was of something suddenly emptying out — a hole being ripped in the side of a spaceship, matter screaming out into the void. The hole inside me was cold and shiny and throbbed for attention. I have been trying to fill it ever since.

The concrete in Côte Saint-Luc was paler than it is in the rest of the city, especially in the high light of the middle of the day. I never wore sunglasses because I was always breaking or losing them. I squinted toward the bus stop, suddenly unable to differentiate spaces particularly well. I walked toward it in a daze. The buses came regularly in Côte Saint-Luc, but no one ever took them. When my dad told me that the first home I had ever known was gone, I just nodded. Children take things for granted. If you present things as normal, they will be accepted as normal. On the bus there were a few middle-aged women and one Hasidic man, holding a Nikon flip phone to his ear under the brim of his beautiful hat. The rest of the bus was empty and quiet. The women had gone pillowy and lovely with age, their faces lined from smiling. I wanted to be an aging auntie on the bus one day. I wanted to overhear more Yiddish phone conversations. I wanted to go on delighting in the contours of languages I loved but did not understand. Some people just get cancer and then they die. Children take things for granted. *I am not a child anymore. I want to live.*

"The King of Carrot Flowers, Pt. 1" by Neutral Milk Hotel.

May–October 2011. Halifax.

The story I want to tell you starts after my first year at Dalhousie University. I guess I have to back up a little. Bear with me.

I had just auditioned for the school's acting program, a program that only accepted second-year students. I'd tanked my first audition, hard: while I'd delivered a good performance of my modern dramatic monologue (the "George and Martha: Sad sad sad" speech from Edward Albee's *Who's Afraid of Virginia Woolf?*, complete with mid-Atlantic accent and fake tears), I had forgotten half my Shakespeare monologue and burst into uncontrollable and very real tears. I had opted to sing one of my friends' band's punk tunes in lieu of learning an actual musical theatre song for the audition — something I thought was very rock 'n' roll at the time. My gatekeepers were not impressed, but I'd gotten a callback audition, anyway. I sighed with relief when I saw my name on the list. Of course, why was I so worried? I always pulled it off in the end.

I'd been saving for university since I got my fourteenth birthday present: a job at the only café in Cannington, Ontario — the tiny farming village where I had spent the majority of my childhood and teen years. I'd spent all of it on one single year of tuition and books at Dalhousie, my dad and stepmother still having to spot me for some of it, and also allowing me to live at home and eat their food. This economy, you know? I had adjusted shakily to the demands of a schooling system where I couldn't pull everything off at the last minute, and had finished the year with my confidence damaged. Dalhousie was raising tuition again the next year, and while we had demonstrated in March of 2011 — inspired by the leadership of student organizers at universities in Quebec — it looked like the powers that be were going to go ahead with the hike, anyway. My dad, my stepmom, and I were renters in our house on Compton Avenue. Most of the money my dad made went right back into his business. "We'll figure it out," he told me. I wasn't sure how.

On my nineteenth birthday, I moved out of my parents' place and into an apartment with my boyfriend of one year. My boyfriend was a banjo-playing bike mechanic almost half a foot shorter than me. He had strong, squared hands and a huge smile. He was kind and innocent and sweet — or at least seemed that way. He also lied to me, all the time, but only to make me happy. He had a classic monosyllabic name — something like Al, or Rick, or Tim. Let's call him Tim.

Tim and I took one of the four bedrooms in our summer sublet, the rest of which were occupied by various members of our friend circle, including Matilda, one of my two best friends. After my parents moved us from Cannington to Halifax the summer before grade twelve, I had to expand the definition of *best friend* to suit the members of my new life. It had seemed wrong, at first — surely my *best friends* were exclusively the friends I had back in the southern

Ontario farming communities I hadn't wanted to leave. I had to admit, though, that the base-level of fucked up that had been established by my mother's death in 2001 had been pushed to some unmanageable levels by my brother's overdose and my sister moving out. I had understood the urge to bail, to head for a coast, to start over, but I had still resisted the move, like teenagers do. My only real friend was our family's miniature poodle, Pip — until I found Matilda and Kate. And Tim. That was when my world opened up — for the first time ever, really.

Tim and I were sharing a bedroom. Two weeks after we moved in, I spiked up my mohawk, put on something skanky, and got a bloody nose at a hardcore show. The next morning, which was actually afternoon, I woke up hungover and tried to get Tim to fuck me, which didn't work.

"Your necklace is gone," Tim said quietly. He was speaking so quietly these days. He always seemed so sad all the time.

I put my hand to my throat. Tim had welded together four links of bike chain and threaded it through a ribbon for me, as a gift. Looking back, it was probably an ugly necklace, but I never took it off, even to shower. My neck was bare for the first time since he had tied the choker around my throat: like a collar, like a promise. It must have gotten knocked off at the show.

Tim turned away from me in bed. I was annoyed. Why was he like this?

"Tim?" I asked, then, half-joking: "Do you love me?"

"Yes," he said, and I could hear he was crying.

"What's wrong?" I was as annoyed as I was concerned. He didn't answer. I called his bluff: "What is it? What, do you hate me? Do you not want to be with me anymore?" It was a joke. I asked this all the time. All the time, he replied, "Of course not! Don't even say that! I love you forever. I'm going to marry you." Setting the stakes this high would usually shock him into telling me whatever was going on.

"I do," he said this time, still turned away, still with tears I could hear in his mouth and his eyes. I smiled. Then: "But I don't think I can anymore."

I felt my smile physically dump out of the bottom of my face.

"Wait, what?"

"Tara! Hi, Tara!" echoed the chorus of girl-voices at work. The staff from the morning was still there, and my colleague for the afternoon shift was early. I stomped down the concrete steps in my combat boots. When I wasn't hanging out with Tim, or Matilda, or Kate, I worked full-time as a barista at Uncommon Grounds Coffee House. It was in the basement of a condo complex: the look was industrial-chic and brightly branded, with very low red leather seating and huge red coffee cups stamped on the floors and the tables, rows of expensive neon French presses and locally made candies lining the walls. I hadn't cried yet. Mostly I had argued with Tim, as if his disinterest in continuing our relationship was some kind of intellectual misunderstanding that I could correct.

My café job, which Matilda had gotten me four months before, was amazing. Very little was expected of me, I had access to a treasure trove of free food, and I was very willing to be friendly to strangers as long as I had enough caffeine — something that made me a mostly good employee, despite being lazy by nature. I worked primarily afternoon shifts, which were slow, and went from two thirty in the afternoon until ten thirty at night. The pay rate was ten dollars an hour — minimum wage in Nova Scotia at the time — and I always walked out with at least ten dollars in tip money, which I spent on weed, beer, or sushi. The staff was mostly cool, alternative, hipster women between the ages of eighteen and twenty-five. We spent most of our time gossiping and trying to eat only a reasonable number of bagels.

"How are you, Tara?" asked Amanda, an angel-faced redhead a few years older than me.

"Tim dumped me," I said, not stopping as I made my way behind the counter, into the back to the bakery and storage room. Amanda's smile fell into an expression of extreme concern. I hung up my navy-blue leather purse in the closet and looked into the mirror. My hair, which was a thick mohawk with grown-out sides and bangs, was still backcombed and full of hairspray, although it was no longer standing on end. I had put it up into a ratty ponytail before I left my house. I licked my fingers and arranged my eyeliner, which was still on from the night before, to look like an intentional smoky eye instead of a recently dumped girl's sudden lack of care about her appearance. Unshowered, I was wearing the first thing I'd found on my floor: a pair of green army fatigue cargo pants and a black tank top. My weight, which fluctuated regularly by about thirty pounds, was at the upper end of the spectrum: I wore a huge zip-up sweatshirt to hide my thick arms and to make myself as invisible as possible.

I had a couple of minutes before my shift technically started, so I pulled out my phone and texted my dad. *Tim dumped me.* Before I could even put my phone back, I got a reply: *WTF? When?*

This morning. I felt guilty, for some reason. My dad really liked Tim. My functional relationship with this nice boy was my most compelling evidence for an argument called *Why I am actually a very mature and responsible person, in spite of the questionable choices I make about hair, clothing, etc.*

My dad texted back: *Do you think you'll work it out?*

Maybe. I don't know.

One email from Dalhousie. I had not gotten into the acting program.

When I left the closet, walked through the bakery, and into the space behind the counter of the café, Amanda was waiting with an oversized mug. It was the same red as the coffee cups stamped on the floor and the tables. "Double shot in the dark with some cinnamon," she said, as seriously as if she was explaining a prescription medication. "Do you think you'll work it out?"

Tim and I decided to stay roommates after a wine-soaked conversation about the logistics of the sleeping arrangement. We talked about how our friendship had been so good before we dated, and our relationship had been so good when we were together, and there was no reason we couldn't still be friends. We talked about how we were mature and responsible people who could handle a tiny little thing like sharing a wall with the first person you were ever really in love with, who you were still in love with, but could not be with anymore. It would be fine.

It was not fine. Tim and I were terse but respectful for a few weeks, and then friendly, and then one rainy day we somehow ended up on the floor of the living room. I can't remember exactly what we were doing. Two separate memories compete for the truth of it: me with his guitar, playing "A Case of You" by Joni Mitchell. Him reaching over, so close I could smell his sandalwood aftershave, to slide the guitar out of my hands, and strumming the chords much better than me so I could focus on singing. I'm a much better singer than I am a guitar player, and he had those solid, square hands for fretting and picking. This was another thing that I felt was evidence we were perfect together.

Another memory: We were setting up his record player in the living room. The day was humid and breezy and we had the door to our back balcony propped open. We managed to successfully make the record player work, but hadn't chosen a proper spot for it: the turntable, preamp, amplifier, and speakers were all splayed out on different parts of the living room floor. We were discussing what kind of mounting setup we'd be able to work out for cheap, or free. What I do know is that we both had the day off, and that nobody else was home, and that music was involved. We were so close to each other, with the breeze blowing in the smell of wet pavement and growing gardens through that open door, the day heady with pot smoke and lavender soap and sandalwood.

I have a friend who says she used to have sex with a guy in her dorm room who would always have her come over under the pretense of watching *The Office*. Years later, she still had a completely involuntary physiological response to the twinkling piano that starts the theme song: fluids moving inside of her like in the mouth of a trained dog. I feel the same way about the entirety of the album *In the Aeroplane Over the Sea* by Neutral Milk Hotel. Since I can't remember exactly what was happening, I would like to suggest that maybe we put on an LP of *In the Aeroplane Over the Sea* by Neutral Milk Hotel and got quiet and lay down.

The pull I had always felt toward Tim was magnetic, and giddy, and carnivorous in its intensity. I didn't just want to kiss him, I wanted to devour his face. I didn't just want to hug him, I wanted to find a way to merge my cells with his cells until we became one unit of matter. Despite talking about sex with a great deal of confidence as a teenager, I sexually matured at an average-to-late-bloomer age. My stepmother had once tried to give me a serious talking-to about sexual health and safety when I was fifteen, noticing I carried condoms around in my purse. I acted flippant and distant about it, because I was fifteen. It was very, *You don't get to tell me what to do with my body!* It was very, *You don't understand punk at all!* I liked that somebody thought I was some kind of wanton teenage sex fiend, but the reality was way less cool: I only had the condoms in there because I had been given them for free by a street preacher on a school trip to New York City and I never cleaned my purse.

"The King of Carrot Flowers, Pt. 1" by Neutral Milk Hotel.

I spent most of my teens in years-long crushes: single-minded in their focus, monogamous in their devotion. I caught a spark for someone and I stayed hooked. It was always unrequited, because I never told them. I would occasionally experiment with a slight variation: only telling them months after it would have been a fair thing to say — when my passion had already mounted to the maniacal. Loving someone who loved me back was still new. There was still a huge novelty in having my desire *yes, and*'d like sexual improv. When it finally happened, I leapt out of the gates of my virginity a star greyhound racer: I wasn't sure what I was trying to get, but my pursuit of it was primal and instinctual.

Tim was not my first partner. I'd started dating him polyamorously, during a period of time that overlapped with the end of my relationship with my first girlfriend. River was an anarchist with a labret piercing, who only ever seemed to wear one pair of pants, which in my memory are made entirely of patches. My affair with River had been a whirlwind: a punk rock fairy tale that should have faded to black after a few dates, the credits rolling with a Propagandhi song playing. However, I had tried to turn it into something long-term, despite every indication that it had already done the work it was meant to do. First mistake.

River and Tim were in a folk punk band together. One day, River and I had a fight about how she was an emotionally neglectful flake, and she promised to do better, and we made a date for the following week. When I showed up at her apartment for our date, I was informed by her roommate that she had gone on tour — with her *other* folk punk band. She would be back in a month.

With River, I felt passionate and dysregulated. I picked fights with her. I cried to my friends about her. She was so hot and so cool. Her far-left politics changed my life, inspired me to read Marx and Lenin and Kropotkin; she was extraordinarily smart, especially for a seventeen-year-old — even when she was cruel and dehumanizing in her extremity. I never relaxed around her. I knew I was not as beautiful as her or the other girls she dated. The less obvious problem was my soft heart, my malleable politics, my will that bent the closer it got to an edge. I was afraid that I was not really a radical, and terrified that at any moment I would be found out — as a poseur or a centrist or a normie, undeserving of her love.

My teenage insecurity, my inability to confidently express my own needs and desires, my manipulative belief that if I just loved her the right way, she would change in some fundamental way, would merge with her interest in sex with other people, and her inconsistent interest in being around me at all, and her lack of follow-through. I felt like there was something wrong with me. She didn't *do* this to me, but I was very attached to the idea that she did. It made me feel like I was powerless, which made me feel like I couldn't do anything to change it, which made me feel less like an idiot. Second mistake.

After I was informed that River had skipped town without telling me, feeling worthless and ugly and numb, I came home and ran a utility knife over my thigh seven times. The pain brought me back into my body. I sat looking at the blood on my leg and decided that, while I now understood why people did this, it wasn't for me. When it had healed enough, I bought some India ink and a Bic lighter and a package of sewing needles. I lit up the end of the sewing needle until it glowed red, stuck it in the ink, and slowly pricked a small heart tattoo over my scars. That pain brought me back into my body, too. A heart, for love — from me, for me, forever. My first tattoo.

Tim and I started kissing one night at the Big G. The Big G was above the Big General Store on South Street in Halifax — hence its name. The landlord was Mr. Kim, who had an experimental style of renovation architecture and a benignly neglectful style of landlordship. Fred, the proprietor of the Big General Store, would be first in line for sainthood if I was the one calling the shots: he put up with our absurd youthful antics, including all-night punk shows that drew crowds that spilled out into the street outside and onto the roof. The only time I ever saw him draw the line was when someone practised the drums so hard they knocked the merchandise off his shelves.

Mr. Kim's renovation job was so cutting-edge, it was almost an art installation. There were two hallways in the five-bedroom apartment that functionally led nowhere: one led from one end of the living room to the other end of the living room, succeeding only in making the living room smaller. Another led from one door to the bathroom to another door, which led to the same bathroom. This bathroom had a third door, which emptied into a bedroom that could only be accessed by said bathroom or another bedroom. In order to avoid being interrupted while doing one's business, one had to remember to lock all three doors, and the locks rarely worked. To this day, I am somewhat laissez-faire about being walked in on while using the toilet, choosing to focus instead on the potential for comedy in such experiences.

It was rare to have the bedrooms at the Big G (which we usually called "the G," to save time) rented out to a single person. Usually there was a couple or a pair of very close friends in one room, increasing the capacity of the five bedrooms to an average of about nine at once. In addition, each of the hallways to nowhere were rented out as bedrooms, for a scant hundred dollars (Canadian!) a month. The closet off of the living room, which I could not fit inside without my legs hanging out into the living room, was rented out to a particularly small person for fifty dollars a month. There was usually at least one person crashing on one of the four couches in the huge double living room, in exchange for buying communal groceries or throwing a few bucks a month against the utility bills. For several months, a guy I called Uncle Green pitched a tent in the living room, poking his head out whenever he heard someone come in.

There was always somebody coming in. Most days after school in the twelfth grade, and almost every day after class my first year of university, I would make my way down Henry Street until it emptied out onto South, open the door that was never locked, and throw my bag over the tangle of bicycles that made the space between the door and the stairs the worst fire hazard I had ever seen. Then I would either gingerly step, trying to find enough space for my feet between the wheels and spokes and handlebars until I got to the stairs, or just kind of lay my body down across it, taking hold of the railing to drag myself over with my arms. There was a time limit on this: the carpet at the bottom of the stairs was also where the cats' litter box was kept, which was always rendered so inaccessible by this stupid way of storing bikes that nobody ever cleaned it enough. Even if they had, the carpet was so ruined it would never smell like anything but cat shit down there. In Dante's *Inferno*, the doors to hell bear the warning *Abandon all hope, ye who enter here.* The stairs to the G had a parallel sign written on a cheese-stained pizza box by a Big G resident, a pixieish tattoo artist named Sabrina: above a Sharpie drawing of a turd, complete with stink lines and flies, were the words *Hold your breath until you get to the top of the stairs.*

At the top of the stairs, light-headed, I would take my first breath. Then, with my first breath, I'd say, "Is anyone home?" From their rooms, the hallways, or the kitchen, the anyone who was home would greet me. Some arrangement of the G's revolving cast of residents would emerge — into the living room with its warm rat's nest of trash on the ground, every inch of the walls covered in punk show posters and stolen municipal signage and vandalized religious iconography — and we'd have a party.

The G was my community centre, my church, and my salvation. I had never been anywhere so beautiful.

One night in the spring of 2010, as high school graduation approached, Tim and I were hanging out at the G. We had not yet begun dating. I was about to turn eighteen, a milestone Tim had already hit that winter. He was planning to move to the G, into the closet off of the living room, after graduation. While he was broad-shouldered and sturdy, he was short enough to physically fit with the door closed. Uncle Green had graciously left his tent to do us a liquor run, and we were passing a quart of whisky around.

My friendship with Tim had recently bloomed. He had always been warm to me, and our relationship had been casual for most of the school year. I had arrived moon-eyed and lonely from Ontario the previous summer, and he had shown me classic East Coast hospitality: eating lunch with me at school and inviting me to my first party at the G to see his band play. That night before graduation, with adulthood and all of its potential in front of us, we were making a list of plans in my sketchbook for cool things to do this summer, like *start a band* and *build a fort* and *buy a motherfucking van!!!* As we got more drunk, our plans got more abstract, and considerably more stupid. The word *fish*, complete with a crooked, sloppy illustration, in case anyone wasn't sure what the word meant. *Set traps!!!* The phrase *return of the son of Awesome Face*, with no further explanation. We were sitting very close. Drunkenness was pooling out into my body: a comfortable, fiery joy. For me, drinking has always felt like falling in love, a warning I would not listen to for years.

I looked at Tim. I decided, hammered, that I felt comfortable around him. Tim and I, we were pals. Tim made me laugh ugly, painful laughs about things I would think about days later, and spit coffee all over my school notes because I was laughing again. Tim wasn't supermodel good-looking, he was a cutie-pie: a few pounds overweight, several inches too short, with an affinity for folk T-shirts and pants that didn't fit him properly. This made him look old, even at eighteen. He was safe. He was very unlike River, with her angular face and her constant criticisms. A few months earlier, I had found out through someone who was not River that River was sleeping with other people. I had asked her, "What the fuck? Shouldn't we have talked about this?" She told me it wasn't something she felt like we had to talk about: non-monogamy was a given, to her. I had been sad, then angry, then grudgingly accepting. I had been going through my Rolodex of acquaintances, thinking that if I was getting something extra, the arrangement wouldn't feel so weird.

So, drunk teenage me decided that this something extra would be Tim. He was safe. Low-commitment. River was my trophy partner: she worked up all of the extreme highs and brutal lows I had read about and heard about and sung about. Surely, that was what love was. Not sitting comfortably on a broken couch someone found in the trash, perfectly at ease, while he jokingly asks me what kind of childhood trauma led to me never listening to Neutral Milk Hotel.

I kissed Tim. When he pulled away, he was shocked. I smiled wryly, alcohol making me bold. He had the pencil we were using to make the list in his hand, and I reached over and took it. "Just throwing this out there," I slurred, and wrote *Stop making out* on our list.

"Uh …" Tim said, shaking his head and its shock of golden hair. He laughed nervously, trying to shift gears. "Yeah, sure, good idea."

I frowned. I leaned in very close to the sketchbook, and added: *… maybe*. I looked up, expectant. Tim looked back. I decided his eyes were pretty: pale grey-blue, full of hope and confusion and something hungry. I smacked the sketchbook onto the floor and pounced on him.

"Oh, Jesus," groaned Uncle Green, zipping up his tent. I don't remember much else from that night, because of the booze. I remember the roughness of Tim's shaved face, his hands on me — his asking, softly, in his low baritone: "Is this okay? Is this okay? Is this okay?"

River had to go. The day she came home, we both ended up at the G at the same time, probably to buy weed. I dumped her on the front stoop. Me and Tim had started writing each other love notes in the time that she had gone — which, might I remind you, was *an entire month*, an *eternity* to an eighteen-year-old — and River hadn't called or texted or even sent me a Facebook message. After feeling so attention-starved for six months, I was feasting and gluttonous and self-important. River seemed genuinely remorseful when I left her behind in front of the Big General Store, but she didn't try to get me back. I went to go find Tim, and we barely left each other's side for a year.

Tim was a punk, but he was more of a Woody Guthrie than a Steve Ignorant. River was handmade patches sewn onto a jean jacket with dental floss, Tim was mink oil worked into a pair of thrifted leather shoes. River played the same four chords on her guitar, Tim played finger-style. He played the mandolin and the piano and the banjo, and he played them all well. River's love language was handing me a stack of half-frozen steakettes she had dumpster dived from behind the Sobeys, warning me about the early signs of botulism like she was reciting me a love poem. Tim came to my house to meet my dad and my stepmother in a shirt he had ironed himself, with his hands full of flowers he'd stolen out of rich people's gardens.

Tim had a classic Nova Scotian accent: the *A* in *car* gliding flatly over the roof of his mouth, *F*s heavy with breath where they ended a word. He forced his accent to pronounce my name properly, *Tah-rah*, the sounds standing tall and round in his mouth like he was making fun of an English person. He was completely sincere, quick to laugh, gentle and forgiving. A foil to the way I had to fight for any of River's attention at all; Tim sought me out tirelessly. Tim fought to be with me and was sad when he had to see me go. Tim was hungry for me.

Next to him on the living room floor, weeks after we broke up, in the first apartment I lived in as something approaching an adult, I felt the magnetic pull of his body. A warmth was stirring in me. I put one bare foot against the hardwood floor and I glided myself closer to him. We used to have sex to the entirety of *In the Aeroplane Over the Sea*. I still think of that album as one to which you fuck someone you love very much. I hear the opening chords of "The King of Carrot Flowers" and I feel imbued with that same possibility: lying in the bedroom he had before we moved in to that doomed Birmingham Street apartment together, which was not a bedroom but one of the hallways at the Big G. He had sprung for an upgrade from the living room closet when he got a job at Subway. In his room, we could hear the Big G residents laughing and talking and smoking through the wall. We were protected only by heavy comforters nailed to each end of the useless hallway. There was garbage thrown all across the floor. We learned what our bodies were for. I tried to work my body into his body, his body into mine, in every way I could — like I was trying to get something back, something I'd been missing since we were separated at the beginning of whatever, something I needed to be whole and now I had found and would never lose again.

But I had lost it. On the living room floor was the first time I really felt him missing from me. We had made all these plans — what, were we going to act like they were just words? That seemed so stupid. The feeling was still there. I could feel it there, between us. Our plans must still be real. Our future wasn't really gone.

Tim moved his arm, as my shoulder made contact with his ribs. We were two continents drifting together, as we should. He put his hand down slowly, gently, on my other shoulder. Huge mountains of goosebumps erupted on my skin. I turned molten and liquid on the inside.

"The King of Carrot Flowers, Pt. 1" by Neutral Milk Hotel.

"Hi," I said, mustering every ounce of girly cuteness in my queer, tomboyish body.

"Are we cuddling?" he asked, his surprise tinged with softness. *See*, I thought. *He feels it too!* There was our love, a thing that still existed in the world. If I felt it, and he felt it, we would be together. We would work it out, after all. I had lived my whole life, up until that point, on pure emotion, talent, good intentions, and gut feelings. What else was there?

I maintain, half joking, but not really, that the best kisses are the forbidden ones. Erotic is, by definition, transgressive. Tim was always a good kisser: holding my face in those incredible hands, firmly and confidently exploring my mouth with genuine wonder and excitement. When we kissed again, I erupted, volcanic. I was home again, but everything was new.

I had been so convinced that Tim was a rest stop. I was young, sexy, brilliant. I would have a long and exciting life, full of many lovers. I had been reticent to be really vulnerable with him, even as he was uniquely vulnerable with me. He had been my safety bet. My consolation prize. I was the goddess and he was my priest — this is what I told myself silently as I said that I wanted to marry him. This is what I told myself while I gave my entire body to him and saw the incredible, genius things he could do with it. Meanwhile, he had been growing up: the poverty of independence had shaved off his extra pounds, odd jobs in manual labour had stacked muscle onto him, cut his jaw like a plank of oak. Out of stress, anxiety, a deep sense of sadness I never really respected him enough to try to understand, he had taken up smoking, and despite my family's cancer history and the stern warnings from my father, I still think smoking is hot. He got a better haircut and thrifted some pants that fit. One day, after he left me but before we had sex on the living room floor, I was stunned to see that he was beautiful: fit, rugged, fashionable, talented, and completely done with my shit.

After we started kissing, but before we had sex, Tim tried to do the right thing. We were broken up and we were still roommates and this was a bad idea.

I thought, for a minute. "We're friends," I ventured. "We do fun things together, right?"

He looked at me. Skeptical. Ethical. But also nineteen. "Right."

"I just think that this is a fun thing we could do together," I said, once again pulling up my Cute Teenage Girl Drag voice, syrupy and Valley girl and innocent and stupid. "You know, just as friends."

This was, of course, a con. I could feel our love between us, this unbreakable bond. It had been there the whole time we were broken up, but I'd been so pissed off I'd been ignoring it. The dumping had been a blip, after all. It was going to annoy all of our roommates when we announced we had gotten back together, but it would be in an eye-rolling, smiley way, before they handed us a beer and clapped us on the back and said, "Of course you did, you crazy kids. Tim and Tara forever!" As soon as he felt it, as soon as he was back inside me where he belonged, he would understand that there was absolutely no version of his life that made sense without me in it. This was a crisis of faith. It happens to every man of God.

After, sticky and exhausted and still bubbling like some kind of unstable land mass, I lay patiently with my face in my hands, gazing at him adoringly, and I waited for him to say it. I waited for him to be like, "I'm so stupid, of course I love you. You're the best thing that ever happened to me."

It never came. A few days later, we had sex again, and then he got dressed without looking at me, said goodbye, and went to band practice. He was treating me like a friend who he was also sleeping with — taking me at my word. Like an idiot! Why couldn't he see the complex, silent, unexpressed desires I *actually* had? I had to dial it up.

I began a systematic campaign of emotional terrorism, usually while completely wasted, bending my life toward the singular goal of manipulating my ex back into loving me, and, very importantly, without having a single adult conversation about it. I went on a crash diet, wore slinky clothes around the house. I couldn't have one interaction with him without dropping some thinly veiled attempt to make him feel bad. It got very, very weird. One night, I went out on a date with a customer from the café. This guy was my type: smart, friendly, funny, not handsome enough to be a real emotional threat. A Tim type! A safe guy.

Me and my Customer Crush had a one-night stand that I would first identify as extraordinarily bad sex, later identify as sexual assault, and then even later identify as a well-meaning but clueless dude who was trying and failing to have safe and consensual sex with a teenage girl, who had only ever had penetrative sex with one person, and could not communicate about her needs or desires to save her life. I left his apartment the next morning at the crack of dawn after failing to sleep, bleeding into my underwear and wondering where it all went wrong. I crawled into bed with Tim. I needed to come home, now. I really needed all of this to be over. I didn't know how to ask for what I needed, so I just put his hands on me. He was into it until he saw the blood.

He was disgusted and I was mute with shame. I didn't tell him what happened. It wouldn't have changed anything, anyway. I went to my room, curled up into a ball on my bed, and I let myself cry, because I knew it was over. I was sure, then, that he would never touch me again. Finally, I was right about something.

A week later, I was still bleeding. I had started drinking even more — drinking before work, staying out until three in the morning to drink even though I knew I had work in three hours. One of those morning-shift mornings, I threw up into the compost bin and felt a stabbing pain between my legs. Suddenly, I felt like the floor was rushing up to hit me in the face. A black circle closed in around my vision. I told people I wasn't feeling well and sat down for an hour. They were concerned, but there was a hint of disapproval. My performance at work lately had not been good, and people had been forced to pick up my slack. They knew I had a hangover.

I made it through my shift, and then I texted Matilda.

That guy I had sex with had a really big dick and it ripped me up inside and I've been bleeding for a week and I almost passed out today and I don't know what to do.

Matilda's reply: *!!!!!!* Then: *WHERE R U*

work

STAY THERE

She came and picked me up in a taxi and took me to the emergency room, where, embarrassed, I explained what happened over and over and over again. I was asked several times if I was assaulted. I had to think about it, but then honestly answered no. I waited for hours while Matilda told me jokes and dumb stories, animated like a beautiful clown. Eventually, a kind doctor examined me, letting me know she had to use a metal speculum that the nurse hadn't had the time to warm up. "I'm sorry," she said, before putting it inside me. It was ice cold. It moved to pry me open and I felt it tear me again. I lay on my back with my feet in the stirrups, staring up at the fluorescent lights beaming down in the sterile white room, tears welling up in my eyes and leaking down into my black hair.

I have thought about this day a lot since it happened. For a while, it felt like karma: like something I deserved, for the crime of wanting to be nineteen and sexually liberated and moving on. I thought of it as the universe really getting me for the way I'd treated Tim: the universe a cruel audience to a horror movie, cheering as the mean slut with the ego gets what's coming to her. Then, after that part of me had healed, I thought of it as evidence that my great karmic treat was coming: evidence of the fundamental cruelty of others, the primary evil of men, my status as a victim who deserved things because look at how I have suffered. In the first paradigm, I hold shame between myself and responsibility: I curl into myself so I do not have to see what I have to see in order to learn. In the second, I turn my attention outward: like I can control other people. Like I can reduce tragedy down into a parable about what kinds of people do what kinds of things, tie it up with a bow, and tell myself I am moving on.

It took me a long time to get to where I am now. I never said, "I don't want to break up and I want to do what I need to do to make this work, but you are allowed to leave me. I need space, even though I really don't want it." I never said, "You hurt me when you touch me like that." I never said, "Tim, I just got really hurt and I am really scared and I'm looking for comfort, and you don't want to be with me and I want to be with you, but right now I'm wondering if you can be there for me." I can wish and wish and wish that I didn't have to say these things. I still do. Immanuel Kant says, for something to be necessary, it has to be possible. We all have disparate and mutually unintelligible maps of what is to be expected and what is common sense. Children normalize what is presented as normal. When I met Tim, I felt like I'd known him all my life, but the truth is that we weren't children together. The truth is that I can't be mad that he didn't read my mind. I can't be mad that any of them didn't do things that I wanted or I needed but were not possible. It doesn't mean that they were bad people, or that they didn't care about me. It doesn't mean anything. It's just a bunch of sad stuff that happened.

When it was done, the doctor and the nurse left and told me I could get dressed. I slid off the table, in a Pat Benatar T-shirt, but otherwise naked. I went to pull my underwear back on and noticed my legs were covered in blood. I looked back at the examination table, which had a huge bloody imprint of my ass on it. The print smeared where I had slid off like the slime trail of some great slug. I stood there, still just wearing my T-shirt, a pathetic and punk rock Winnie the Pooh, and I cried for a long time.

When our four-month sublet was over, everyone hated me except for Matilda. She and I got a cheap two-bedroom on Agricola Street, just off of the Commons. She drew pumpkins on the walls in chalk pastel. We called it the Punk-in Patch.

I was disappointed and embarrassed and frustrated about the spot in the acting program, which I still felt like I deserved, even though I blew my audition. I refused to sign up for any classes that year, on principle. My intentions were not entirely unreasonable: I also refused to go into debt for school, and definitely would not let my dad. I spent the fall of 2011 slacking off at my café job, smoking massive amounts of weed, getting drunk, and feeling sorry for myself. I dated a series of people who just seemed like studies in Things That Are Not Like Tim.

Tim had asked me nicely, because he was a nice person, to give him space and allow him to move on, something that I steadfastly refused to do. I called him, I texted him, I tried to get him alone. When he took pity on me, or I convinced him I was acting normal for long enough, I would switch: tearfully pleading with him, all attempts at subtlety exhausted over the summer, pulling out the big manipulation guns to try to guilt him into loving me again. It didn't work. I could see whatever affection and respect he still had for me dwindling, but I couldn't stop. During one particularly egregious episode, I confessed about that morning after my bad date: cloaking the truth in awkward wordplay and long glances in order heavily imply that the whole thing was Tim's fault. This was bullshit — but my heart was broken, and I felt like this fight for his love was the fight for my life. Tim had a panic attack. Then left. Then never spoke to me again.

I made half-hearted attempts to get my shit together. I bought happy, lilac-purple paint for my bedroom walls and painted about a third of them, before I gave up. I started organizing my clothing, before I gave up. My room was a barely painted box of sadness, a sea of mess with a mattress and box spring floating in it. I volunteered every once in a while with Food Not Bombs, handing out free meals to the homeless with some of the other radicals. I got into occasional, spirited political discussions on punk house couches. I talked cute drunk people into kissing me. River and I briefly rekindled our affair, but while she was still beautiful and cool and fascinating, everything that didn't work about our relationship before was still not working, and it fizzled out without a lot of fanfare. I felt a deep, burning loathing for all men, even though I was still very attracted to them. I wondered if I would ever sleep with one again. Worst of all, the Big G got evicted. Mr. Kim was free to keep pushing the limits at the cutting edge of apartment renovation further and further into functional sculpture meditations on the human condition. I regained all the weight I'd lost trying to starve myself into someone Tim could love, plus another ten pounds. One day, at work, my manager, Shannon, took me aside.

"We're doing performance reviews," said Shannon. I loved Shannon. I am a very friendly person, but Shannon was so friendly that when I met her, I thought she was making fun of me. It took me almost a week of seeing her every day to realize that that was her normal personality. She knew how to chastise me without my even realizing I was being chastised. I'd do something wrong. "Tell me how you just did that!" she would say, excited. Clocking me. I'd do as I was asked. "That's so funny," she would say. "I would never have thought to do that. Here's how we're supposed to do it here," she'd say, seamlessly, taking over.

Between expertly prepared coffees and casual, efficient, glowing interactions with customers, she would share bitter little details about her life: her relationships, her friendships, her frustrations with school. I would complain about my failures — Tim, the acting program, weight loss — and she would let me know about her failed relationships, the classes she flunked. We had so much in common. Pretty much the only thing we disagreed on was that she didn't like "What I Am" by Edie Brickell & New Bohemians.

"Not even the guitar solo?" I asked, incredulous.

"It's not my thing," she said, as she went into the back and put on a playlist of the saddest songs I'd ever heard: wailing indie boys covering ancient country songs about dead children, murdered lovers, beloved animals who left one day and never returned.

"Lately, I only want to listen to sad music," she said, beaming, throwing herself into the minutiae of the detail-cleaning I never bothered with when I worked without her. I picked up a cloth and got to dusting, as if I did it every day. I hummed along to the sad, sad music, anticipating the next note. A seasoned choir girl.

"I have some feedback for you," said Shannon. I was one of two on-shift baristas. She was on managerial duty — checking stock levels, ensuring someone was doing the detail cleaning I never did, assessing the continued safety of the industrial espresso machines. As usual, I was unshowered and hungover. "Uh-huh," I said, my body and soul preparing for praise.

"Well, as you know, you are probably our best customer service person." Yes, I was expecting that. I am a delight. "And you show up to all the shifts you commit to, and you call if you're going to be late, and you do everything on the task list." Check, check, check. "But ..."

But? I was pre-emptively hurt. Gentle criticism, my only weakness.

"You don't try very hard. You get by on how charming you are. You show up, but then you're just sort of here. I think you could be applying yourself more."

Shannon was being too nice to me. Currently, I was not even applying myself to standing. I was slumped over the prep counter in the bakery because there were people in the café and I didn't want to look at anyone. My phone was in my apron pocket because I had been texting with Margot right before Shannon showed up instead of doing any work. Not interested in critically examining myself at all, I went through my mental list of Reasons I Should Not Have to Do Anything Different. Minimum wage, minimum effort. I don't own these means of production! Et cetera.

"You're doing a lot of the same things," said Shannon. "You should try doing something different, if you want something to change."

One day, arriving for another shift at Uncommon Grounds, I saw a message waiting on my phone from Matilda.

"Hi," she said. "Hi, I was just thinking about you, and wondering if you wanted to move to Montreal together. Okay, love you, bye."

In Canada, people tend to do one of the following things when they don't know what to do next: move to the Yukon, go tree planting, or move to Montreal. The Yukon was too far, and I didn't have the work ethic for tree planting. Montreal seemed like the obvious choice.

I sighed and looked around at the afternoon sun streaming into my little café. The rush, the worst part of the day, had already happened. It would be a long, slow, easy shift. I loved Halifax. Plus, I had no money for school, no motivation to do it. I was shell-shocked from heartbreak — all blasted out on the inside. I could spend years like this, waiting for an opening — waiting for the money to add up, for the weight to come off, for the feeling to strike me. Then my dad walked into Uncommon Grounds with his arms full of roses. His eyes were bright and joyful. Behind him, my stepmother and my grandfather, head still full of white hair.

"Your papers," they said. "Your papers came in."

"Bury My Heart at Wounded Knee" by Buffy Sainte-Marie.

October 1492–October 2011. Occupied Turtle Island.

My dad came into the café with his arms full of roses because of the Indian Act. I have to back up a bit, here, again. Bear with me.

Genocide is a term coined in 1944 by Polish lawyer Raphael Lemkin, who defined it as

> *the destruction of nation or of an ethnic group.... Generally speaking, genocide does not necessarily mean the immediate destruction of a nation, except when accomplished by mass killings of all members of a nation. It is intended rather to signify a coordinated plan of different actions aiming at the destruction of essential foundations of the life of national groups, with the aim of annihilating the groups themselves.*

The objectives of such a plan would be disintegration of the political and social institutions, of culture, language, national feelings, religion, and the economic existence of national groups, and the destruction of the personal security, liberty, health, dignity, and even the lives of the individuals belonging to such groups.

Lemkin lost forty-nine relatives to the Holocaust and died in poverty in New York City. At the time of his death, he considered his work on preventing genocide to be a failure.

Years earlier, Adolf Hitler mused approvingly about the success of the genocidal project that settled the Americas. The process by which land was "cleared" — the inhabitants slaughtered or displaced to make room for European immigrants — was the template for the Nazi concept of *Lebensraum.* The European colonization of the Americas killed 56 million people. It's still the largest human mortality event ever, if measured relative to the world's total population: 10 percent of the entire planet, at the time. How many prayers were sent up to God then? How many little girls, unheard?

The settlement of the Americas eliminated 90 percent of the human life on my home continent. It was the immediate, or relatively immediate, destruction of not one nation, but dozens: the Beothuk, the Koroa, the Acuera. Westo. Ababco. Calusa. So many others. Those who survived posed a legal and logistical issue for the expansion of European settlements. These legal and logistical issues were compounded, for the English, by Indigenous allegiances with the French. The Royal Proclamation Act of 1763 attempted to remedy both problems. The Royal Proclamation Act was not the Indian Act — it predates it — and it set in motion a series of events that led to my dad walking into Uncommon Grounds with his arms full of roses. I really am getting there, I promise.

The Royal Proclamation Act laid down the first colonial written declaration of the rights of Indigenous peoples on occupied Turtle Island, and, with it, a series of steps by which the English would appropriate the remaining Indigenous-controlled land. It also contained a bunch of stuff that really pissed the French off, but that does not have anything to do, really, with why my dad ended up in my work with his arms full of roses. It asserted that wide tracts of Appalachia be retained as Indigenous-controlled reserve, which bothered many colonists in what is now the United States, and contributed to the onset of the American Revolutionary War. That also doesn't have anything to do with my dad, or the roses, it's just funny.

In 1831, the Anglican ministry at the Mohawk Institute in what is now Brantford, Ontario, began to take boarding pupils, in what would come to be known as the residential schooling system, and began a 160-year legacy of the physical, psychological, cultural, and spiritual torture of children. In 1850, the euphemistically named *Act for the Better Protection of the Lands and Properties of Indians in Lower Canada* defined an "Indian" using a very new concept called *race*.

Race, if you do not know, is fiction written in the late sixteenth century by the English — who are a pale group of people who live on a windswept rock in the ocean — as a justification for the murder and colonialism of the Irish — a nearly identical pale group of people who live on a nearly identical windswept rock, in the same ocean, but slightly to the left. The fiction of *race* is quantified by *percentages of blood* — even though anyone with any rudimentary knowledge of biology or liquids could tell you that this is not how blood works. *Percentages of blood* is then tracked and measured by breeding lines — the way we do it with unreasonably expensive dogs — as if that is what a family is.

In order to be considered an "Indian," one must also be a member of a "*body or tribe of Indians*" — be recognized as a member of a community. This, at least, makes a modicum of sense: family is, after all, who you love. One was also an "Indian" if they married one, or if they were adopted by an Indigenous family. This, too, has reason. We are what loves us.

The Gradual Civilization Act came in 1857. It offered Indigenous people a bargain: get full citizenship, the right to vote, and some of the land that was recently murdered away from you if you give up your legally recognized status and the rights that came with it. This was called *enfranchisement*, which was also a euphemism. Only one person voluntarily enfranchised, which is also funny. This was the end of the era of voluntary enfranchisement.

The Indian Act, which contained bits and pieces of the before-mentioned acts, was signed into law in 1876. *Generally speaking, genocide does not necessarily mean the immediate destruction of a nation.* The Indian Act did not affect *a nation* — it affected dozens, the more than fifty culturally and linguistically distinct groups who survived the immediate destruction of so many others. *Genocide is intended rather to signify a coordinated plan of different actions aiming at the destruction of essential foundations of the life of national groups.* The Indian Act followed the tribal customs of lands distant and unhappy, forcibly imposed European governance structures on Indigenous communities, forbade women from tribal politics, rendered religious ceremony and collective cultural gatherings illegal. *The objectives of such a plan would be disintegration of the political and social institutions.*

My heart breaks for these colonizers — these lonely, wandering children, who were taught by other lonely, wandering children to look at two like kinds and see only the minor differences. They were people, sure — with agency, like we all are — but also victims of circumstance. Like we all are. Survivors, themselves, of hundreds of years of murder and persecution, from and against nearly identical groups of people worshipping the same God, from nearly indistinguishable holy places. I am getting to the roses. Hold on.

As the sun wound around the earth in 1894, great-grandfather's twentieth year, the last legal sun dance was held. In 1914, it became illegal to dance off-reserve. Dancing was banned outright, for Indians, in 1925. Three years after that Adolf Hitler clucked approvingly at the great rearrangement of the North American continent. My grandmother was born the next year. *The objectives of a plan of genocide would be disintegration of culture, language, national feelings, religion.*

Duncan Campbell Scott, a civil servant working to expand the residential school system, wrote, "I want to get rid of the Indian problem.... Our objective is to continue until there is not a single Indian in Canada that has not been absorbed into the body politic and there is no Indian question, and no Indian department, that is the whole object of this Bill." It's in my best interest to forgive him.

Scott was born in 1862 in Ottawa to wandering children. He was a poet and he played the piano. I am a poet. I play the piano. He and I had a lot in common, probably. He wanted to be a doctor. He normalized what was demonstrated to him as normal. What is the point of a quarrel with a man who had been dead twelve years when my father was born? *The objectives of a plan of genocide is the destruction of the personal security, liberty, health, dignity, and even the lives of the individuals belonging to such groups.* We know the names of 2,800 children who died inside the schools. Imagine, surviving a mortality event like the great dying that settled North America, only to have your great-great-grand babies snuffed out in a school with a slur for a name. How many prayers did those babies send up to God? How many more ugly parking lots to be dug up where those schools were torn down, to find what's left of the ones who went uncounted? How many more graves, hidden without the dignity of names, or numbers, or red sheets in ceremony?

I don't think Scott actually wanted the *children to die*, he just wanted the *Indian problem* to go away. Canada's colonial history has made a lot of the moment when the body count of European invasion and occupation stopped being the result of a gleeful hack and slash and became the result of a lot of paperwork, and hand-wringing, and convenient negligence. *Generally speaking, genocide does not necessarily mean the immediate destruction of a nation.* Scott just wanted the *Indian problem* gone, absorbed, and normalized: *a coordinated plan of different actions with the aim of annihilating the groups themselves.*

There's an argumentative benefit to defining something in writing — you have parameters, then, to prove its negation. An Indian was "any male person of Indian blood reputed to belong to a particular band," as well as his children and wife. The negation of the Indian problem was achieved through *enfranchisement*, when that Indian graduated university, became a minister, became a doctor, or became a lawyer. The negation of an Indian daughter was marrying a non-status person. This was my grandmother's negation. Only a few years before she had her status stripped for marrying my grandfather, Raphael Lemkin died in poverty, convinced his work on preventing genocide had been a failure. He died in New York City. Lenape territory.

My grandfather washed up in Newfoundland in 1949. He had left Scotland, a windswept rock in the ocean, and stepped sea-beaten and nauseous into the port of St. John's. He was horrified to find another windswept rock, in the same ocean.

"If this is Canada," he muttered, in his thick Highland drawl, "then I'm going back."

When he got to Halifax he relaxed, a little. He got on another train, to Montreal — drawn there like it was a shimmering light. In Montreal, his proficiency on the war pipes would lead to his being invited to a party at the Douglas hospital to fill in for a bagpiper with the flu. There, I know he met a dark-haired psychiatric nurse-in-training named Marie Pictou, and they'd marry, and they would have children, among them my father. Now, we're getting to the roses: when my grandmother married my grandfather, she was *enfranchised* and lost her status. My grandfather didn't know she was an Indian until they'd been married for eight years. When my father was born in 1960, he was not born as a status Indian. The next year, in 1961, status Indians were granted the right to vote.

Amendments to the Indian Act made in 1951 brought the sun dance and the potlatch back but also laid down the laws that led to twenty thousand Indigenous children being placed with non-Indigenous families with no training, no access to cultural resources, in what's become known as the Sixties Scoop. *Our objective is to continue until there is not a single Indian in Canada that has not been absorbed into the body politic.*

The objectives of a plan of genocide would be the destruction of culture, language, national feelings, religion.

Further reform in 1985 sought to identify Native women by something other than their marriage. My father was twenty-five. My brother was three. My grandmother had her status reinstated. By extension, so did my father. I was born at home in Toronto in 1992. In 1996, when I was four years old, the Gordon's Indian Residential School ceased operation in Punnichy, Saskatchewan, 165 years after the Mohawk Institute started taking the first Indian children as boarding pupils. It was the last fully funded federal residential school. *Generally speaking, genocide does not necessarily mean the immediate destruction of a nation.*

The process of applying for my own status documents started. One of the benefits for Status Mi'kmaw in my ancestral band is a stipend for the funding of post-secondary education, now without the penalty of negation. I was so sad that day, in 2011. Then, my dad walked in the door to my work with his arms full of roses. My whole future pressed its head out of the ground, like a living thing budding after a long winter.

After my shift at Uncommon Grounds, when my father gave me the roses, I went back to the apartment I shared with Matilda and I poured some tap water into a big pickle jar. I set my roses on my coffee table and I sat down on the couch. I looked at my phone and I read the news. I had a sense I was at the beginning of something, but I didn't really want to think about it.

The news told me that unrest was mounting in Quebec: thousands of students were on strike, blocking trains, shutting down major streets, demanding not just an end to tuition hikes, but completely free post-secondary education for all. I thought about some different timeline, with a different version of me who was not protected by treaty, different versions of me not fought for by my father and my grandmother before him, the two of them thorough and passionate and determined. I thought about everyone I had so much in common with: the children blocking trains and the children writing policy and the children who sat around talking about the doing of things and then not doing them. I thought about how I should try doing something different if I want something to change.

"Train in Vain (Stand by Me)" by the Clash.

February 2012. Halifax.

This new boy was fine.

He was almost a decade my senior, with a grown-up job in animation and an apartment in the outer reaches of Dartmouth. I couldn't fall in love with someone who didn't live in one of the hip parts of the downtown Halifax core, so I was safe. There would be no repeats of the mistakes I'd made with Tim. I flounced into the spice-thickened air of the Indian restaurant with my comic book–printed dress and my date night makeup. He was already there — I was late — and he was doodling idly in a sketchbook propped on the nice white tablecloth. When I arrived, he looked like something terrible had happened — like my hair was on fire, or I was his cousin.

"Sorry I'm late," I cooed over the Bollywood soundtrack, trying to be charming. His face was still fixed in terror. "Are you okay? What's wrong?"

"Oh! Oh, it's just, I, uh —" He laughed, nervously, then pushed his glasses up his nose, then laughed again. "It's, uh. Um, it's just. It's — it's, uh …"

This continued for quite some time. It continued for so long that my happy-surprised-concerned expression started to cramp. *Spit it out, you nerd.*

"I just like your dress."

Oh, he thinks I'm hot, I thought. I smiled, girlishly, then sat down. *Good.*

"I'm Tara," I said.

"Sandy."

I met Sandy on the internet. I was just looking for something to pass the time. My foray into internet dating had, up until this point, been depressing — my standards were *not* high, I just had a few simple guidelines: I needed the person to be decently fun to get along with. I needed him to be good-looking enough that sex was possible. No punks.

My time-waster needed to be a man — this was me being pickier than I normally was. Thinking about dating men at all made me break into cold sweats after the one-night stand that had sent me to the emergency room over the summer. I knew myself well enough to know that an attraction to men was an inherent part of my identity and personality. The extent to which *my feelings about men were complicated* was already, honestly, boring me. I was ready to sort through this trauma, and the internet offered me a generous sampling menu of potential partners to join me on my self-directed therapy.

It was imperative that I not develop even a modicum of feelings for this man: I had just gotten an acceptance to Concordia University, in Montreal. Matilda and I were going to spend the

summer in Europe, and then we were going to move together. I had
a savings account, which was growing every day. I'd gotten a credit
card. I was stubbornly determined to leave the city undamaged, and
unattached. I was going to enter the new phase of my life *a modern
woman*: intellectual, independent, and sexually liberated.

Digitally, Sandy appeared to be the cream of the crop. He was
not someone I recognized from the tiny, incestuous subcultures
I ran in, but he had alternative leanings — he listed punk music
and metal shows among his interests on the dating site, along with
various visual arts, but he dressed like an adult and had a job. He
had gotten points for suggesting an actual restaurant for our first
date and additional points for the fact that it wasn't a major chain
— I was still salty over wasted time with an economics major and
a Boston Pizza. I liked that he was an artist, and that he wrote me
messages in full, funny, grammatically correct sentences. Across
the dinner table, he was definitely handsome enough — he was
tall and well-muscled and slender. He had reddish hair and a full
beard that was still flattering, despite being styled into the weird
pointy end that was common amongst *Dungeons and Dragons* en-
thusiasts and metalheads. His glasses were so thick they shrunk
the appearance of his eyes. He took them off to clean them when
he was nervous, which was all the time. When he did that, his eyes
were bright blue — wide, and innocent, and marvelling, and much
too large for his face. Like a cartoon.

"Anyway, yeah, buses, you know!" I said, ending a long-winded
diatribe explaining my lateness, all of which was a lie — I had
smoked a bunch of weed and spent too long on my makeup. Sandy
laughed nervously again, but then sat in complete silence. He opened
his mouth, as if to speak, but then he didn't. I watched, amazed,
as he panicked. He started twitching, his eyes darting around the

room. I should have stepped in — out of pity, or mercy — but I was curious about how long this would go on.

It went on for *a while*. He opened and closed his mouth, fiddled with the linen napkin — first absently, then somewhat violently, knocking his cutlery against his water glass. The longer I let the silence go on, the more he twitched. He was aware he was being weird and could do nothing to stop it. When he could no longer delude himself about this behaviour being normal, he forced himself to speak — and only a small fraction of what he said had any semantic content. His sentences floated in a sea of *erm*s and *uh*s and *aah*s while he thought, far too hard, about what to say next.

"So, uh. Do, uh. Do you. Do, uh, you, uh … do you … do you, uh. Uh. Do you, uh, go … erm, to … do you … to Dalhousie?" As he said it, he slowly collapsed — like the matter of his body was being sucked into the gravitational centre of his shame.

I squinted, staring at him hard. His cheeks were flushed pink in two perfect circles. Was it some kind of speech impediment, or was he just afraid of me? Neither was a deal breaker — I just had to know which one I was dealing with.

"No," I said, syrupy with sweetness. "No, I work at a coffee shop. My turn to ask a question now: What are your top five favourite movies?"

The shame-collapse immediately reversed. He didn't think about his answer, he just sat up bolt-straight and said, "Great question. *The Treasure of the Sierra Madre* is a masterwork of cinema. That's on there, for sure."

Bingo. "I've never seen it."

"I have the special edition on DVD. We can watch it. Okay, next, I have to put a Star Wars film in there, so *The Empire Strikes Back*, definitely. And then I'll say *The Good, the Bad and the Ugly*, *Evil Dead II*, and then …" He took a sip of his Cobra beer, staring off at nothing in the distance behind my head. "Then there's that tricky fifth one."

He did not have a speech impediment, he was just a nerd, and *terrified* of me.

"I've got a sci-fi, an action movie, those cowboy movies I like … no comedies, I guess, which is not accurate to my tastes. I watch a lot of comedies. I've watched *Jurassic Park* probably more times than any other movie, but is it *a favourite*, per se?" he asked, philosophically. "Okay, no, yeah, *Jurassic Park*. There we go, five." As if waking up from a dream, he shook his head, and then blinked. "Do. Do, uh." He started to collapse again. "Do … do you, uh, live … uh …"

"I live in the north end with my friend Matilda," I said, quickly, before I lost him. "Ask me another question, but make it more stupid."

The waiter arrived, to take our order.

"How do you feel about spice levels?" he asked me.

"Oh," I said, "I'm a masochist."

He laughed and then turned to the waiter. "Hi, can we get naan, rice, papadam, a mango lassi for the lady — and the three spiciest things you have?"

I sat back in my chair and swigged my beer. Yes. This one would do nicely.

I waited a whole three dates to sleep with him, which was the picture of prudence and chastity for nineteen-year-old me. I *meant* to wait longer, but our third date was to an open mic and Tim was there.

I hadn't seen Tim, or spoken to him, since that night he had a panic attack. I was extremely frustrated and pissed off to see that he looked good — even more so when I saw he also had a girl with him.

With Sandy next to me, I'd tried my best not to stare at Tim and this mystery girl. They were just sitting together, across the room — and Tim had lots of friends who were girls, so maybe it was nothing. I drank my drinks too fast and tried to give my date the attention he deserved. *Tim was obsessed with me,* I thought. *There was no way he's moved on this fast, or at all — if I'm not over it, he sure as shit is not.* But then I looked up, stole another glance over, and I saw Tim has his arm around this girl's shoulders. I saw him whisper in the ear of this girl, who was pixie-small, and laughing, and blond, and — worst of all — *thin,* and I knew they were together and it was the real deal. I knew I had to do something drastic.

"I wanna play," I slurred to Sandy, now very drunk, as I made a stumbling exit from the booth where we were sitting. I staggered to the bar, took several more shots, and then went to the stage.

I don't exactly remember how sign ups worked, or how quickly I got on there. Let's say I got on right away. I know I took a borrowed acoustic and strummed up a song I'd been working on since my earliest, most desperately horny years — when I came into slippery, fretful pubescence among the cow patties and hay bales and tween farmhands of rural Ontario — an angry, screamy acoustic cover of "Train in Vain (Stand by Me)" by the Clash.

It was the final act in the distinguished drama of Tim and Tara. I raged, in Joe Strummer's voice, about my job and my apartment and the other poverty-stricken humiliations of youth, all of which would be rendered fair if only Tim would bless me with his love. It was a completely genuine swan song, my bitter reputation for a cruel *you* who could not stand by me — whose love I still felt like I deserved, I still felt was my rightful property, still felt was the only fair consolation for a childhood spent begging a God who never answered and an adolescence spent twitching and swollen with the kind of want that only grows where needs are never met.

In the shadows, Sandy was standing, unbuttoning his blazer, trying to look natural, while making sure he was at the perfect angle for me to get a good look at the shirt under his jacket — which was faded, and vintage, but where I could see *The Clash* still written across the front, thirty-odd years after it was printed. Sandy and his T-shirt got my attention — like a signal, or a symptom.

When I finished my song, my lost love still had his face nestled squarely in the thin shoulder of another woman. I claimed my consolation prize. Begrudgingly, I welcomed the future.

"Let's go back to my place," I said to Sandy, and we did.

On the cold walk there, I asked him another round of the never-ending litany of questions that kept him strong and upright.

"How many siblings do you have?" I asked.

"Two brothers and a sister." At twenty-eight, he was the oldest.

He experimented with asking me questions: "What's a good movie memory you have from when you were a kid?"

"Watching *The Princess Bride* and seeing my mother nearly die of laughter at the wedding scene where the priest keeps saying 'Mawwiage.'"

"What is something about a movie you like that always came across as a plot hole?" he asked.

"When I first saw *Ghostbusters* as a kid, it seemed absurd that Zuul, the demon, was repeatedly referred to as looking like a dog. We had a terrier, Gertie, and she had a moustache and baby eyes and a body like an ottoman. Zuul looked nothing like any dog I had ever seen."

"I think that's the joke."

"That's what my dad said, but I replied, at the time, that the gap between reference and subject was too large and, as such, forced the viewer to abdicate from the agreement of suspended disbelief — but, you know, I said it more the way a six-year-old would say that. What is your favourite comfort food?"

"Tacos."

"Who was the first person you knew who died?"

"My friend Rosemary had an aneurysm. Then my train was so late I missed the wake."

It was a good answer, so I let it ring out into the night for a little bit. We walked in silence, until I asked, "Do you have any secrets?"

We were outside my apartment. He looked genuinely thoughtful before he said, "I don't think so."

I unlocked my door. "Good."

On my bare mattress, floating in my mess, he held my hips in his hands. Breathless, he said, "I thought of my secret."

Fearing the worst, on top of him, I stopped moving. "What? What is it?"

He hesitated, then said, "I've never done this before."

"Oh, baby," I said. I couldn't help myself. I doubled over and kissed him on the mouth. "Baby," I said again. "You shoulda told me. I woulda lit a candle, or something."

It was three in the morning when I saw the headlights of the cab pulling down Agricola Street. Sandy had me pushed against the side of my apartment building, kissing my neck. I was giggling. I was happy.

"Your cab's here," I said into the hair above his ear.

"That's stupid," he said into my skin, his hands grasping at my thighs.

I let out a peal of manic giggles. "You have to go," I said, as the cab slowed to a stop in front of my door. "I have work in the morning," I said. Something about him made me want to be good — something about him made me know I was allowed to start now. It wasn't too late. He sighed and he kissed me on the mouth. It was February, and cold.

I walked him the few steps to the cab. "I'm moving away in three months," I said, as he opened the door.

"Three months?" he replied. He was quiet for a second, and then said, "I can work with that."

I kissed him, and then he climbed into the back seat of the cab. "I'm going to study philosophy and write poetry and join the revolution," I explained. I crossed my arms over my chest. I wasn't wearing a jacket. The Atlantic wind whipped down Agricola Street, whistling into my bones, chilling me from the inside out. I was so cold but I needed to make sure he understood. "So, don't fall in love with me, okay?"

He smiled, said okay, closed the door, and drove away.

"If Love Is a Red Dress (Hang Me in Rags)" by Maria McKee.

March 2012. Halifax.

Something was wrong with Matilda.

It wasn't just that she had up and quit her job at Uncommon Grounds — and so soon to our European departure date. It wasn't even just the drinking, or the drugs — those were more or less par for the course with her. She had almost completely given up on sleeping in her bedroom, opting instead to spread out on the couch in our living room — it was closer to the food, and the bathroom, where she could smoke. Her life had become a circuit of couch, bathroom cigarette, kitchen for more beer, and back to the couch for bong hit after bong hit after bong hit. None of that was really what worried me.

The thing that I actually found most disturbing was that she had downloaded *Pulp Fiction* and was watching it more or less on repeat. I'd wake up for my shift in the late morning and find her nursing a cup of cold coffee and a day-old Uncommon Grounds wrap or sandwich, clouded in the smoke of several bong hits, watching *Pulp Fiction*. On the screen, our heroes would be up to some hijinks involving anal rape or armed robbery. She would acknowledge me, or she wouldn't, chewing her sandwich or grinding her pot and loading her bowl to smoke. I'd leave her there, watching *Pulp Fiction*, and come back ten hours later to find her still there, still watching *Pulp Fiction*, curled around her bong like she was clinging to a life raft. She did this for days, then weeks, as winter turned into spring.

"Are we going to have enough money?" I asked. "You know, for Europe?"

"Of course, Tara," she reassured me. "That's so silly. Don't even worry about it. I have so much money. I just need a break." Then she'd press play on *Pulp Fiction*, and I'd go to work. I believed her. I always did.

Matilda was small and feminine and beautiful. Her dark-blond hair fell down her back in a long braid, the very end dyed blue like an in-use paintbrush. In high school, when I met her, she was an anachronistic dresser: she wore lace blouses and maxi skirts and lace-up heeled boots, like a distinguished lady in an old movie. She wore tiny black miniskirts and huge men's cardigans. I couldn't stop looking at her. Sometimes, when she got up, there was a few pieces of glitter where she had been — a bread crumb trail of tiny stars and moons.

When she'd taken a shining to me, I took it very seriously, like it was a kind of education. She texted me coordinates, and I came with offerings: cigarettes and dark rum, tea and red wine and marijuana. When I arrived, she would be there, with Kate — her twin moon, her best friend. They were artists, both of them — painters and musicians and poets. The art I admired most was the way they moved through the world. I didn't feel like I knew how to be a girl — I knew I was one, but I felt like a cat who had been raised by dogs and then couldn't stop panting and barking. I was a woman *culturally*, but I didn't *practise*. I didn't know how. No one had taught me. I watched Matilda and Kate, in all their grace and beauty, and I tried to mimic. I tried to understand.

Matilda was my first favourite poet. Once, after a devastating breakup, she had woken up at her ex's house and gone to their dresser to write:

> *soon, you'll wake up*
> *and I'll have to leave*
> *and nothing will be different.*

I was awestruck. Matilda wasn't just my friend — and my colleague, and my roommate — I genuinely believed she was a wise woman.

So, I believed Matilda when she said it would be okay, as the days passed, and she watched *Pulp Fiction*. I believed her when she stopped cooking for herself and the takeout containers piled up around her. I even believed her when she stopped commenting on our *travel plan*: the British Isles, then France, Germany, Spain, and the Netherlands. The Czech Republic. A quick bit down into Croatia, maybe, then back around through Italy, back to Spain, and home again. Is it too much? Matilda? Fuck, haven't we watched that movie enough?

When the birds started to announce the dawn chorus and spring warmed its way across the Maritime coast, she announced that she had no intention of leaving Halifax. She had no intention of going to Europe or Montreal. She was going to stay there — right there, probably, on that very couch.

"But I dropped out of school," I said, aghast. "I've been saving all of this money."

"We'll still go, I just can't go now."

"How do I know you won't bail the next time, too?"

"Tara, you can't go alone, and I'm not going, so get over it."

I would hear this a lot, in the following weeks. My friends: *It's too bad, but you know, Matilda's fickle. And, you know, you can't go alone.* At work: *I know you were excited, but my buddy knew a woman who went backpacking in Europe alone, and her parents had her FedExed back to them in three separate bags.* The parents of my high school classmates who came in to order coffee cooed, *Oh, your friend isn't going anymore? She's sick? Well, that's too bad, you know. Because you can't go alone. Your dad would never let you.*

My parents had me over for dinner and I complained the whole time. "It just sucks," I said, pushing my pasta around. "Because I can't go alone."

"Of course you can," he said, without looking up from grating Parmesan.

I tested the waters: "You'd, like, *let me* do that?"

He scoffed, like that was ridiculous. "Tara, you'll be twenty years old in a few days. You work full-time and you live on your own. You're an adult," he said. "Obviously, I'm always here for you, but your victories and your mistakes belong to you and they have since the moment you turned eighteen. You can do whatever you want."

"Lots of women backpack alone," said Brooke, my stepmother. "You could get murdered in Paris or murdered here, you know," she said, pragmatically. She spiralled the pasta around her fork. "There are risks to everything."

As serious as if he was explaining the basics of economics, or the laws of physics, or our family history, or any other key to my future, my dad said, "Risk is the only way to have an interesting life."

I smiled. Fuck everyone. I was going to Europe.

April 2012. Montreal.

"Lots of natural light," said the globular, grey man — my prospective landlord. My dad had taken me along for a work trip to Montreal. He figured we should go there in person before my move, to look at apartments. My dad, the musician, could hop two provinces as casually as if he was running an errand. He didn't look like a man who had just driven for two days from the North End of Halifax to Outremont. He was bright-eyed and serious, illuminated in the powder blue and thin honey gold of the early spring light, from his dark hair to his nice Italian boots.

"And the bus passes just by here, yes?" my father said, examining, and walking, his boots echoing in the high ceilings of the empty room. The walls were so fresh with white paint that they glowed. On the other side of the long rectangle of an apartment, away from the windows, I was looking hard into the shadowy bathroom.

"*Comment?*" asked the landlord, and my dad shook his head and smiled apologetically.

"*Ben, j'ai commender s'il'ya un route d'autobus très proche, en fait?*" repeated my dad, in his thick Montreal East End accent.

"*Ah, t'es Montréalais,*" said the landlord, visibly relieved.

"*Oui. Anjou,*" said my dad, naming his childhood neighbourhood. He listened to the landlord, who excitedly professed the luxuries of the local bus lines, in French, while I flipped on the light in the bathroom.

My anguish over Tim's departure from my life had dulled to a quiet sort of ache, soothed by the balm of Sandy's ample attention. I was mad at everyone, but mostly at Matilda. I'd been able to use my heartbreak and anger to trigger another episode of crashdieting, and I was delighted — I could fit into clothes at American Apparel now. I stood, feeling fabulous and hungry, in my sheer black tights and my striped bodysuit, my gut only slight pinched by the top of my ultra-high-waisted jean shorts, examining the tiny bathroom — a half-sink practically on top of the toilet and a shower with a shallow basin that was only *designed to look* like a bathtub. That simply would not do. Since I was *thin now* — and likely to only ever get thinner, and never gain the weight back ever, not this time, *goddamn it* — I needed a space to take lots of long, luxurious baths. I was fairly certain that this was a thing thin girls did.

"And it's six-fifty, right?" I called out, in English, to the two men in what could have been my room.

"*Oui*," said the landlord. Then, in English: "Plus hydro and gas."

I pursed my lips. It was a lot to pay to not be able to take a bath.

The Lincoln Avenue apartment had a cracked marble floor in the foyer. The wood of the railing on the grand curving staircase had been lacquered and re-lacquered so many times it looked like it had turned to stone. The tenant, Katherine, emerged out of the fourth-floor walk-up from a door set into brand-new drywall. She invited us in and explained the specifics of the lease transfer: *Once you sign the paper, it's yours, I'm leaving in May, the lease renews in July, and you can move in any time after May 1 ...*

Everything in the apartment was in miniature, to accommodate the smallness of the space — it was a slip of a thing, the result of one larger apartment being divided up into several smaller ones. It ran in one narrow line, less than the width of a train car, from the apartment door to a fire escape fed by a window so small it would never have saved me — I never would have made it out, even now that I was thin. I beelined for the bathroom as soon as we got inside. The bathroom door was original — heavy wood and set into an ancient and many-lacquered moulding. There was a wisdom to the door — real personality. I pushed it open, and inside was the original cracked marble and black tile floor, and a claw-foot tub, and a wide open mirror to gaze at myself. The unit Katherine was showing me had gotten the original bathroom in the split that had divvied up the place. It looked as grand as a ballroom.

"The rent is four hundred dollars," Katherine explained. "Everything included."

I heard my dad whistle, unable to tamp down his excitement.

"It's small, but I love it here — it's right by the metro, there's so much good food around, dozens of grocery stores …"

"And location, location, location," said my dad's voice. It was a two-minute walk from school. My monthly stipend, as an Indigenous student, was nine hundred dollars, so I'd have money left over for booze and food and my cellphone — maybe even transportation, or American Apparel. I could fill this bathroom with candles and be thin and naked and beautiful.

I told Katherine I'd be running off to Europe, and that I'd be heading straight for the city for the first of August, so she could leave all of her stuff until then, if she wanted. I signed the lease transfer papers right away, and paid the rent for the whole summer. It was official, now: I was going to go back to Halifax, tie up a few loose ends, sell off the rest of my old stuff, ship a few boxes and pieces of furniture to Montreal, and then I was leaving Halifax — forever, maybe.

"The Ruins"
by Max Steiner.

Later in April 2012. Halifax.

I was angry at Sandy, but I didn't know why. *The Treasure of the Sierra Madre* was playing on his computer. He'd made me dinner, and our dirty dishes were piled on the floor. I think part of me was angry because I'd made some crack about a punk house and he'd let it slip that half of the residents used to be his roommates — he *was* a punk, just an old one. He had *broken* one of my *two firm rules*: no punks, no falling in love.

His black rescue cat, Hexadecimal, was perched on his desk, next to his computer, beaming her green eyes into me with unadulterated hatred. She swished her tail back and forth. She didn't trust me. I guess she didn't really have a reason to.

Sandy and I were watching *The Treasure of the Sierra Madre*. Humphrey Bogart, as Fred C. Dobbs, was trying to justify the theft of his comrade's gold. I wanted to talk to Sandy. I learned forward to pause the movie, but when I did, Hex the cat hissed and swiped hard at my hand.

"Ow!" I barked. "Fucking — Hex, ow."

"Hex, buddy," said Sandy. At her name out of his mouth, she sweetened — stretched, and pawed her feet forwards. He scratched her behind her ears, and she purred loudly, arching into him in pleasure. Hex the cat had been a reject from two homes — cast out for extreme acts of aggression and violence and being an asshole — before Sandy had taken her. Where she seemed to genuinely enjoy causing pain and misery in all other living creatures, she loved Sandy — she curled up with him at night to sleep and let him pick her up. When he was gone for too many hours in a row, she sat on his bed, shaking and shedding, until he came home. She woke up every morning to wreak havoc. Sandy loved her anyway.

Hex and I didn't get along. She started it. In the movie, Dobbs was sitting by the fire with a man named Bob Curtin. Dobbs was staring, unblinking, while Curtin tried to convince the paranoid Dobbs that he wasn't a threat.

I was hurt from Hex's swipe — but more emotionally hurt than physically. I sat back on his bed and crossed my arms, pouting like a child.

"What is it?" Sandy asked. "Baby, what is it?"

I *loved* that he called me "baby" and I *hated* how much I loved it.

"I like you," I said, angry.

He laughed. "I like you, too," he said. God, he was cute. He wasn't stumble-muttering anymore. When we could pry our hands off of each other, we talked art and music and movies. He had diverse, surprising, well-justified tastes — Richard Pryor and *X-Men* and *The Magic School Bus*, *Gargoyles* and N.W.A. and Joni Mitchell's *Blue*.

"No," I said, louder. I was really mad now. "No, like — like, I *really, really* like you."

"I *really like you*, too."

I fixed him with a withering stare.

"How much?"

His smile faded. He understood. We sat in silence, looking at each other. On the screen, Fred Dobbs had sunk into madness from paranoia and greed. He said, *I bet you a hundred and five thousand dollars you fall asleep before I do.*

"I think I love you," Sandy said.

Tears blurred my vision of him.

"Aren't you going to ask me to stay?" I asked.

He broke eye contact and made a small, bitter laugh — barely audible, and out his nose. He pushed his glasses back up against his face. He set his mouth in a hard line.

"Of course not, Tara," he said, looking at me again. "You need to go to school."

"Enough to Be on Your Way" by James Taylor.

May 2012. North of Milngavie, Scotland.

"Where're ye goin'?" rattled the voice of the man in front of me. He had stopped to watch me, concerned.

Where I was going was down the rocky dirt road of the West Highland Way, very slowly, carrying my backpack with its hundreds of straps. The backpack easily weighed sixty pounds. I creaked under its weight, laboured beneath it. I huffed, puffed, stumbled to the side to catch myself when I was knocked off balance and almost dragged down by its magnitude.

The Scotsman in his shirt jacket and slacks had his hands in his pockets, his clothes red and brown and stark against the bright green grass and low shrubbing trees. Above him, the sky was blue after a week of rain, thick with globs of fat cloud. If the Scotsman carried anything, I couldn't see it. He was unencumbered, so quiet a long-eared jackrabbit hopped up almost to his ankles before noticing him and bolting away. His only burden was his concern for me.

"I'm hiking the Way," I said, squinting against the early sun so hard I had to screw my whole face up. I had a laptop, a party dress, and ten books in my backpack, but I didn't have any sunglasses. It would have been better to clear some of it out — I'd had to buy some camping gear and, out of space, the tent and the sleeping bag were lashed to the outside of my pack with bungee cords, like bulbous tumours. The bag was twice as wide as me, sticking two feet over my head — soft detritus like underwear and sweaters and the arm and face of my teddy bear straining out of every available orifice. It would have been better to abandon some of it, but I *needed* all of it, and while I had blood relatives in Scotland, I didn't *know* any of them, so I was hiking the Way anyway — burdened down with pounds and pounds of things I could not let go of.

The Scotsman shook his head, then continued past me — light, and almost impossibly quick. "Not with all tha', yer not," he said. "What's yer name, darlin'?"

"Tara McGowan-Ross," I said.

He laughed.

"Good Scottish name," he proclaimed, trudging along past me — deciding I was fine, or giving up on me. As he passed, he pointed at my teddy bear. "At least make him help."

June 2012. Paris, France.

The whistle was so sharp it wrenched me from where I was nestled into my paper map, trying to get my bearings. I looked up and across the street, to the man there, leaning on a bike rack and staring in my direction. I looked behind me, but there was nobody. I looked back and he was laughing, pointing at me. He started to clap his hands.

To my shock, more men stopped walking to work or their errands to join the whistling man — also whistling, clapping their hands, knocking the first man on the back like he had accomplished something noteworthy by discovering me. The shock wearing off, I tucked my hair behind my ears with one hand, flapping my hand at them in a false-modest *go away* gesture, which just made them cheer and clap and whistle louder. I laughed — out of nervousness and genuine delight. I threw my leg over my bike. I cycled away.

I knew all women got catcalled in Paris, but my shorts had recently started feeling tight — which had made my bulimic mind so uneasy that I was sincerely relieved to still be recognized as a woman. I was relieved the same way I had been when I'd politely declined the invitation of a handsome Italian to have sex in an Irish hostel bathroom, or when Sandy and I had broken down and said nasty things in hushed tones over a Skype connection. There were still men who wanted to fuck me. And thank God for that. Thank God.

Sometime in the heat of the afternoon, the effects of the bottle of rosé I'd smuggled into Montmartre cemetery began to make themselves known. I had been admiring the grave of Alexandre Dumas, and I poured the last of my wine out onto it from the Sprite can I'd emptied for this purpose.

"Pour one out for you, homie," I slurred, and saluted the grave before stumbling away and out of the cemetery to unlock my bike.

With the bike in one hand, I climbed the hill toward the Sacré-Coeur Basilica — wandering, rubbernecking, drunk. Looking for something. At the top of the hill, I looked out and saw the huddled centre of the ancient city. I thought about how Dumas, Foucault, Sontag, and Baldwin were all dead. I thought that maybe what I was searching for didn't exist anymore.

I found another cemetery — small, full of trees, with young families and laughing babies relaxing among the headstones of the departed. I let my bike fall over onto the ground between two headstones. I put down my purse in the grass, lay my own body down, tucked my bag into the crook between my hip and my ribs, for safekeeping. I looped one arm through the body of the bike, clasped my hands together over the hard-working button of my shorts, and relaxed into the soft earth. In the park, a small blond baby reached his fat fingers to his father's face. His young mother laughed in her T-shirt and jeans, took a drag of her cigarette, watched her partner's face brighten as his baby ran his fingers over his nose and his mouth. My eyes fluttered closed, and I thought of my father — as he was when I was young, with his long Native hair and Scottish freckles and his Anjou accent. I fell asleep, and I dreamed of men and the plans they make.

When I woke up, there was someone near me. I turned abruptly to face what I assumed would be a pickpocket, suddenly alert and awake and ready to defend my purse, despite the throb of a hangover between my temples. Laying next to me, on his side, one hand on his hip and one under his head, was a man. At the sight of me, he smiled, proud of himself.

"*Bonjour,*" he said, with a wiggle of his eyebrows.

June 2012. Amsterdam, Netherlands.

"I can't send you a lot," said my dad. "But I can lend you a few hundred dollars to change your ticket and survive until it leaves."

Relief started to pool through me. I was down to my last fifty euros. I blamed Edinburgh, Paris, and now Amsterdam — much more expensive than any of the other places I'd been to. The money would be enough to change the plane ticket, hide out in a hostel until my departure date somewhere cheaper than *fucking Amsterdam* — Prague, maybe. The South of France. Maybe back in Spain — Spain had been cheap, and hot, and nice. Once I got home, the apartment in Montreal was paid for, so it was just a matter of holding out until then, really. My father was saving my life again. At least he wasn't mad.

"I'll pay you back, I promise."

"I know," he said, nodding, and smiling. "Why are you crying?"

"Because I'm so ashamed," I said, sobbing so loudly that I could see people looking up from their computers out of the corner of my eye. "I saved for so long." A whole year of double shifts, weekend shifts, careful budgeting, my blooming savings account. Gone in six weeks, on a Eurail Pass and a plane ticket, and then on one-euro wine bottles and nibbling-bedbug hostels and late-night cab rides with dishonest drivers. "I don't know how it happened." I did know — slowly, and then all at once.

"Baby," said my dad, shaking his head. "Baby, you're in western Europe. Do you think you are the first twenty-year-old person in history to have run out of money in western Europe?"

"I've done it!" yelled my stepmother from somewhere behind him on the call. I laughed.

My dad laughed, too, beaming warmly at me over the Skype connection. Then his smile fell a bit, and he got another far-off look. "If I'm being honest," he said, "so have I."

July 2012. Madrid, Spain.

"So there are six of you?" I asked. It was technically a question for the three of them who were crowding the balcony with me in downtown Madrid's second-cheapest hostel — but mostly it was a question for the red-headed rugby player I was eye-fucking.

"Yeah," he said, his accent gliding across the roof of his mouth: *Yee.* "But Australia's really hard and expensive to leave, so you have to make a whole thing of it."

"It's not just the plane ticket," said the redhead's equally cute dark-haired brother. He had his arm around his fiancée's shoulders. "I mean, the continent is covered in shit that wants to kill you."

"There were ten of us, when we left," said the fiancée — a pretty blond who had been generous with her tequila. "Four of them got eaten by sharks, though, while we were trying to leave."

Our laughter cascaded off of the balcony and down into the narrow cobbled street below. It echoed off of the wall of the apartments across from us, with their twin balconies holding smoking *Madrileños* and flapping white linens on laundry lines. Our laughter went with the hot dark-haired one and his hot girlfriend off of the balcony and stayed with me and the redhead as we loitered there and moved closer to each other in the hot Spanish air, weaved our fingers together, checked to make sure the room was empty.

I woke up at 4:00 a.m. and climbed naked down the steel ladder and into the room full of sleeping people. I found my shorts but could not immediately locate my underwear, and abandoned it. I rescued my shirt, bra, and purse off the ground. I went to my room, in another part of the hostel, where my backpack was laying on my lower bunk, packed. I tightened the straps, hauled it on, and went to check out. It would have been nice to say goodbye to the generous, good-looking Australians, but I had a plane to catch. I was headed home.

July 2012. Montreal, Canada.

"*Pardon*," I said to the bus driver, and to the people around me, and, to a certain extent, to the universe, while barely managing to hoist my overstuffed trekking backpack onto the city bus. I kept one hand on it performatively. I knew that it was too large and too annoying of a piece of equipment to be bringing with me on public transit, and I wanted everyone to see me at least trying to contain it as I reached deep into my filthy black shorts to find my bus pass. That took me too long. "*Pardon*," I said again.

By the time I scanned my bus pass, I could feel the annoyance of the driver and the long line of passengers behind me pressing against my skin like a hot wind. "*Pardon*," I said, to no one and to everyone, as I turned down the narrow city bus, using both of my arms to prop up my backpack slightly on my thighs. I just sort of half-walked, half-kicked it back and forth as I hobbled down toward the skeletal luggage carriage, the straps of the backpack making a percussive beat — deafening and rhythmless — as I did so.

The luggage carriage was metal and welded to one side of the bus. It secured the bags of city-bound travellers by way of a series of elastic straps. The other passengers' luggage was set up neatly — politely pushed into the back corner to make it easier for other people to put in their own stuff. My backpack had so many *straps*. Despite having stared at them every day for two months, throughout my escapades in Europe, I had no idea what most of them were for, except maybe to get caught on things like door frames or subway turnstiles, or in the elastic borders of this luggage prison.

As I did my best to load my backpack into this contraption, seven or eight of the straps attached themselves to the elastic. I tried to work them free, quickly and violently, with a series of shoves and wriggles. The weight of the backpack was so oppressive and impractical that I had only a very small rage of motion in which to work. I attempted this, saw it wasn't working, and then attempted it several more times in the exact same way — seeing the aspects of my plan that were getting in my way and changing none of them. Several more passengers had boarded by this time, and my useless struggle was causing a human-body-traffic pileup. Due to the silent social pressure of the gathering horde, I was forced to admit that I was not making any progress. Their frustration was hot, and physical, and very present. *"Pardon."*

I put the sole of my combat boot against the backpack and held on tight to the metal parts of the luggage confinement device. With a sudden and violent display of lower body strength, I shoved the backpack into the stockade. The jingle-jangle of my four hundred backpack straps erupted into the bus, not tempered in the slightest by the low bestial roar of the ventilation system. They clinked their plastic ends together in an obtuse cascade of claps and slaps. My backpack smacked into the neatly assembled luggage of my cohort. It knocked a smaller bag off of where it was perched on top of a larger one. It came to a rest — diagonal, but mostly sideways — occupying altogether too much space in the keep, in clear violation of the social contract. There were so many people, carrying so many bags, assembled behind me. *"Pardon,"* I said, like it mattered. I tried to shimmy the backpack over to the far side, but it was too heavy. Somebody cleared their throat in a "get on with it" sort of way. I gave up. *"Pardon."*

I took a seat while people clucked their tongues disapprovingly at the bad job that I had done. I had another bag with me: a smaller side bag that was so overstuffed that it was giving me nerve damage that I would not know about for years. I rummaged through it for my phone, which was dead: I had only been charging it to use the maps feature on Wi-Fi for the last two months. I stared at it, anyway, feigning interest in the glossy black screen, peering into it like a scrying mirror. I put on this performance to distance myself from the backpack, until the demographics of the bus shifted and the ones who knew about my mistake became a minority.

We lurched away from the Montreal–Pierre Elliott Trudeau International Airport and started heading downtown. I was twenty years old — the same age my grandfather had been when he stumbled across the Atlantic, all the way to Montreal. My grandmother had been three years younger when she arrived from the reserve by way of Halifax — already a mother to my eldest uncle, a veteran of five years of full-time work. I hadn't had to grow up as quickly as she did. She had worked really hard to make sure of that.

I had about twenty dollars left in combined overdraft and loans, much of which I had spent on the day pass on the metro. I was two thousand dollars in debt, and I had no job and no family wealth to back me up. I was in Montreal, though, which had to count for something. The low suburban buildings of Dorval gave way to the long and snaking grey highway. On the overpasses and guarding walls, graffiti germinated and sprouted and reached until it was technicolour and solid in my peripheral vision. I watched, transfixed, as the buildings got lower and darker. Then, suddenly, we were around the corner, and my breath hitched in my throat. The Sud-Ouest was a dark stack of sooty red brick buildings licked all over with graffiti paint. The distant chrome and glass ship sails of the downtown skyscrapers. The copper church spires crowding the skyline like pine trees.

I dragged my backpack off the bus at the terminus of the 747 express from Pierre Elliott Trudeau to Centre-Ville. The bag made a clattering cascade of plastic clinks as I pulled it free from the luggage carriage, as I dragged it down the aisle of the bus, as I avoided eye contact with the bus driver, and as I plopped it onto the sidewalk outside Berri-UQAM metro. The bus pulled away, and I looked around. The metro entrance was a wide glass and concrete cube, and inside I could see escalators heading down into the abyss.

Next to that, a park. Across the street, a tall multi-level music shop called Archambault. The sky was stark and blue, and the concrete of the sidewalk was heating up from the midmorning sun. It had been such a long morning. I wondered, briefly, what time it was in Madrid — how my redhead had slept, if he missed me — before the enormity of the space between us struck me, and I let him go.

Goodbye, sexy rugby boy, I thought, as I kicked and shoved my backpack toward a city bench. *Don't cry for me, Australia*, I thought, as I folded the top of my backpack over the bench and leaned enough pressure onto it to raise the bottom a couple of inches off the floor. I looped my combat boot into the gap between the sidewalk and the backpack and heaved the bag onto the bench. *Maybe one day I will see you again*, I thought, as I sat down on the bench in front of my backpack and weaved my arms through the straps. *If the sharks do not eat me on my way to your weird country*, I thought, giggling, as I half-leaned, half-deadlifted the thing off the bench, all of its weight cutting into the space between my shoulders and neck, threw it up onto my hips, and clipped up the padded hip straps.

I stood, laden again, for the final stretch. It would be fine, as long as I didn't stop moving, or think about it very much. I took a step, and the button of my shorts gave up — snapping off to *ping* off the concrete and disappear forever.

"Do They Owe Us a Living?" by Crass.

*July 1967. Somewhere between Montreal and
Prince Edward Island.*

My grandparents, Ron and Marie, used to drive the two youngest
boys back to the East Coast to go camping. They drove out of the
greyed skies of the Montreal summer, the windows drawn against
the pollution that choked out the blue and sent my father to wheez-
ing when he was a little boy. They made nests out of blankets for
the kids, in the back of the Dodge Polara, and headed east toward
the home Marie left, toward the Atlantic and the home Ron left
beyond it. They drove along the highways and the pounded dirt
roads. Marie sat with her legs folded to one side, in her blouse and
her nice brown slacks, her plum-painted mouth and her crown of
dark curls. On top of her vacation clothes, in the space between her
and her husband, was her work ID: *Marie (Pictou) Ross. Psychiatric
nurse.*

Her mother, my great-grandmother, had done whatever she could to make money, including reading tea leaves for the white folks in town. She was careful only to tell them happy things. White people didn't take well to Natives with bad news — even less well if she was a woman. I'd heard it told to me somewhere that her mother, my great-great-grandmother, was a basket weaver, and that in December of 1917 she was there when two ships, one laden with explosives, collided in the Halifax harbour. I remember hearing that the largest man-made explosion before the atomic era killed 1,782 people, and injured 9,000 others, and among them was my great-great-grandmother. I remember hearing that the blast threw her, blinded her, and shattered both of her arms, and that her arms knitted themselves back together, but she never recovered her sight. But when she picked up two lengths of maple splints with her healed hands, she found that she could still weave them in the dark — fluently, off by heart, like a mother tongue or a lullaby. I asked my dad, and he said it wasn't true. It was my great-grandmother, thrown, blinded in one eye. Who told me that first story? What else did they tell me?

What I know to be true is that when the money ran out my grandmother and her mother would scrape roadkill off the highway and dry it out, mash it with foraged berries and rendered fat. My grandmother still made cracks about it, in the front seat of the Polara, with her good work ID, and in her starched shirt and nice wool slacks. When the boys called out "Eww!" about the animals mashed into the road, she was ready.

"Mmm," Grandma said, eyes glittering and full of darkness and good humour — beautiful and empathetic and determined to survive. "Pemmican."

After Mom died, my dad started building us little nests in the back of the car, driving the long drives back to the reserve, to go home to his mother and his father, seeking council and refuge. I'd fall asleep somewhere in Ontario and wake up in New Brunswick with the hum of the earth rushing under me. Out the window, the dawn was breaking through cracks in the clouds in long straight beams to the earth, the long fingers of God blessing the crop fields of oat and wheat and yellow canola. It looked like a gap, between this world and the next. It looked like a brief glimpse into heaven. I breathed my hot breath on the window. I wrote, *Hi, Mom*, in the condensation there, with the tip of one extended finger.

July 2012. Montreal, Canada.

"Hi, Katherine!" I said, when she picked up the phone.

"Hi, Tara," she said, kindly. "How is Europe?"

"Oh, I'm ..." I looked around the Lincoln Avenue apartment, which I had unlocked and entered to find it still full of Katherine's things, because I told her I would be back at the end of August, and she could wait to move her stuff out until then, and she had taken me at my word. Like an idiot.

"I'm actually back now," I said, moving aside a sheet covering a pile of her things to peek underneath — a bicycle and a pile of boxes.

"Oh, great. Yeah, it's important to say goodbye to Halifax."

"No, like ..." I turned around to look at the glorified hallway of an apartment, barely manoeuvrable stuffed as it was with boxes packed with her belongings. "Like, I'm in Montreal."

She was quiet, on the other line.

"I'm at the apartment!" I said, excited. I leaned against my backpack, on the floor by my feet, as the zipper on my ruined shorts started to slide open without the support of the button. "And I'm, uh ... well, I'm wondering ..."

"Oh God," she groaned.

I knew a few people in Montreal. I crashed with one of them for a few days, while Katherine rearranged her life to suit my failure. When she let me back in, my first order of business was to look for work.

In Montreal, you need to be bilingual for even the least glamorous and most entry-level positions. Masters of three or more languages work back shifts in fast food while they wait for their Ph.D.s to transfer over. Newcomers from countries where English or French are not spoken have twice as many languages to learn at a base level in order to ease themselves into their new lives. Bilingualism is just good citizenry, for everyone to whom it is even remotely accessible — an objectively useful civic duty taken up by the overwhelming majority of Montreal residents. No one understands this less than the anglophones who move here from Alberta or Ontario, excited to take up the mantle of the oppressed speaker of a minority language at a moment's notice. The majority of the world's population can work in at least two languages. I wonder how much of the remaining monolingual minority are anglophones.

My mother and my father were both born in Montreal. My father lived in Dorval in his teens but grew up in Anjou — an almost exclusively francophone neighbourhood in the deep east of the island. His French is as comfortable and unaccented and effortless as his English — his voice, when he switches, drops an octave, his diction moving to the back of his throat where his vowels get long and flat and his consonants become barely audible fricatives, his *R*s bubbling where they roll in his throat. I see a personality shift in him, as I do in all bilinguals. To learn another language isn't just to speak to a new set of people — it's to find, within yourself, another version of yourself, relating to the world through a new set of terms.

My mother was born in Snowdon, a neighbourhood in Notre-Dame-de-Grâce, in 1958, to anglophone Irish and English parents from Saskatchewan. She died in 2001, in Toronto.

The year she died, I was in the third grade, in French immersion. It was important for my parents that I learn to speak French — Quebecois identity permeated their lives. My sister and I have French middle names. Sometimes, in francophone company, I experiment with going by *Tara Elise*, as a sort of apology for the difficult jumble of British Island consonants that is my last name. *Mack ... Mack-goh ... Mack-goh-wahn? Irlandaise, ouais? 'Scuse moé, mademoiselle ...*

When my mom died, my dad brought my sister and I along on his work trips, and spent a year home-schooling us. We wandered the earth shell-shocked and grateful and ravaged with loss. A touring musician, my dad took us to Belgium, France, Italy, Mexico — I missed my mother, and I missed her in parts of the world some people never get to see. I didn't work on my French that year, but I did learn some rudimentary German, running up and down the aisles at the concert halls in Berlin and Frankfurt. I can say *hello* and *I'm sorry* and *where is the toilet* in all of the appropriate languages for the thirteen countries my sister and I and my father all wandered to, trying to outrun the sadness that followed us like a lost dog.

When I had to go back to school, I wanted to go back to school in English. I was behind enough in math, without having to work out how to say everything in French. I took core French, like all Anglo-Canadian kids, up to grade nine, and was terrible at it. Most core French curriculums in English Canada are bad — they are painfully boring, focused on drilling children full of verb conjugations, as if that is something children find remotely interesting. I found *French* interesting, but my enthusiasm did not extend to the drilling of verb conjugations. I have been cursed, since childhood, with a steely determination to not do a single thing I do not find interesting. I was always sick with this delusion that *I could speak French, anyway,* even though all of the evidence — every single scrap of it — pointed to my being a monolingual anglophone.

I would occasionally nail something in French class. My reading and spoken comprehension were both reasonably good. I had a weird little bastardized Quebecois accent that made me sound more natural than most of my peers. This fed my delusion that I could speak French. The near-failing grade I got in the actual class, I decided, was no reflection on my abilities.

In Montreal, in those first few months, I came to the sickening realization of just how deeply held this self-delusion actually was. People stopped me in the street, asked simply for directions, and my brain went completely blank. *How do you say, "I have no idea"?* I would open and close my mouth a few times, the person looking on wide-eyed.

"English?" they'd say.

"*Way,*" I'd reply, in an awkward forgery of my father's accent.

"Where is the metro entrance?"

I motioned wildly with my hands in a generally leftward direction. "*Lah-buh,*" I'd say, not even pronouncing that right, as if I could fool a native French speaker. They would walk away, bemused. I would burn a hole into the sidewalk with shame.

I can speak French, I can speak French, I lied to myself, as I failed to speak French over and over. *I can understand French just fine,* I lied to myself, as I nodded along to people's conversation with no idea what was going on. Eventually, I admitted it: I didn't have it. I was nowhere near good enough. I had been able to ignore it in

English school. I could not ignore it in Montreal, where French ran the buses and stoked the fires, unlocked the doors, welcomed you inside, and told you belonged. French was what was shouted by the Algerian shopkeepers to the Haitian businessmen, before they both cracked into raucous laughter. It was what was drawled by the Parisian bakers to the Vietnamese entrepreneurs, as they exchanged knowing looks. It was in the mouth of the Cree busker, my Moroccan landlady, and my apartment building's ancient Acadian custodian. French was the lifeblood of the city. French was the rule of law. Without it, I entered a kind of underbelly — a strange sort of parallel world to the real francophone one.

When I got into my apartment, I spent the last of my money. I got popcorn, dry beans, rice, coffee, oatmeal, a few cucumbers, and a French press. At the Salvation Army, I bought a pot and a bowl and a mug and a glass and a single set of cutlery. At the drugstore I bought a Diet Coke and a bar of soap. Rent was paid, but there were six weeks until my stipend came in. I unpacked my bag and found some treasures from my adventure — Italian olive oil, Czech absinthe, Belgian chocolate, a beeswax candle from Germany, and a bag of salt from France. I poured myself an absinthe, drank water, and ate rice and beans and olive oil while I assembled my Ikea daybed and I tried to crunch the numbers in a way that made sense. *This isn't going to work*, I thought, comparing the six weeks until my stipend came in to my caloric needs, even if I was dieting, which I'd need to — considering what had happened to my shorts and all that.

I lit the candle by holding the wick against the bright red burner on my half-size electric stove until it burst into flame. I carried it gingerly into the bathroom, stripped my clothes off of my gathering curves, and ran a bath in my claw-foot tub. I put a handful of salt in the water, put Keith Jarrett on my laptop, and sent Sandy a picture of me posing and naked in the bathroom mirror. I opened the window and listened to the sounds of the city as I sunk into the tub, lathered the soap on my hair and all over my body. I imagined I was scrubbing off Halifax and Scotland and Spain and the couches I'd crashed on before I'd gotten into the place. My muscles warmed where they had tightened into little knots to hold up my bag with everything I wouldn't set down. I put my hands over all of me, and sunk into the water, imagining I was an ugly girl stealing a pretty girl's dream like a pickpocket. I tried to marvel at that. What a brave impostor I was. What a trickster.

The next morning, sipping coffee out of the same bowl, trying to ration the chocolate, I started looking for a job. I didn't find a job for a long time, but I did find things to do for money, which is different. It would do. It would have to.

August 2012. The Plateau, Quebec.

"Approximately how big do you need this hole?" I asked, lowering myself into the earth underneath the strange man's house. I was there to dig a hole for forty-five dollars, in the floor of a basement that was in another apartment — one that looked like it was abandoned, years ago, while people were still living in it. It was dank and poorly lit, but I could see through two open doors that there were sheets and comforters on the beds, with boxes and piles of old newspapers stacked on top of them and a thick layer of dust on top of all of that.

I knew that this man was a hoarder of some description. Everything smelled musty, wet, and rotten. The hole I was digging was in the kitchen of this basement apartment, where a manhole was hand-broken out of the concrete. There were still dishes in the kitchen cupboards. Even though it was summer, it was cool and dark and moist in the earth under the house. There were so many layers of concrete between me and other people: the concrete of the floor, the thick walls of the basement apartment, the long stretch of space up the street and into the Plateau.

The man was very small and wore a wig. He told me he was arthritic and couldn't dig the hole himself. "I need it six feet by three feet," he told me. The size of a grave.

I blasted music and tried not to think about John Wayne Gacy, who buried the boys he killed under his house and hired workmen to dig the trenches and sprinkle lime in order to accelerate the decomposition of the bodies. In the seventh grade, I'd gotten a computer in my bedroom, which had been hooked up to very slow rural Ontario dial-up internet. I did all the normal things that a seventh grader would do with a new device: I visited Harry Potter chat rooms and I took my first confused glances at pornography. I wrote *Pirates of the Caribbean* fanfiction and my first attempt at a novel. I also engaged in the oddly common little-girl pastime of embarking on an extensive self-directed education program about serial murder and other horrors, primarily on Wikipedia. I would scare myself until I couldn't sleep. Then, when I couldn't sleep, I would keep reading late into the night.

I'd seen pictures of the crawl space, where a monster had stored what was left of the children he tortured: low pipes, dirt floors, three feet or so of crawling space, thick concrete walls. It looked exactly like this one. I dug my way through the earth, uncovering rocks and worms, and, once, a small white bone. I planned to pocket the bone, loading that dirt into the bucket I'd been using to haul the earth out of the crawl space. When I got to the broken opening, there was the man, wielding a huge shovel in both of his hands. My heart leapt directly into my throat. He smiled, and then reached out with one hand, holding the shovel. "I thought you could use a bigger one." I laughed a too-loud, nervous laugh.

He watched me pour the bucket full of earth onto the pile outside, where I'd been accumulating it. I engaged in polite small talk about how new I was to Montreal, and he suggested things for me to do. It was getting close to the end of my allotted work time. He told me that if I squared off the edges and cleared off the last of the dirt, he'd pay me, and I could leave.

I didn't go back for the bone. I buried it deeper under more and more buckets full of earth. I didn't find any more, even though I was looking. The work went much more quickly with the larger shovel. I only need another half an hour or so to finish what I'd started, and I tried to reassure myself. *He's just a sweet, tiny, arthritic old man.* Besides, the bone had been so small.

As I was leaving, he handed me a piece of paper. He'd noticed that my sweater — a gift from River — had a big circle-*A*, the symbol for anarchism, sewed onto the back. He told me there was an anarchist bookstore on Saint-Laurent, and if I was new here maybe I'd like it. I was surprised — I would like that, actually. I thanked him, was paid my forty-five dollars, and headed back to my tiny apartment. I turned the paper over in my hands, laughing at myself for how nervous I had been. The bone was probably a raccoon or something who had died under there. On the back of the paper were simple math equations — basic algebra. He'd reused a piece of scrap paper. What did an elderly man need with elementary algebra exercises? I stopped dead in my tracks in front of the entrance to the metro. Unless they weren't his? Unless they belonged to someone else — someone small-boned. Like a child.

"A Box Full of Sharp Objects" by the Used.

2002–2009. Ontario.

I was on my knees, at my bedside, with my elbows on the mattress, like she taught me. She'd been dead for a few months. People kept telling me, *She is still with you,* and *If you pray for her, she will come to you.* I kept praying and she kept on not coming. I must not be have been doing it right. I was going to try again. I had my hands clasped dutifully in front of my face.

God, I thought. *Hi. It's me.* I shifted on my knees, trying to get comfortable. *I know you had to take my mom, for some reason.* I felt anger rise in my nine-year-old body. I thought that, probably, I wasn't allowed to be angry with God, so I pushed it away, down inside me, as far as I could. I pushed it down past my throat and my diaphragm, where it burned me. I pushed it neatly down into the skin around my stomach, into the muscles of my thighs.

I don't really understand, but whatever. I mean, that's okay. I mean, like, I don't like it, but ... I shifted on my knees again, readjusted my hands. *Well, anyway, apparently you can do anything, so ...* I felt a swelling in me. Heat ran up my throat, flooded my head. *So maybe it was because I wasn't good, or I didn't pray enough, or something.*

The guilt of a lonely, bargaining child filled me with anger and desperation. *I'm just wondering if I can talk to her.* The tears bloomed hot in my eyes, made my vision of the wall blur. *It doesn't have to be for too long, just like ... just like, a minute. Thirty seconds. Please.*

I waited, gripping my own hands so hard they were shaking. My nose filled with snot. The world swam, cloudy and underwater, where my eyes filled with tears. I waited, digging my fingernails into my own hands, shaking with concentration and the intensity of my need.

I didn't think she was going to die. I didn't say goodbye.

I took a deep, shuddering breath, and the tears ran down my cheeks. I was listening. My eyes darted, wild, around the room. Nothing.

Please. I tried to pray for her. To live. I did it wrong.

I collapsed into myself, driving my head into my bed.

I need to tell her I'm sorry.

I waited for a little longer, and then I sobbed, and then I beat my head and my ears with my balled up fists. I didn't want to hear the nothing anymore. I didn't want to feel the incredible depth of the silence.

I stood. I tried to move on. Every so often, for reasons I did not always understand, the parts of me where I'd buried feelings I didn't like swelled and ached and called out for attention. While puberty hit me like a speeding car that year, I was still just a little girl, and I didn't know how to take care of myself. The only thing I knew how to do, when I was hurting, was eat, so that was all I did.

My brother, who was already an addict by the time my mother died, faded even further away. He left for Vancouver, where he found the light and got sober and came back to us. Then he felt some sorrow that seemed, to him, too heavy to carry alone. He asked for help from the spectre pacing the streets of the Downtown Eastside. It was such a human request, you know? It's nothing a tall boy with sad eyes should have to die for.

He was only twenty-five. I was fourteen, with black rings of eyeliner and long triangular bangs. I was carrying several suitcases' worth of extra weight around from eating to soothe myself, every time I missed my mother, every time I felt the crushing silence of God. I resented needing to take up the work of another trauma, as my time was heavily occupied by my first one. What remained of my time was taken up by high school, an encyclopedic knowledge of mid-2000s second-wave emo music, my monogamous one-way crush on an oblivious boy at school, and my diverse cast of bullies. The day after he died, somewhat resigned, almost begrudgingly, I went through my regular prescription of eating, and then headed to the bathroom as if guided by some invisible hand. I stuck a finger down the wet hollow of my gullet, and prodded, searching, until I'd triggered my stomach into motion, and vomited every last morsel into the toilet. It was simply the most efficient way to deal with it.

Overnight, I was a raging bulimic. I wished I was an anorexic, but I had to live with my character defects. I was a slave to desire, which could never be satisfied, no matter how much I wanted to be emaciated, redeemed, cured of want. I wished I had the constitution, and I wished I didn't wish for these kinds of things. Honestly, it would have been nice to wish for normal things, like a boyfriend or driving lessons or for my mom to stop nagging me. Sometimes I would say the words I'd never get to say, like an incantation, smiling at their incredible beauty: *Oh my god, Mom, you're so annoying! You're so embarrassing! I hate you! I wish you were dead!*

Other girls talked about their horrible relationships with their mothers, and I was sick with envy. I fantasized about good things, but also about having someone with whom my maternal relationship could deteriorate. I fantasized about her crossing her arms over her chest, not angry, just disappointed. In my fantasies, her chest was scarred from the procedure that had successfully cut the problem out of her. Sometimes I would have a dream where she was alive and we fought so much we never spoke again. *Your parents are very different,* people would tell me, in my dreams. *And you're just like your dad. You don't even look like her.* In these dreams, I walked through my life, angry at a woman who was my origin, and out there somewhere in the big wide world, so different than me I couldn't speak to her.

I woke up. The last time we spoke I kissed her weak body, her soft skin, ran my hands over her blond curls with their halo of grey roots, and there was not a shred of animosity or anger or sadness. I wanted her alive. I would take any bargain. I would take her, alive, even if she rejected me, hated me, never spoke to me again. *You don't even look like her.* I'd go to the mirror and look for her and I couldn't find her.

When I hear people speak, disgusted, about the burden of addicts, I want to kill those people. When I hear them say there can't be a safe drug supply, that we should not distribute naloxone, I want to rip them apart in my vomit-slick fingers. I think, *My brother was an addict and a good person, and he died, and you are sober and horrible,*

*and still here, and what a waste. What an injustice. If there is a God,
and He has a plan, He has a terrible plan. His plan is so bullshit.*

I wished my mother was alive and annoying and ruining my
life. I wished my brother was alive and addicted to drugs. Mostly, I
wished I believed he was going to meet her, somewhere.

I ate until the ache was rubbed out. I knelt in the bathroom, in front
of the toilet, to beg for forgiveness.

"Un Canadien Errant" by Antoine Gérin-Lajoie.

August 2012. Berri-UQAM Metro, Montreal.

I put my dad's old guitar, the one he gave me, back in its case. I only had a few more minutes before my allotted two-hour busking set was over. The man who was to take my place was already impatiently plucking the strings on his violin — tuning, but mostly waiting for me to leave. I'd probably already hit my money goal — another week's worth of bus passes, and some cash for beer and fresh groceries — but I liked to finish with one in French. For the fans.

I cleared my throat and whipped out my best choirgirl posture: shoulders back, chin lifted, knees slightly bent. Power from your diaphragm. An invisible string from the bottom of your pelvis up through the top of your head.

> *Un Canadien errant,*
> *Banni de ses foyers,*

Parcourait en pleurant
*Des pays étrangers.**

The song was written in 1842 about the Lower Canada Rebellion. French militants attempted an overthrow of the British ruling class, the political power in Lower Canada, despite being a demographic minority.

The battles that became known as the Lower Canada Rebellion effectively began after the catalyst of a major street fight. The Doric Club, a social club slash paramilitary organization, disapproved of the gathering of *Les Fils de la Liberté*, which was also a social club slash paramilitary organization. The French ones, who *just wanted to have a party*, had to flee the city and disband. The English ones, who vandalized houses and broke a guy's knee, and also *started it*, got jobs in the rebellion that followed. This is what historians refer to as *extremely fucked up*. I'd probably write songs about it, too, if that happened to me.

Un jour, triste et pensif,
Assis au bord des flots,
Au courant fugitif
Il addressa ces mots: †

The rebellions were huge failures. The overwhelming majority of the rebellion's casualties were the swaths of Patriotes who were executed — turned into a metaphor, defined and negated. The ones who weren't killed were exiled to lands distant and unhappy: to the United States, or Australia. They wandered along the banks of the

---

* A wandering Canadian, / banished from his homeland, / travelled, while weeping, / unfamiliar lands.

† One day, sad and pensive, / by the banks of the fleeting river, / to the fugitive current / he spoke these words:

shark-infested waters and sang sad songs. They started the complicated process of returning. They had to pay their own way back, if they made it back at all — all the way across the great expanses of ocean, maybe with a stop somewhere in Asia, or to an inn in Spain to meet a dark-haired girl who looked like home.

People at the Berri-UQAM metro station ate it up. *Bravo*, they said, emptying their pockets. They muttered approving things in French that I still didn't understand. I could sing the lyrics without a hint of an accent, mimicking the way my mom and dad had played it in their band, the Harbord Trio. I did an impression of my mother and her Montréalaise accent. I had a recording of her singing it — as crisp and real as if she was standing in my living room, with my dad's voice on harmonies and their friend Oliver on the violin. They used to practise with my brother, a little boy, running around at their ankles. Now all of them are gone, except my father — from some sickness, or another.

I sang my song for Matilda, who I hoped had gotten off the couch. Or was at least watching another movie. I sang for Tim, the bastard. For my brother, my other parent, eleven years older than me, who was my friend and my comrade and a sweet, sad boy.

> *Si tu vois mon pays,*
> *Mon pays malheureux,*
> *Va dire à mes amis*
> *Que je me souviens d'eux.‡*

---

‡ If you should see my country, / my most unhappy country, / go and tell my friends / that I remember them.

"Pagan Poetry"
by Björk.

October 2012. Concordia University.

My first year at Concordia, my poetry professor was Leslie. Leslie was a small, soft-voiced woman. She had a steady gaze that saw through my bullshit but did not judge it. She had beautiful hands, which made small marks on my manuscripts in tidy script. Her salt-and-pepper curls were perfectly defined and shiny. She made me want to sit on the floor when she spoke. She made me want to shut up, for once.

I was a procrastinator. My apartment was in a constant state of disarray, and even when I was in class I worried the people around me could smell my mess on me. I woke up exhausted every morning and struggled to sleep every night. I arrived late for my classes.

I covered for my perpetual embarrassment by remaining in a constant state of confession, trying to shrink my shame in the forgiveness of people I barely knew, or liked. I was the first one to say the horrible thing about myself so no one could surprise me. I wore my worst fears and insecurities on my sleeve. This way, no one could dig them out of my computer hard drive or the mouths of my snitching comrades. I erupted into class fifteen minutes late, already laughing. I wanted to give off an impression of being in on the joke.

My poetry was scattered and insecure. I was afraid to work too hard and still be found wanting, so I handed in first drafts. I lived and wrote in a state of excess. I kissed strange men on dance floors, took new friends home to drop MDMA in my tiny apartment, walked in late to class and handed Leslie the literary equivalent of a hole pic. I found new words for all the old ways I had to hate myself. I dared the reader to judge me for the worst things I had ever done.

My cohort in poetry class devoured my bullshit. It was 2012, and though I didn't know the name for it, I was standing in the cultural centre of what was termed in journalism the *first-person industrial complex.* The writing that was getting attention, getting people noticed, was brash and upfront, harrowing and traumatized. Writing by women like me was *going viral*: fat women, women who did not so much experience lapses in self-control as they did occasionally surface from the vast ocean of *more.* I showed up to class hurting and handed in a blueprint for how I did it and planned to do it again.

All I heard was *more of this,* until Leslie told me, frankly, that I was writing what was easy. *Not emotionally,* she clarified, in her notes. *Formally. You need to let the work do some of what you are leaving to the content.* She underlined some of my more revealing work, and she wrote, *Be careful what you give away.*

I got the notes back and I was embarrassed. I ran through my useful list of excuses. *You don't get to tell me what to write about. What do you even know about aching, or emptiness, or love?* I was fronting. I knew she was right.

Leslie told me that my poems didn't know what they were doing. They didn't know what was at stake. A poem, Leslie told me, must always have something at stake. Ultimately, a poem must always be a matter of life and death. People write because there is no alternative.

She also told me I had to be careful about what I gave away. A poem is an offering. Once you let go of it, it is no longer yours. Artists make things, which are material, but are also ideas. Ideas want to touch things, change them, and be changed. There is no way to control an idea, protect an idea, prevent an idea from getting out. That's just what ideas do.

I've spent my whole life trying to learn how to communicate as well as possible: at first, I thought that if I could explain myself perfectly, if I could march a thought from point A to point B, stare at it long enough, cut out everything ambiguous and curious about it, I could avoid being misunderstood. The truth is that there is an eternity inside of me, and language is a box with a ceiling, a floor, and its own walls. If you try to put eternity in a box, how much of it fits? I keep getting boxes handed to me by people desperate for me to understand. I can only receive what's inside of these boxes in relation to what is already inside of me.

Habermas writes, "Language limits as it opens, imposes as it discloses." I am misunderstood for mostly innocent reasons, by people who are doing their best. Children normalize what is demonstrated as normal. I think I understand what Leslie meant when she said, *Be careful what you give away.* I'm such a slow learner.

I studied form. Villanelles and tercets and what a line break is for. I started writing second drafts. I printed my first drafts, cleared off my tiny card table in my glorified hallway of an apartment. I sat for a moment, very still, and wrote *WHAT IS AT STAKE* in big letters above my drafts. I peered over the little black marks until I could read the second meaning underneath. *Life and death, and also honour.* Or *salvation.* Or *responsibility.* And so on. I sighed, and I wrote a third draft, even though I didn't want to.

Kafein was the first place I overheard workers speak in English to each other. The Concordia University hipsters who worked Kafein didn't seem like they spoke much French at all. I was at a table, listening, siphoning Wi-Fi. I hadn't heard the baristas utter so much as a *syllable* of French, to each other or to the customers. The clientele appeared to be 99.9 percent Anglo Concordia students: coming in for a caffeine fix or a hot date between study sessions at the library. But the Kafein hipsters had something else that I didn't. The Kafein hipsters were *cool.*

Coolness. In Montreal, coolness was king. In Montreal, coolness meant something altogether different than it had in Halifax. Halifax had been warm and friendly and hospitable: all of Halifax's flaws, of which there were many, were hidden under a baseline of politeness and warmth. My dumpiness and lack of fashion sense were written off as second fiddle, in Halifax, to my confidence and my good attitude. My bold fashion choices were lauded as brave: among them, my feathery mohawk hairdo, my punk-patched army fatigue pants, and — God forgive me — *a bright-blue John Mayer hoodie.*

"You are an icon," said Halifax, about my outfits that clashed and did not fit. "A visionary!" said Halifax, when things did not flatter my figure. "Work it, girl."

Montreal did want the girl to work it. Kafein was populated by the type of hipster whose personal dramas and good looks outranked the needs of any customers to do foolish things like exchange money for goods or services. When I went in to follow up about my CV, the good-looking hipster behind the counter was engrossed in a retelling of some story — *rife* with *exquisite* drama, I'm sure — and not doing any work. I waved, and she did not respond. I waved again, and she glanced over, but kept talking. I caught her eye, and smiled, and she did a short body scan of me. She was calibrating how nice she had to be to me. *God, that's so mean,* I thought. *I wanna work here so bad.*

"*Bonjour*-hi," she said, bored.

"Hi! I'm actually just following up about the CV I dropped off. I'm wondering if you're still looking for anyone?"

She did another, deeper, body scan, and pursed her lips. While I would be in denial about it for a few more years — rail against it, swear it must not be true, swear that no civilized society would operate this way — this was actually all of the information I needed. I was not going to get the job. I wasn't *cool* enough. She might not be the one calling the shots *exactly*, but she was telling me, based on the information she already knew as a working professional, that I was not up to snuff. I was pudgy from a summer spent sitting around eating popcorn because it was cheap and I had nothing else to do, reading books, thinking hard about exercise, and then, exhausted from thinking so hard, not exercising. I walked, sure, but mostly I drank beer, started *Infinite Jest*, gave up, and read *The Mists of Avalon* instead. I was very clearly not cool, in the way a Montreal twenty-year-old was supposed to be.

I was retreating, dejected, when I saw the flyer on the counter: POETRY NITE AT KAFEIN. I picked it up. EVERY SECOND TUESDAY. OPEN MIC.

It was divine intervention. There was place at Kafein for people like me, after all.

Just inside the Kafein doors, one set of stairs lead up to the café, while the other led into the bar. I stomped my boots to shake off the droplets of cold autumn rain stuck to them, entering the establishment on the requisite Tuesday. I took my hat off and shook it, opened and closed my hands over and over again until the feeling came back into them.

The basement of Kafein was low-ceilinged and dank. Kafein was filled with curving vintage couches made of threadbare velvet and old wood. It was a hookah bar before it was a café and a bar. The basement was still haunted by a heady sense of tobacco — more of a ghost than a smell or a stain. The ghost remained after many hands ran wet things across every surface to lick the resins away, damp cotton coming away brown and then yellow and then clean.

The metal stairs gonged under my boots as I descended into the warm dark and warm murmur of conversation. String lights twinkled off of the mahogany of the bar, the liquor bottles, and a big mirror. Tea light candles on every table threw warm, whispering, inconsistent light. The decor was made of so much old, dark wood, that in the muddy image of my memory, even the air was brown as melted chocolate.

People were shuffling their papers and sitting in a state of excitement, or fear. Everyone was turned to each other in excited expectation, leaning forward on age-worn couches in blush pink or mustard yellow, lifting their highball glasses from the low tables, in their American Apparel or similar. There were other reading series happening in the city at the time. *Matrix Magazine* ran the Sparrow reading series on St. Laurent. Ashley Obscura with This Is Happening Whether You Like It or Not. Poetry was being read at cafés and libraries and music venues and parties in people's living rooms. A francophone city, it was bursting with English poetry — the city of Irving Layton and Leonard Cohen carving a whole culture out of *poetry*, of all things! One of the least profitable artistic mediums on Creator's good green earth!

When I saw Andrew by the bar, before I knew his name, I saw what the coffee shop girl upstairs had not seen in me. *Ah*, I thought. *Ah, yes, that is what it looks like.*

Montreal cool. Six feet, thin, with a jaw so wide and sharp it protruded out over his long neck. He had bleached white hair, stark against his ubiquitous all-black clothing. He had a look on his face like he knew something — like he was always on the brink of laughter, barely managing to bite it back.

At this point in my development, I was working on my sense of irony. I had started to understand the winking subtext of things that had flown over my head when I still needed art to spell everything out for me. I found this so thrilling that I applied my newfound sensibility everywhere, even when it was wildly inappropriate. If I encountered something dangerous, or sinister, I assumed there was some kind of commentary being made about danger, or sinisterness. I lived in a constructed reality, where nothing was actually what it seemed to be. It served me very well, sometimes.

It also made me a harsh critic. I found the vast majority of the work being presented at my first Poetry Nite at Kafein painfully sincere: people saying exactly and precisely what they mean, their metaphors over-explained, their literary devices afterthoughts. Most of the time, when somebody read, they read something that was at once unrevealing and a public display of vulnerability so saccharine it grossed me out.

"My soul ..." started one poet, and I sat up on my bar stool, expectant. "... is like a flower," they continued, closing their eyes as though unable to fathom the enormity of their own profundity. I slumped in my chair, sipped my beer. I wasn't angry. I was just disappointed.

"My heart ..." began another poet, and again, I sat up, ears pricked like an attentive dog. "... is a muscle." The poet stopped, and smirked at the audience, knowingly. People went "mm," snapped their fingers in approval. I looked around, in shock. *What the fuck.*

I interpreted it all as an attachment to *being understood*, which I read as cowardice, or at least not poetry. *Write an essay*, I thought, bitterly, *if you want to make a point*. I looked for ambiguity, for space — for the gaps where interpretation could fall, and fall, and never land. I didn't find it. None of it made me curious.

When Andrew walked up to read, he was cheered on by his entourage: A curly haired white girl in a vintage flapper dress, with a long strings of pearls and a perfectly painted little rosebud of a red mouth. Next to her was a tall Ojibway man, with a full face of airbrushed makeup, a dozen facial piercings, and the perfectly coiffed barrel curls of a 1940s housewife. Next to him, a kind-faced redhead, a person who always had the air of someone who was headed to the library.

"Oh, shut up," he said, playfully, to his friends.

"No, seriously, shut the fuck up!" he snapped, suddenly angry, at the whole crowd.

A nervous hush fell over everyone. He waited, making us squirm. Then the control behind his perpetual smirk gave out, and he broke into peals of high-pitched laughter. The crowd laughed along, relieved. Some people looked pissed. I took a handful of dirty bar peanuts, shoved three in my mouth without looking away from him — wide-eyed, delighted, enthralled.

Andrew began,

Christmas is coming again, sooner,

His eyes were laughing at us, but then his face fell, and he said, more seriously,

and I see you everywhere. Your
head, just the back of it. Not your face.

Then the anger that had been there when he screamed at us was back in his voice, when he said,

That stupid shape. Every tall, freaky,
lanky blond is you, and I wonder,
how I would respond if you appeared,

A wave of softness, tenderness, ran through his body, when he said,

if I turned the corner to my apartment,
and you're there. Standing, waiting.
So nervous.

He swallowed.

I can't speak.

He built momentum,

I can't even breathe, I spit out
my Adam's apple, instead of the words,

A pause. A look out into the crowd, a sense he was making eye contact even though he wasn't actually looking at any of us.

I love you.

Three more peanuts in my mouth. I had not blinked, this whole time. I was chewing, nervously, wondering what was going to happen next.

Words I've been meaning to say,
But I can't, because they're just
letters, strung together. They
won't express, convey, explain away,

the electric charge, tearing through
my body. Burning as fire, on
the surface of my skin or pushing tears
from the corners of my eyes …

We were all leaning in, swooning. All of our defences were down. We're right there with him, on the sidewalk, with the tall lanky freaky blond, when Andrew suddenly bellows, in something that no civilized person would describe as an indoor voice,

OH FUCK YEAH GIVE IT TO ME THIS IS
WHAT I TRULY WANT

The crowd starts, terrified. We burst into a murmur of giggles — nerves, relief, fear. Delight.

I went up with my poem, something I was working on called "To All the Girls Who Have Not Lost Their Mothers Yet." I began:

You will.

The room went quiet and uneasy. Someone looked up at me, shocked, which is what I wanted.

Your family will want to speak about it,
In the car, or in the frozen food aisle.
They will not listen. You will say
you are not ready to speak about it
yet, and they will not listen. God
will not listen.

I paused.

God doesn't listen to little girls.

In the audience, some people went "Mm." Some people snapped their fingers. Most people looked queasy. In the back, with his friends, Andrew stared me down, his perpetual smirk broken into a huge smile.

"We're going to start a magazine," explained Andrew's friend, the white girl with the pearls. "Do you want to be our editor?"

Many of my sensibilities were offended by Andrew, and would continue to be, for years. He was grumpy, manic, depressive, obsessive. He was *extraordinarily problematic.* He took up too much of my time. I was in school full-time, picking up gigs whenever I could, and I didn't know it yet, but work was about to pick up — I was about to meet Abdul, the best boss I ever had. The white girl — whose name was Hannah — and Andrew and the others weren't just describing a magazine. What they wanted to build was a multimedia empire. They insisted they had the connections — stylists, photographers, philosophers. Poets and drug dealers. Everything we needed.

I simply did not have the time, so I said yes, of course.

"Blessings"
by Chance the Rapper
(feat. Jamila Woods).

December 2012. Montreal.

I wanted so badly not to seem desperate to this nice family in this coffee shop.

"So, yeah," I said, fingering the side of my espresso cup. "As you can see, my police check came up clean."

The dad, Anwar, was across the table from me, eyeing the envelope in his hands with one raised eyebrow. It was torn open on one side. When I'd picked it up from the police station I had been overwhelmed with a *need* to see what was inside. I knew I had never been charged with a crime — but what if there was some way I could have a criminal record without knowing about it?

He looked back up at me, kindly, deciding to let this one slide. "Great."

"We're really happy to have found you," said the mom, Maryam. They were an unreasonably beautiful couple. They were no more than a few years older than me. They both had perfect, clear skin and youthful eyes. He was a medical resident at the McGill teaching hospital, and she was taking English classes at Concordia. They had a brand new baby — only three months old.

"He's a really good baby," she said. "He can be a bit slow to warm up to people. And, of course, he's a little underweight right now ..."

"Because of his skin," said Anwar, softly.

"We think it might be the climate," Maryam said. "It's really dry and hot in Saudi, so it's a big change."

"Oh, yeah," I said, waving my hand. "The weather here's hard if you've lived here forever — and you guys have been here what, like ...?"

"Three weeks," said Anwar.

"Oh, wow!" I said. "Welcome to Canada!"

"Thank you!" they said, in unison.

"So it would be two times a week, when I have class," said Maryam. "And then, if that's good, we might also have you on the weekend so we can go out, or on weeknights so I can go study with friends."

"That's perfect for me," I said.

"You like babies?" Maryam asked, seeming worried. "You won't get bored? Even if he's a bit cranky at first?"

"I have loved babies since I was a slightly larger baby," I said, very serious. This made the both of them laugh, which woke up Abdul in the stroller between them. He opened his eyes, which were Maryam's eyes — huge, rimmed with lashes so long it seemed impossible they were real. His brown skin was patchy with eczema, and his small pink button of a mouth was open in awe and horror as his eyes darted around the room — overwhelmed, on the brink of tears. Flabbergasted, at the enormity of being. *Same, kid*, I thought.

"Hi, boss," I said, smiling at him. Abdul looked at his mother, his head wobbling slightly from the effort, and then looked at me,

"Blessings" by Chance the Rapper (feat. Jamila Woods).

from the shade inside his stroller — sizing me up, deciding what to think. I caught his eyes, abruptly broke into the largest and most exaggerated smile I could force onto my face, and froze it there to wait for his reaction. This was my move with all kids under three, and about seventy percent of the time it made them laugh — when it didn't, however, they *were* afraid of me forever.

Abdul stared, his huge eyes assessing me, his face unsure, his little button mouth agape, and then his face folded into a series of tiny circles and his mouth widened into a beaming smile.

January 2013. Montreal.

"So, uh … yeah," Sandy said, sheepishly. "I could start at … at, uh, Concordia. In the fall. If I wanted."

I was sitting in my shitty Lincoln Avenue apartment — the one I loved, which was not large enough for two people. Which was hardly, really, large enough for one.

"Are you going to?" I said, staring hard at the screen and the person on it.

He was quiet for a long few seconds, staring back, but not at me — because he was looking at me, but it was the me on the screen, which meant he wasn't looking at his camera. I wanted to see his eyes. I flitted mine back and forth. I wanted to look at his face. I wanted him to see my eyes.

"Yes," he said.

"Do you want to get back together?"

I saw him take a breath: a short, high, chest breath. Like he was in pain. "Yes."

The music in my body, which had felt cold when it started, was getting so comfortable running through me it was heating me up. I was hot from the inside. I felt sweat under my knees, in the hollows of my elbows. One long, hot trickle of sweat ran down from between my hair and my right ear, snaked its way down over the crest of my collar bone, and disappeared into my shirt. All along the way, the ends of my nerves perked up. I thought of desert plants blooming after rain, or in a tiny circle of moisture from a trekker's emptied water bottle.

"You will have to meet all the other people I'm fucking," I said, teasing. He took another breath, but deeper this time, shuddering slightly, his mouth set firmly, his eyes dark and full of want. I was pissing him off. He said nothing. Fully performing now, I set my eyes directly at the camera. I couldn't watch him watching me, but I needed these lines to land.

"If you don't want me to be with anybody else," I said, slowly, pausing, and then, "just tell me."

"Tara," he said. I wanted to see what he looked like. I wanted to watch him watching me. I needed him to see my eyes. I held the line, looked at the black lens of the camera, heating inside like water on to boil. "I don't want you to be with anyone else."

Not long after, the pipes above my ballroom of a bathroom exploded. They dripped directly into the toilet, which was lucky, but in order to use the toilet I needed to open an umbrella. The building fixed them, and they exploded again. They fixed them again, but took much longer — then they exploded a third time, and they didn't fix them for a long time. I complained about these things to Andrew, to Sandy, to Kate and Matilda, and in Leslie's poetry class, to my new friend Gregor. He told me he had an extra room in his apartment.

I moved in in April, preparing myself for my first summer in Montreal. Still mostly broke, and now without my living stipend, I increased my maxed-out credit card to five thousand dollars to pay for things. That summer, Sandy made plans to follow. He had quit

"Blessings" by Chance the Rapper (feat. Jamila Woods).

his good job, one of the last Canadian jobs for classical animators in a rapidly changing industry. He'd sold off most of what couldn't fit into a few rolling suitcases and some Rubbermaid bins. He'd gotten tranquilizers for Hexadecimal, for the train. He'd bought a one-way ticket to Montreal, and we were going to be together.

"Miss World" by Hole.

Late May 2013. Westmount.

"So, how long have you worked here?" I asked the live-in grounds-keeper, as I helped carry in the ladders.

He seemed surprised by the question. He made eye contact with me, for the first time since my window-washing crew had arrived at the mountainside mansion. He was a short, work-weary Filipino — he looked the kind of tired that could only be cured by several years of vacation.

"Three years," he said.

I whistled as I set the ladder up by a wall of windows on one side of the house. The place was massive — built into the side of Mount Royal in the old-money Anglo city of Westmount. Through the wall of windows, you could see the entirety of the rest of the city — the broad expanses of low-lying buildings and copper church spires, the chrome-and-glass Jenga blocks of the business district, the coal-and-graffiti burnished red brick of the southwest. I could see the joyful arc of the Ferris wheel in the old port and the snaking antique roller coasters of La Ronde, and, off in the distance, the rolling drumlins of the hills and the outer reaches of the Laurentian Mountains.

The house was also, to my delight, extremely tacky — everything was in a hideous, beige Regency revival style, from the curving antique couches and chairs to the wrought and mangled gilded frames that held hideous paintings on every inch of wall space, like a terminal malignancy. The paintings were artless, too flattering, devoid of style or a point of view. Doughy white women and ugly children held fish, posed at garden parties. *You can't buy taste*, I thought, as we loaded in the ladders and buckets and cleaning solution, navigating drifts of tables and cabinets crammed to bursting with so much silver and fine china it could only register as detritus, every inch of table space too occupied for so much as a champagne glass, let alone a sit-down dinner. The only difference between the house and an episode of hoarders was several millions of dollars.

I was setting the ladder up over one of several homely sculptures — the twisting body of a headless and armless woman, carved entirely out of glass. It was set against the glass wall, and it was my job to clean behind it. My cohort and I made eleven dollars an hour, and as we cleaned the mirrors and glass and windows of the house, we were informed over and over again the exact value of what we were cleaning around, and that if we *so much as scratched it we would be held personally liable* — "Your boss's insurance doesn't cover this, it costs two thousand dollars, if you damage it you will be held personally liable," or "It costs eight thousand dollars, if you damage it you will be held personally liable," or "You see this plate? *This plate is worth six hundred dollars*, okay, and as you can see there are *stacks* of plates ..."

"That sculpture," said the man, as I climbed the ladder, "is worth *twenty-five thousand dollars* ..."

"Great," I said, as I started cleaning the window. "Do you like working here?" I asked, cheerfully.

The man blinked, surprised — then laughed a slow, bitter laugh.

Maddie was steadying the ladder for me. She was, at that point, the title holder for *most horrifying window-washing work experience*. We worked mostly outside, on less ostentatious, normal-people houses — climbing ladders and clambering over roofs and rendering the outside-facing windows shiny and clean. The agreement made at every job was that we could come inside and use the toilet if we needed to. We had gotten so used to it that when Maddie arrived at a newly minted McMansion in the West Island, she had just used the toilet without asking. She had emerged to find a horrified maid, who had screamed upon seeing her.

"Get out!" the maid pleaded. "*Please* — oh God, please ... you have to get out!"

"Ohmigod, I'm so sorry," Maddie said, running out the front door, but not before seeing the maid spring into action, ripping out heavy-duty cleaning products and a vacuum and throwing herself into erasing any indication that she had been there. In the work van, heading home, she'd retold her experience to her crew boss.

"Fuck," her crew boss said, shaking her head. "Yeah, that's the Bonetti mansion. Sorry, I shoulda told you."

"What the fuck does that mean?"

"Oh, you don't know?" Her crew boss laughed. "They're gangsters! Major Mafiosi."

Maddie had peed in the bushes for a few shifts before she was ready to go inside a job again.

Now she was holding the ladder, watching me as I got to the top and carefully stepped over. My keys were clipped to a belt loop with a carabiner, and as I stepped my leg over the top of the ladder,

I didn't see my keys get caught. Even at the weight I'd starved and vomited myself down to, anxious and displaced and lonely my first year in the city, I was more than heavy enough to knock my keys off without breaking my stride. Maddie didn't have a chance to warn me — plus, she didn't want to alert the attention of the grounds-keeper, who had temporarily looked away to threaten somebody else. Which is why he didn't see my heavy set of keys fall directly from my hip, at the upper pinnacle of the ten-foot ladder — he didn't see them tumble, picking up speed, glinting and glittering in the hot, late spring light as they cascaded down with shattering speed toward the ugly, extremely breakable glass sculpture beneath me.

I felt their absence right before I heard them hit, and froze, halfway over the pinnacle of the ladder, clinging and unsteady and cramping. *Twenty-five thousand dollars.* I heard a crash as they hit — but no breaking glass. They hadn't hit the sculpture. Poker-faced, I quickly and quietly descended the ladder to find Maddie pale and sweating.

"Where are they?" I asked, whispering.

"I saw them hit the top," she whispered back.

"But it didn't break," I said, looking. I quickly examined the base of the sculpture — no keys. I climbed back up the ladder, and saw an opening at the top of the sculpture — it was hollow. My keys were inside.

Seeing the groundskeeper doubling back around, I lifted my wet cloths and started washing the windows like nothing had happened. "How does that look?" I called down to Maddie, fronting.

"Oh, great," she said, too loud. "Yes, very clean! *So* clean, good cleaning ..."

We finished our work, carefully removed the ladder, and moved on. The only person I told was little baby Abdul, at my next baby-sitting shift.

"And that's the story of how my keys ended up inside of some rich dude's ugly statue," I said, sweetly, while he gurgled. He was propped up on my knees, swaddled — a heavy, warm brick that made me glow with love where his weight pressed down on me. I was slowly and deliberately smoothing cream over the eczema on his cheeks and nose while he blew spit bubbles and looked excitedly back and forth from my left to right eye, taking in everything. Learning. "For all I know, little buddy, that is where my house keys will stay forever."

The week before Saint-Jean-Baptiste weekend, 2013. Snowdon, Montreal.

"What makes you want to work at our day camp?" said the man with the white hair.

I was in a summer dress, my hair up in two buns on the top of my head. I was trying to look whimsical, and full of joy, and not at all desperate. I smiled.

"Oh, uh." I swallowed, and then smiled bigger. "I, uh. Um."

The truth was, I was tired of masturbating for strangers on the internet. I'd been unemployed for about a week before I signed up for a cam site. Camming paid a lot better than window washing. Every incidence of my putting my naked body on the internet was recorded and disseminated on a tube site. I had to swallow the idea that that could ruin my ability to do other kinds of work — that it could permanently damage my relationships and my chances at securing any more work with children. But I'd been fired from the window-washing gig and I couldn't find anything else.

Paula was one of my regulars — respectful, very into me. She made me think I didn't mind the job that much. I was actually thinking about Paula's many virtues when she said, *Tell me about your dad.*

"I, uh." I stopped what I was doing. I sat down, suddenly shy. "I don't … uh, I think that's against like, some rule, or …"

She was quiet for a minute, then logged off.

I sighed, blowing a flop of my heavily coiffed bangs out of my face. I thought maybe this line of work was not for me.

"I just love kids," I told the white-haired man at the job interview, finally. "So much."

He nodded, cast his eyes down, made a note. "What kind of kids?" he asked, and then looked back up at me quickly. "Please say 'little ones.'"

"Oh, yeah," I said. He started furiously scribbling notes. Encouraged, I said, "I started babysitting when I was twelve, so I have like, nine years of experience with kids." This worked him up into a frenzy. He wrote several more notes, pulled open one drawer and then another, took out two brightly coloured Duo-Tangs, shuffled through them for papers, started annotating them.

Encouraged, I went on. "Most of it with children under the age of …"

He looked up, delighted. "Five?"

Sure, I thought. "Yes," I said.

"I got it," I was telling Sandy, on the phone. I'd taken the long way home on foot, cutting through the cemetery on one side of the mountain to climb up, among the dead, to the peak. I got Sandy on the phone near the fence that sectioned off the highway running down the centre of the dead volcano. I was walking along the fence, in my Birkenstocks and summer dress, through the dense brush and boulders dappled as it was by the solstice sun filtering in through the leaves on the trees. I'd just finished my weeping, and I was raw on the inside. Hearing his voice, I relaxed.

"I'm so relieved," I sighed. "I'm such a terrible cam girl."

"I still think you're hot," said Sandy, lovingly. "I would pay you to do stuff on a webcam."

"I do stuff on a webcam for you, for free.

"I have this feeling," I told him. "This feeling like everything's about to change. Get better. Easier."

"I think you're right," he said.

I found a passage bolt-cut in the chain-link fence. I said good-bye and hung up the phone. I clutched my purse close to me, looked both ways as well I could on the long, curving road that disappeared close on either side of me, and I ran in my sandalled feet across the road that broke the mountain into one side for the living and one for the dead.

"Love in the Time of Human Papillomavirus" by AJJ.

Autumn 2013. The Gay Village, Montreal.

Sandy arrived in August. He moved into my room in Gregor's apartment and started art school in the fall. I finished up at the camp and walked away with more babysitting clients. In September, my stipend started up again. I was still making half as much as I'd have to in order to put my head above the poverty line. It was hard not to feel decadent, though, for the way love filled my life.

Sandy practised his figure drawings on huge pads of newsprint, with sticks of sharpened charcoal. He drew me reading my course work: Karl Marx and Tomson Highway and Immanuel Kant, Eden Robinson and Eileen Myles and W.H. Auden. I lay prone and half-naked, on piles of soft things on top of the Ikea bed we were breaking by fucking so much. He let me cut the point off the end of his beard and practise barbering on his wild mop of hair. Sandy got charcoal on the walls, on the refrigerator, and on the doorknobs. It came off on our hands — I undressed to shower and found charcoal on my hips and my thighs and the inner curves of my breasts.

We lived handsomely, the hot yellow light of the sun glowing through the green of the trees that cooled Saint Christophe in the high heat of the summer. When the snow came, it wasn't so hard, with Hex the cat stalking through the drifts of mess on our bedroom floor — stacks of philosophy and poetry books, the sketchbooks, the cast-off clothing, and with our laughter and Gregor's filling up the apartment from the inside, and with a depanneur and its cheap wine barely a stone's throw down the cold street. Had winter ever been hard, I wondered, or was that just something I'd told myself so I didn't forget to enjoy the summer?

I had become the thinnest I'd ever been, in my loneliness and anxiety, the year after I moved. Love filled me up and filled me out. Love piled food onto my plate, drew me down into the bed, chased away the bad feelings I'd wandered the streets for hours and hours trying to outrun. When I started to hate my body, I caught love looking at me over the thick rim of his glasses.

"What?" I asked him.

"You're just ..." He looked away, shook his head, nudged his glasses back up, cleared his throat. "You're just so fucking beautiful."

"Genesis" by Grimes.

February 2014. Montreal.

I will tell my children that the parties were great at the end of the world.

Andrew and Hannah and I were having a party to announce to the media that there was a *new magazine* to watch out for. We had not actually *made the magazine yet*, but we would. On the morning of the apocalypse, I woke up somewhere around ten and I drank black coffee and I smoked weed and cigarettes. Salvador Dalí said he woke up every morning and experienced the singular pleasure of being Salvador Dalí. I experienced the singular pleasure of being myself, and got to work in my Gay Village apartment.

The apartment was too small for three people, especially one serious person (Gregor) and two very not-serious people (Sandy and I). I knew this was a problem, but I didn't do anything. I performed for Gregor, trying to sell the fact that our roommate arrangement wasn't working out. As a performer, I have always been talented, and my talent has always been augmented by a heightened ability to self-delude. This is not self-depreciation. It keeps me alive. It's one of the best things about me.

I looked at myself in the mirror: all wild black bed-head and pudgy tummy. My weight gain was the result of my mental health improving. I was getting better. I didn't hate myself all the way down anymore, I just hated the surface of me, just the way I looked. My eating disorder made me feel this was an unfair trade: a whole life for a thick body. I hated every ounce of my new body, but I was relieved by the knowledge that talent was essentially the mirror inverse of good looks: if you have a good amount of self-delusion, you can fake your good looks to everyone but yourself, which is the opposite of talent, the absence of which is obvious to everyone — except for the mercifully deluded individual. I've never doubted my talent. I am a delusional person. What does that mean, do you think? Don't tell me.

First, I needed a theme. An inspiration. A style icon. The two figures I was fixated on — with the same kind of monogamous and obsessive dedication that underwrote my romantic crushes — were Candy Darling and Hunter S. Thompson. I loved Candy's doe eyes and her thin brows and her bold, anachronistic, old-Hollywood beauty. I loved her slinking vulnerability and her silver-tongued audacity. She was my kind of girl. Hunter was the American moralist — by way of alcohol, drugs, and insanity. Hunter was a man who destroyed himself to expose the rot at the heart of the American consciousness. Hunter was my kind of guy.

I decided on Candy. I did not feel like I was pretty — what's more, I felt like my unprettiness was a fact that I would be foolish and stupid not to accept. I wanted so much to be pretty. Candy was so pretty. Candy and I could not have more different figures — she was a waif, like a fashion model or an underfed teenager. I selected a black dress for myself that had fit, once, but was by this point too tight, and I laid it out on my bed. I built an outfit around it, and threw all of its requisite parts onto the bed alongside.

The dress was boat-necked and, when worn, hugged all of me extremely tightly. It clearly exposed my lumps and my bumps, the places my flesh gathered and then rippled in a cascade of corpulent little gatherings. This was not inherently a problem, but I wasn't deep enough into recovery to be able to live with it. My internalized fat-hatred still ran bone-deep. To suck it up, I would need underwear. Lots of underwear.

To prepare for the underwear, I rendered myself naked, and stepped into the shower. I had to scrub myself down and pat myself all over with harsh astringents, slather myself in thick, whipped body butters and mineral-infused oils. Most importantly, I had to make sure that anything on me that could, at one point, generate any kind of smell, was neutralized and covered in heavy-duty deodorizers. I was not, after all, going to be physically capable of nudity for quite a long time.

A dress this tight necessitated very small private-part-covering underpants, and additional huge compressing layers of public-part-covering underpants. I selected my smallest thong: a tiny, seamless, red thing, and then tore through my dresser looking for appropriate tights. I found control-top nude tights and non-control-top semi-opaque black tights. I tried on my outfit: the thong, my most push-up and padded bra, which unified the divided states of my boobs, my flabby chest skin, and my rib fat. I added a big pair of shaping panties over top of the thong, which began a negotiation to flatten my generous stomach.

From there, I stepped into a tightly constricting full-body-shapewear number that provided additional diplomatic support to the aforementioned divided states of my upper body, and brought them into conversation with my lower body, smoothing over the abrupt line left by the tummy-sucking-in underpants. The shapewear was slightly too small for me, for additional "support" (squishing). Wrestling myself into it took a considerable amount of time. Over that, I put on the control-top nude tights. Over that, the semi-opaque black ones. Finally, the small, slinky dress. I looked in the mirror. Two dress sizes slimmer, or so, due to compression alone, I looked back at myself. I occupied less space, with more mass, like a black hole. Except for the subtle line of the control top, visible through my sheer tights, and the slight shelf of fat caused by the double-layering of tights *over* the shapewear, I almost looked like a real girl. The dress barely covered my ass: I'd have to keep checking to make sure the gusset of my tights was not visible where the skirt stopped off abruptly. I couldn't feel anything through this many layers. *A lot of work to look mostly naked*, I thought. *But it is what it is.* It would do, as long as I never had to pee.

Next, face.

I washed my face — really scrubbed it raw — and then I used astringents to strip it of any remaining moisture, and then reapplied new and better moisture. I painted my face one even colour, a flat circle of beige. I removed all of its variant human colours — the ruddiness of my cheeks and nose, my freckles and birthmarks — and then I reapplied them in different places: the red a bit higher, the shadows a bit more defined. I drew on a completely new face. I patted out the edges of my lips, blurred their borders, redefined them — annexing a not-negligible section of my chin as I did so. I darkened my lash line, extended it into a fine point.

I glued fake eyeball hair over my real eyeball hair: my eyes suddenly heavy, feminine, sweet. I filled in the sparse patch in my eyebrow — if I was really doing Candy, I'd make them thin and arching, Dietrich-esque, but I don't have the requisite waif face. I can tell I'm looking good when I start making eyes at myself in the mirror — pouting and squinting and checking my angles. Nice.

I brushed all the curls out of my hair, burned in better ones, arranged them on my head so they looked intentionally and grace-fully dishevelled. I filled my hands up with mousse, squeezed it into my curls. I went into the bathroom, still squeezing with one hand, and rummaged through the sink storage for the hair dryer and the diffuser attachment. I needed some tunes. I also got myself another coffee, from Gregor's bougie espresso machine. Humming to the tunes, I couldn't help but notice it had gotten dark. I checked the time. It was six.

"Fuck!" I said out loud. How did that happen? I was nowhere near ready. I hadn't eaten anything. My hair still full of rapidly drying medium-hold mousse, one hand sticky and still against my skull, I threw open the door to the refrigerator. The first thing I saw was a half-eaten leftover falafel. It was not mine. I scrunch-dried my hair and dropped pieces of the inside of the wrap far inside the borders of my delicately-made-up mouth. I left the wet pita bread, afraid the bread would cause me to burst like a pierced sausage.

The clock read six twenty. *Okay, okay, maybe it'll still be okay*, I thought, slipping around the apartment in my nyloned feet, grabbing the last of the essentials — phone, almost dead, as always, charger, headphones. Makeup, for touch-ups. Wallet, keys. Notebook. Pen. Laid out on my bed was that outfit's pièce de résistance: a real, vintage mink shrug, which I had bought at a Halifax thrift store for thirty dollars when I was eighteen. It was dishevelled, had a hole in it, and smelled bad. It was the coolest.

It was still winter, but winter was ending. The winds had a humid breath to them now. I put my short black peacoat on, my shrug over my coat. I chose to protect my hair and didn't wear a hat, and I put on fingerless gloves, even though it was too cold: that night was all about *looking good*. I'm *Canadian. Canadian girls* don't *get cold*. It was all about the socks, anyway. I sat down on the wooden chair near my apartment door and put on two pairs of tightly woven wool numbers, so warm and so thick that I had to partially unlace my most formal pair of combat boots to fit my feet inside. The boots gave me a bit of lift that, with the ultra-short skirt, provided me with the *illusion* of legs. As I was lacing them up, Gregor came home.

"Happy Ragnarok," he said, stamping his feet free of snow on the mat by our door.

I laughed, pulling my laces tight around my ankles. "What?"

He was smiling, hanging his coat up. He was handsome, smart, well-educated, and gay. A few years older than me. His apartment was very nice: recently renovated, modern, tasteful. He kept me there like a rescued feral dog — I scuffed his floors, tracked dirt everywhere, left bobby pins in the shower to rust and stain the enamel. He was fond of me, anyway.

"Today," he said. "It's the Viking end of the world, or something."

My boots were tied up, and I was arranging my bag and my shrug and my coat. "I gotta go. How do I look?" I asked, and Gregor fixed me with an intense blue-eyed stare. He nodded. "Fabulous. I'll be there later. Have you eaten?"

"Yeah," I said, opening the door. "You?"

"I have a falafel in the fridge," he said as I left.

As you can see, I am late, I was texting to Andrew. It was 7:13. *This is because of …* I stopped in my tracks, looked up to think of an excuse, and then wrote, *my personality.*

In 2014, William Street smelled like horseshit. The neighbourhood held one of the stables for the city's calèche industry: an ancient relic of a tourist trap in a city full of ancient relics and tourist traps. I trudged on the sidewalk and was passed by a great beast, his stirrups and chains jingling as he headed home to food and water. I waved at his master, who waved back, as I made my way to the loft building where *the performance* was to happen. The night was fresh and cold, the sky a fresh navy blue, the neighbourhood all red at the edges, the snow white at my feet. I cut into a domed opening in the old industrial building: a carriage passage, into a courtyard, where a door was propped open. On it, a sign: *THE BOOM ROOM*, with an arrow, leading to the warm glow of the inside.

The St. Lawrence Warehouse Company is still performing today. They're a folk band, and at the time they were one of those sprawling multi-instrumentalist outfits: guitar, flute, violin, accordion, and so on. I heard their sound check before I got in the door — the meandering hum and whine of strings being eased into place. The hallway leading to the Boom Room was long and wide, illuminated by long strips of fluorescent lights that filled it with an artificial glow. I didn't have to check my nearly dead cellphone again for the exact apartment number; I heard it before I turned the corner, the instruments as well as the conversation. I rounded the corner of the old building. Stylish people were standing in front of an open door. One of them looked at me and squared their shoulders at me. "Doors aren't open yet."

"I'm with the House of Grizzly Andrews," I said, and they let me in.

A soft and pillowy bloom of coats had already exceeded the capacity of the rack just inside the door, so I didn't bother. What struck me first were the lights: all blue, washing up against the far wall of the loft, where the work-worn red brick disappeared into the shadows somewhere short of the twenty-foot ceilings. The space had been barely adapted before it was put to use by a crew of ambitious young people with a more thorough grasp of sculpture than actual carpentry. Tucked into the back, with makeshift walls and approximated soundproofing, was a recording studio. The space had a mezzanine arching like a cave over the entranceway — you could stand on the mezzanine to watch the show. Below the windows, against the far wall, was the stage, washed out in navy blue.

Hanging down in front of the stage, dark against the light, was a wooden swing. I had swung on swings like that, under huge curving trees, where they struck out into buggy summer air and over the lake water, where I'd throw myself and find firm-packed sand and smooth, warm rocks. Or frigid muck, maybe, that buckled under my feet and then sucked me under. Or hard rocks — shiny and sharp with zebra mussels to cut me up into long thin ribbons.

I confirmed my name with the beautiful person taking tickets at the table to the immediate left of the door. *I'm with the House.* They were in the middle of setting the merch table up — they sorted through the piles of burnt CDs wrapped in butcher paper and the handmade patches to find their cache of Sharpies. I pulled one glove down, and they drew a five-pointed star on my wrist.

I wandered into the space, brushing shoulders with busy young people, rubbernecking at the sleeping space being converted into a lounge on the mezzanine, and the small crew of caterers ushering servings of vegan pad Thai into four-inch mini takeout containers, until my eyes landed on Andrew under the merch table directing the unloading of a massive haul of liquor.

We'd talked about an open bar. "It's what will set us apart," said Andrew. I had thought he meant some cheap beer and boxed wine. While supplies last, wine and cheese style. What I saw under the mezzanine was something altogether different: bottles of vodka and rum and whisky, a hip-high stack of cases of beer. We're talking *variety.*

Andrew was as broke as I was. He was a grocery store stock boy, and Hannah was a cashier, and I was a babysitter, and these were the combined salaries on which we were attempting to start a media empire. In spite of my now almost two years of effort, I had never managed to pay down the credit card debt I'd rung up in Europe.

How can we afford all of this? I thought, marvelling as I approached. The men helping him unload had a different *look* than the lithe, stylish twentysomethings who made up the rest of the pre-party party: aged and greying and dark-eyed.

"Hi!" said a voice, very clearly at me, from immediately next to me. I stopped in my tracks where I was marching toward Andrew, trying to remember I was supposed to be a host, trying to smile as I made sudden eye contact with another wide-eyed artist type. He was a twinky redhead with a five o'clock shadow, smiling like he knew something.

"Hi!" I said. "I'm Tara. I'm with —"

"I know!" said the boy, and he laughed, and I laughed. I felt famous.

"I'm Will, I live here." He pointed to the space behind the bar, where there was a mural: an otter, a stag, and a crow. "I'm the otter," he said. He was. The doors were opening, throngs of people milling into the already assembled throng. I watched as Andrew and his bartender volunteers were swallowed behind a wall of young people mewling in approval over the open bar. No time to talk to him, I guess.

The St. Lawrence Warehouse Company played music that sounded like the folk punk I'd heard in Halifax. I couldn't help but shout harmonies along to their final chorus, of the song I'd only just heard for the first time, a mythologization of the metro system that made me want to cry. When the set was ending, I found Andrew at the bar, clutching my fur shrug tighter around me.

"Where did we get all this?" I said, looking out over the rapidly diminishing small fortune's worth of alcohol. He reached behind the bar, grabbed me a bottle of red wine out of a case of red wine, and handed it to me. "Don't worry about it," he said with a smile. I opened my mouth to protest, but right at that moment a short man with a sketchbook appeared out of nowhere, smiling under his black beanie, saying something that I could not hear through the boom of the speaker system and his thick Quebecois accent.

"What?" I screamed in his face, over the noise. He shook his head, then waved with his hands toward a corner with a couch. I did as I was told, sat down on the couch. "I could draw your portrait," he said, and I could hear him this time. He opened his sketchbook on his knees with their black jeans, flipped through portrait after portrait of partygoers in thick, confident cartoon lines. "The only catch is that you have to tell me about your life."

"Oh, my life's not that interesting," I said, cracking the screwtop on the wine bottle, barely managing to even feign humility as I put the bottle to my lips and took a deep swig.

"I am sure it has been fascinating," he said, squinting at my face and then starting a long, black line on his paper. I agreed with him, and I started talking, and Andrew was free from my questioning for another good, long while.

Andrew performed next, and we taped it for a spoken word performance called *Andrew Jamieson Live at the Boom Room*. On the recording, between many references to the smoking of cigarettes, Andrew and I scream insults and declarations of love at each other: he on the stage with a whole bottle of white wine, and me in the audience with a whole bottle of red. The bar was slamming drinks into people — the strange, out-of-place *real adults* had disappeared, leaving only us kids with our booze and our drugs and our smokes. When Andrew was done, as the next act was getting ready, I asked him again.

"Where did we get the drinks?" I demanded, in front of the bar, with another bottle of wine in my hands. The bartenders were labouring in front of jars overfilling with bills and change, labelled *donations* or *tips.* When asked, they said, "The drinks are free, but you can make a donation!" The attendees shoved bright-blue fives and whatever pocket change they had into the jars.

There were enough partygoers to drain the bar somewhat quickly: Andrew, Hannah, and I had all worked very hard to drum up as much drama and hype as we could to surround the event. We soaked labels off of wine bottles in Andrew's Plateau bathtub, dabbed the remaining adhesive off with cotton balls soaked in nail polish remover. We printed off a *select number* of invitations and signed them ourselves. We hand-delivered them to every independent media personality we could get access to. We handed off still more bottled invitations to *cool people*: the underground glitterati, the tastemakers of Canadian *subculture haute couture* — the ones who pulled in eight thousand a week from their online vintage shops, who had sunk their trust funds into indie media empires and played poor until it turned a profit. The New York imports, the L.A. rejects, the crème de la crème of the great Canadian urban migration, which all turned toward the last great bohemian city. At least, I *think* this is who we gave the invitations to. This is who we *intended* to give them to.

The intention was to *raise some buzz* for the magazine we were starting: *The Court.* We had done everything we needed to do to launch the magazine, except for the vast majority of, like, the *work.* We figured we'd get to it.

We made it very clear to the receivers of these invitations that they got *one plus one*, and that *entry was by invitation only*, and then whispered in private that this would pique the interest of party-crashers and clout-chasers. The city was full of people who only wanted into a space because you told them it was *exclusive.* It must have worked: we had hand-delivered forty, maybe fifty invitations. The space was packed: at least two hundred people were crammed in to the rafters, all trying to look like they belonged there, everyone taking pictures or whispering meaningfully or writing something down on a piece of paper. A few of them moved to dance in front of the stage as a two-piece electronica outfit moved us into the next phase of the night. Will, the otter, did a covert uniform change into a red panda onesie for his set with a pop band that had his name — the Willing. They were so surprisingly and genuinely good I almost forgot to ask Andrew, again, about the booze.

"An'rew," I slurred. I was hugging my red wine bottle. My lipstick had transferred onto the spout of the bottle, and the liquid had stained my lips a clashing sort of berry where the makeup had rubbed off. "Where we get drinks at?"

"Oh, right," he said, and then he took the joint out of his mouth, and leaned close to me, so I would actually hear. "The alcohol has been provided by the Hells Angels," he said, like it was not a big deal.

Admittedly, I knew almost nothing about how the Hells Angels functioned, except that they were *bad guys* who did bad guy stuff. Illegal stuff! I, of course, also did illegal stuff — but they did the *bad guy* kind. And now I had to keep a fucking secret? *Fuckin' An'rew.*

Somebody tapped me on my mink-covered shoulder.

I spun around, sure I was about to *get knifed*, or whatever those motorcycle dudes did. I saw a very thin girl, smiling too big.

"Hi!" she said, but it was also a laugh. I gave her a once-over.

"Hi," I said, narrowing my eyes. She was an itty-bitty little waif of a thing, with long hair and some generic hipster outfit. I thought she looked just a little *off* from the rest of us. She looked like she was *trying* too hard, you know? But also not standing out, you know?

"Someone told me you might have weed?" said-laughed the waif-girl, a little too loud.

Very carefully, and too slowly, I said, "I might."

"That's so cool!" she said. Was it? "I was wondering if I could buy some off of you."

I did another, longer body scan. She was wearing some kind of slip dress, Doc Martens, a cardigan. She looked fresh out of 1994.

The look was off, I decided. It was like she'd gotten all of her pieces today at a thrift store and hadn't thought about how they all *worked together.*

"I can give you some," I said. "Later. I'll have to find it."

"Oh, no, I *really* want to *buy* it from you."

Now I was really suspicious. I narrowed my eyes, got icy, unfriendly. *Yeah and I really want to know that you're not a cop, you cop-looking bitch.*

"I'll find you later," I said, firmly. "And *give* you some."

"Okay!" she said, and immediately left. I saw her, a few seconds later, grab another waify girl and start dancing aggressively to the next band — who were called Tofu Stravinsky, a name that still makes me stop, every so often, shake my head, and say "great name" out loud — and then I didn't see her at all for the rest of the night.

I know from an article I wrote about this night that the next band was called Jijune, but with my apologies to Jijune, I was wasted, and I remember none of their set, and could not tell you about it if the alternative was getting knifed by a gangster. The finisher was Zebrat, a gossamer electro-pop duo, composed of the other two residents of the Boom Room — the stag and the crow, by process of elimination. Honestly, the whole end of the show was upstaged by the very last act. Burlesque dancer Gigi Marx, the most beautiful woman I had ever seen, brought the swing back down and performed aerials on it, ending the night standing in nothing but a G-string and nipple rouge.

We were all gathered together by the end: on the couches, obscured by shadows. We talked. We discussed dolphin dialects. We talked rising sea levels. We talked about how animals would take over the world after the end of humanity, if we were the ones calling the shots. I do think the world ended that night — some version of it, at least. I guess it does every night.

The party built some real momentum for Andrew and Hannah and I. We needed to keep it going. Andrew didn't want to put together a quarterly, or even a monthly magazine: he wanted several articles a day, every day. The content, the actual meat of it all: that was my job. Running on this momentum, and full-time school, the hours and hours and hours of work I needed to do to try to bring my debt down, meet the necessary ends, feed the *sheer, mounting number* of bad habits I was picking up: I took all of this and I really ran with it. I ran it right into the ditch. I didn't get it done.

I missed deadline after deadline after deadline, until one morning I woke up to an email from Andrew, firing me. The magazine — whatever of it we had actually *developed*, which was mostly email addresses, a website with a splash page, and a whole lot of hype we couldn't live up to — folded soon after. The House of Grizzly Andrews, built on shaky foundations, was demolished before it was ever truly inhabited. I drank and studied so I didn't feel my shame.

Andrew and I didn't talk. We didn't see each other. Some of my school notes turned into poems. My poems were about Andrew. They were angry, defensive, blaming, and self-aggrandizing. One night, at Kafein, I read one of them. The door was opening and closing and opening again as people came in.

I read the line *I don't owe you anything, I don't owe you one Grizzly Answer.* This was pregnant with so much Andrew-specific symbolism that it would have been impossible to deny its implications. It caused a sharp caw of laughter to echo from the staircase. I glanced over, and he was there, laughing into his hands where they were over his face. Adrenalin shot through my face, chest, and stomach. I didn't falter. I finished my work. In the couches, with my friends, I was looking at the table when two long-fingered hands with chipped black nail polish placed four shots of tequila down on them. I looked up — defensive, or scared, or something. There was no malice in his face, though.

"Nice poem," he said, and pushed two of the shots over to me.

"Thanks," I said, and I motioned for him to sit next to me.

"So, what else have you been writing?"

"I Want You Back" by the Jackson 5.

March 2014. Montreal.

When Abdul cried, I thought my heart would burn up, fall out of my chest, float away. His beautiful little face crunched up into hundreds of little folds. He would ball his hands up into tiny fists and swipe at his own forehead — like he was trying to bat the sadness or the frustration away, send it out of his head where it couldn't hurt him. I wanted to send the sadness where it couldn't hurt him. I tried stories and lullabies and it didn't work.

"Once upon a time," I started, and he cried harder.

"Baa, baa, black sheep," I started, and he'd be quiet for a second. "Have you any wool …" Then he'd scream, thrashing in protest.

"Okay, jeez," I would say, pacing around, thinking, my hand patting his back and his little behind through his onesie and from the space next to his crib. Not leaving. "You're a harsh critic, kid."

Out of ideas, I just started singing, "I Want You Back" by the Jackson 5, because it was what was stuck in my head. Abdul wailed, but then he sniffled, and his crying dulled to a whimper. My voice was creaking and breathy, a whisper compared to the power Michael Jackson had, even as a little boy. Abdul seemed to like it. I looked into the crib, and he had stopped his crying, although his bottom lip was still firmly out, trembling, his eyebrows furrowed and grumpy. I giggled, still singing. He looked like a tiny little man.

I followed the lilting curves of the Motown melody. Abdul's expression softened, his breathing slowed, and got heavy. Then he fell asleep.

Later in February 2014. Montreal.

Thomas was a Mi'kmaw from Listuguj. We met online, and met up at his Notre-Dame-de-Grâce apartment to smoke weed and watch cartoons and talk shit. He was very tall, and had long black hair in a straight muscle down his back. He leant me a T-shirt when I got caught in the rain on my bike on the way to his apartment, and books when he was sure I'd have a dry ride home — Lee Maracle and Leanne Betasamosake Simpson. It was easy and comfortable — an instantaneous friendship, like we were made out of different parts of the same old dead star.

We discussed progress, capital accumulation, with great frustration. On his couch, under the Bob Marley poster and the Mi'kmaw flag, his research from his nearly completed Ph.D. and our dinner dishes on the coffee table, my hair still wet and my heart full, I listened to him.

"I don't think it's unreasonable or uncivilized to use something when it's useful and then let it go," he told me. "Our ancestors built a whole civilization out of birch bark." I think he saw the wonder on my face, and he continued, "You make it into anything, you know?

It's waterproof, malleable ... as long as you don't take too much, it will be there forever. And then when you don't need it anymore, it rots into the ground."

He looked at me, very serious.

"When you have children, their inheritance — you know, all you really need to pass on is your stories."

"Die Young"
by Sylvan Esso.

Even later in February 2014.

When I arrived at the Cock and Bull for the party, arranged by the student organization at the philosophy department, my friends were on the front porch, smoking. I stopped to talk to them. Antoine emerged, looking for one of them. I remember his serious blue puppy dog eyes and his mop of blond hair — the way he seemed to curve at awkward and impossible angles from height, and thinness, his neck perpetually craned. A tall, freaky blond. I remember the way he told me his name, shook my hand, leaned in a little too close. He smelled like woodsmoke, and cigarettes, and sweet vinegar. There was a look of urgency on the face of this man I'd never met — like he'd been waiting for me to get here, for a while, and now we had to get on with it. Whatever it was.

He was friends with another female philosophy student — the program was, at this point, still mostly men, and sticky with casual misogyny. Much of Western thought dealt with the intricacies of the processes and opinions of people writing at a time when the secondary status of women was a given — a tightly woven part of the inherent fabric of the cosmologies we studied. The women in the department spent a great deal of time entertaining insulting ideas. One had to quickly develop firm values of charitability and mercy and patience while people worked out what seemed like they should be obvious stupidities.

And they were stupidities: the basis of most of the rhetoric that props up the subjugation of women is a mistake, which is the assumption that women are incapable of reason or rationality. An absurd error, so boneheaded and clearly false, so unmoored from reality it seems impossible that it was ever believed in the first place. A worryingly solid pillar of thought, so ubiquitous and insidiously believed, that it proves how any falsehood, once uttered, takes on a life of its own. It spreads, like a fire: burns in the heart of the villagers, masks the complex and varied reasons for strife or disagreement. It lights the torches, illuminates the way to the pyre and the stake. It catches and kills the sacrifice, tied there — an offering, an example, a metaphor.

What happened to me, the first time I saw Antoine, was like witchcraft, or a chemical chain reaction. Something similar had happened when I'd seen River for the first time — when she had swaggered in, late, to our twelfth grade philosophy class, five feet and three inches of bulldozer with a labret piercing and teenage white-girl dreadlocks. Something bloomed in my head at the sight of Antoine — caught, and bloomed again in my throat, trickled hot down into my chest. Sudden familiarity. Recognition. Like we'd met before. Complete, overwhelming physical desire. *Yes*, my body said. *Yes, correct, you have found it, and that is it.*

As we entered the bar, he didn't split off — didn't go off to talk to our other friends, didn't wrest his attention on to some other girl.

"What do you study?" he asked me.

Ohmigod, he's talking to me. "Philosophy," I said, laughing, twirling my hair, feeling sparks go off in my body. "This is a philosophy party, *silly.*"

"Yeah, but I don't recognize you."

"Yeah, well …"

"And I'd recognize you."

Spark ignited. Synapses fired. Dependency activated. I was hooked — an addict at first exposure. We slunk to the back of the bar, away from it all, to talk philosophy and depression and his now-ex-girlfriend who was still his roommate. We drank, excessively. When I finally left, I left with his number and in a daze. *I think I have a crush on your friend Antoine,* I texted that mutual female philosopher friend during my cab ride home. Our instant connection was bolstered by his connection with my fellow female philosopher — another descendent of Hypatia, so bored of and accustomed to commonplace misogyny, one eye always nervously on the oyster shells. We were tough critics. This granted him credibility. I think I was already in love.

Maybe I'm wrong. I'm trying not to have a feeling and then call it reason, because it's happening to me. So maybe it wasn't love. Maybe it was just the beer. Maybe it just *felt* like divine intervention, or a natural disaster, something so major we split the calendar up into what came before and all the time after.

"Somebody up There Likes Me" by David Bowie.

April 2014. The Plateau, Montreal.

Andrew's apartment wasn't a safe space. I was uneasy. Something was different.

When Andrew looked at me, I was rebuffed by a physical wall of resentment. He had the air of a big, strong dog who had been hit, a mother who had been disappointed. I needed him, and I needed us reunited, but I was wary.

He poured me too much wine into a jar while I thought about him. I was thinking about him like one spouse thinks about the other when the rough patch is really rough. We had stayed together for the kids, sure — our kids were the art, and Hannah, and his straight boyfriend who was always around. I knew that everybody at the country club could see we had problems.

My relationship with Andrew was a romantic one in every way except for the romance: we had fallen in *art love* quickly, maddeningly, and forever. The eroticism of our union is creative, intellectual, generative, sexless, but still physical. He cut me like a spouse. Our conflict bruised like the words of an old lover. In his apartment, with its low-lying furniture and its religious decor, everything in abrupt lines of white and black, I tried to keep him close but out of swiping distance. He was beautiful, like a jewel-toned amphibian. He was beautiful like a raptor. I felt safe in my distance. To congratulate myself for my distance, I threw my head back and opened my throat to welcome the wine: too much, and all at once.

"I just don't understand how you could not like *Young Americans*," said Andrew, bent over his massive white Ikea desk, trying not to lose too much weed in the peeling finish as he laboured over an enormous joint. Andrew loved David Bowie.

"The issue isn't with *Young Americans*," said Dorian, Andrew's straight boyfriend. "The issue is that I don't really like David Bowie."

The fact that Dorian wasn't much of a Bowie fan had long since eclipsed Dorian's heterosexuality as the central tension to their relationship. Andrew struck the table with his open palm. I started at the noise, jumping as tiny marijuana bud particles were launched into the air.

"Well, as you know, that's unacceptable," said Andrew, very quietly, his palm still against the desk, without looking up. Dorian clearly did not understand the gravity of the situation, leaned back in the low futon couch where he was sitting just to the right of Andrew's desk. He had a wide-brimmed fedora crowning his pretty little elfin head, his long hair escaping out from under it in a shiny brown cascade.

"It's just how I feel," he said, taking a deep swig from his own Mason jar full of too much wine.

"How you feel is *unacceptable*," seethed Andrew through his gritted teeth, just calm enough to continue rolling the joint. He licked the edge of it too quickly, eyes going wide as he twisted the joint smoothly and expertly up from the base, before beginning to aggressively push weed down into the cylinder with a takeout container chopstick.

"He just doesn't do it for me," Dorian said, slurring slightly, his wine jar almost empty.

"All twenty-five of David Bowie's albums —" Andrew shoved the joint in his mouth and swivelled his desk chair abruptly to face Dorian and fix him with a withering stare. Muffled by the joint, he said pointedly, "— *just don't do it for you?*"

Dorian didn't find any of this aggressiveness disturbing. He blinked slowly and then turned to face Andrew, smiling when he saw his face so close. He reached into the pocket of his vintage black tuxedo slacks and took out a Zippo, flicking it to burning a few inches away from where the joint hung out of Andrew's mouth. Andrew's look of complete seriousness cracked. He leaned forward and puffed in a few times, the joint blooming into a solid smoulder in front of his face. "Thanks," he muttered through the joint and the smoke. Dorian kissed him on the cheek.

"Gotta pee," Dorian said, and stood. Andrew followed him with his eyes, reaching up to curl his fingers around the joint, take a big inhale, let the smoke curl out of his mouth. He turned his chair to zero in exactly on Dorian's retreating back. Dorian had to pass next to me, where I sat awkwardly on a wooden chair that was missing its back leg, propped up against the wall next to the bedroom door.

Andrew stayed staring at me as Dorian left. He had mostly been ignoring me up until this point. This was on purpose. He wanted me to know he remembered what I did.

He offered me the joint.

"Not tonight," I said, and he smiled really big and took a deep drag. We sat in silence for a minute while he smoked. I wished Dorian would come back.

"Where are we going?" I asked.

"Oh, you'll see," Andrew said, and for the first time, I was not intrigued by his performative vagueness, but annoyed by it. I looked over at Hannah. She was on her phone. I had the sense that wherever we were going, we were late. I was uncomfortable. White wine gives me heartburn.

Dorian came back and Dorian was very drunk, almost too drunk to stand. "Guys," he said. "Guys, look." He held up his finger, and on it was a tab of acid.

"You sharing?" asked Andrew, grinning. Dorian took it all in one fell swoop. Hannah and Andrew started talking about the theatre.

When we did leave, Dorian was passed out cold. He was lying on the mattress, not moving. "Are you dead?" I asked, only half joking. He said, "Eh," and turned over. I got my stuff. We were going to leave.

"One second," said Andrew, in a singsong innocent voice. He got a water bottle and an empty Mason jar, put those next to the bed. He took off Dorian's hat and laid it gently on the couch. He turned off the overhead light, threw a red scarf over the lamp. The room's air muted, filtered, and suddenly warm. It was cozy. I was touched by his sweetness. "That's nice," I said. Andrew was fiddling with his record player. He reached into his small collection. He was going to put on music for his fucked-up boyfriend. He put on *Young Americans* and then said, grinning wicked, "Let's go!"

I laughed, in spite of myself. "Are you trying to CIA PSYOP him?"

Andrew's door locked from the outside. I guess it was never meant to be a bedroom. It was never meant to hold a sleeping body, or at least not a trusting one. Andrew closed the door, rested his finger on the lock for a second, and then barred it, locking Dorian in with Bowie.

Waking up felt like pushing myself slowly through some kind of tight, hot, sludgy hole. The headache was a burning in my eyes, and the skin of my cheeks, a fever in the place where each of the hairs of my eyebrows rooted themselves into my pores.

I was face down on a loveseat, my head twisted to wedge itself against the armrest. My hips were twisted sideways, my legs cramping where they'd been stuffed into the not-enough space. I peeled my face off the couch, and my hair and skin tugged in the places where my drool and a tiny dribble of vomit had affixed me to it. More little fevers erupted in my neck when I moved it. There were sudden, bright stabs of pain that warned me not to move too quickly. I had to push myself up with my arms. I realized, distressed, that I was not even sure where my arms were. It took a few moments of opening and closing my eyes, loosening crumbling goobers like dead flies being washed off of a windshield, to find them. One was against the wooden floor, numb from cold. The other was wedged under me, numb from a lack of blood flow.

With the cold hand, I heaved myself down and away from the armrest of the couch. I turned myself sideways. I moved my head back and forth, the nerves and muscles crackling and erupting into a glittering light show of pain. I did this for long enough to determine that my neck was not broken. Pins and needles cascading through my cold arm informed me that the sensation loss was not permanent. I was not dying. I had just gotten too drunk and passed out all crumpled up. I had just been too drunk to wake up when my body stopped sending blood to the ends of me.

When I could move my neck, I rolled onto the floor. More fevers erupted as I hit the ground. They were in my joints, as they woke up, groggy and cawing out in protest. The fevers were in my flesh where they collided with the ground. Each isolated incident would have been manageable, but inevitably, they all met up, the pain building and spreading like a forest fire.

Down there, I picked up the numb hand in the cold one. My own numb arm was alien, soft, and too heavy in my cold hand. I shook my dead arm: once, twice, three times. It didn't react. The pins and needles were spreading down my arm: the cap of my shoulder to my tricep and down toward my elbow. They were moving slow. Nowhere near my hands.

Saturday night palsy is a colloquial term for an injury caused by the compression of the radial nerve. The term is a reference to the tendency to carouse on Saturday night. It's often the result of someone falling asleep on a chair with their arm hanging over the back. The condition is usually temporary. Sometimes, normal functioning doesn't return for weeks or even months. In some cases, it causes cell death. Severe cases can require the amputation of the limb.

I had the sense that I was tipping backward and then forward, even though I knew I was lying there on the ground. I shook my dead arm over and over. I was trying to move my hand, but I couldn't. I shook it again. *Oh God.*

Suddenly, sensation bloomed in the core of my arm, warm and spreading. My fingers twitched. There was a sense of relief, burgeoning despite the devastation in the rest of me. Then, over top of the relief, was the cascade of a million tiny pinpricks of pain. I dropped my hand. The room pitched to one side. I slapped my cold hand to my mouth, and it barely managed to hold back the vomit that erupted there, hissed out in pressurized streams from the cracks between my fingers and my cheeks. It seared its way up through my sinuses and out my nose, all over my icy hand, and slapped hot and burning onto the ground.

In the bathroom, over the toilet, I was racked-through with convulsions as deep and desperate as sobs of profound grief. My hand slipped off of the toilet seat and I pitched forward mid-heave, my head resting against the toilet seat, riding the waves of relief and unease and sickness again and again. I could smell nothing but the sharp acid smell of my own insides. When I was done, I was empty of everything but pain. I lowered myself to the floor and curled like a baby around the toilet, counting my shuddering breaths until I could reach up to the tank lever with my slick and ruined hand.

"Good morning!" said Andrew's voice from behind me. A visual would have been impossible. I was sure that if I got up, I would die. I groaned. He laughed.

"Poets, man," he said. The way he said *poets* was clearly meant as an insult. He was leaving for work. He was fine. Andrew always seemed fine. He never slept and he was always *fine*. I hated how fine he was, as I felt his presence leave the doorway without seeing it. He returned with a jar full of water, which he wedged between me and the toilet.

"Stick around, if you want," he said. "Dorian is still asleep."

When I drank the water, I felt joy. My body erupted into desperate pleasure wherever it was touched by the water. I gulped the water down. The water gave me strength. *Nothing is more beautiful than water*, I thought, sucking the water deep down into my body that was mostly water. I lay flat on the floor, a cool pool of water in the centre of me. I got back on my knees, and vomited again, but even that made me feel a bit better — better enough to stand and wash my hands at the sink, and then cup them together and bring more water to my mouth. I stuck my fingers inside my mouth and rubbed them hard into my teeth. I spat blood and water and saliva into the sink.

Stronger now, my body started to put me back together. I cleaned the filthy little space where I had been lying, and then washed my hands again, splashed my face. *Drink more water*, screamed my body. I tried to put the jar Andrew left me under the sink, but it clinked against the faucet and didn't fit. I left my shame in the bathroom and walked, renewed, into the kitchen.

When I had downed three more glasses, I became acutely aware that I needed to leave. Water was only going to do so much. I needed stronger stuff: Pedialyte or Gatorade, some kind of egg-based sandwich, a half-gram of good weed, and a stupid TV show. I heard the toilet flush as I headed out to gather my things, and as I walked past the bathroom Dorian emerged, looking dazed. We exchanged *hello*s and *I feel like shit*s with one another, and then filed into Andrew's bedroom. I could feel the dawning creep of dread in my throat and the pit of my stomach. I needed fresh air. I needed a shower. I needed Sandy. I was sweating, my body purring with tremens. I was sure I was acting weird — not that Dorian noticed. Dorian seemed to be somewhere else.

"What happened last night?" he finally asked.

"You passed out," I said.

He was setting up the record player.

"What are you putting on?" He didn't answer.

The opening chords of *Young Americans* struck up, and Dorian looked up from the spinning record to stand, staring, at the wall.

"Sympathetic Character" by Alanis Morissette.

May 2014. The Gay Village.

Sandy's presence was bothering me. I wasn't so sure about *us*. I used to be so skinny, and so slutty, and now look at me — domestic and doughy and *happy*. Like an *idiot*. And what if it doesn't work out? Boys will never want me like this. What if it does? Can I live the rest of my life knowing I let it all fizzle out when I was *twenty-one* because a guy I met when I was *nineteen* who's *old and stuff* moved to be with me?

It had only been eight months, or so, of living with me, and he'd already spent the lion's share of his savings. He needed fast cash, and quick. He got onto an internet forum for tree planters and found a crew boss who needed people. He'd be leaving for North Bay in the morning. I was delighted. I pictured a perfect version of myself who would emerge: modern and sexually liberated, from this summer of independence. We'd talked about monogamy, again, and I was wearing him down. I was sure if something happened, it wouldn't be the end of the world. And if it was the end of our world — I was only twenty-one. I would build a new one.

He left on a bus for North Bay, in the morning, a week before my twenty-second birthday. At thirty, he'd be the oldest person on his crew — planting was a young man's game — but he was determined.

"I want to make you proud," he said.

"Aww," I said, not looking up from where I was texting with Antoine.

I saw Sandy off, on his bus. I smiled as the bus pulled away. I came home to our apartment, empty of him, and I lay down on our bed, and I barely stood up until he came home.

I started my days intending to do things. *Today's the day I really get my shit together.* Then I would take too long on the first few tasks of the day. I would lay down, mentally exhausted, to take a break. I would look up, and it was 4:00 p.m., nothing done. Any semblance of a schedule slipped away in the long, lazy days as spring grew strong and bold into summer. I had enough work to cover my bare expenses — babysitting, busking, postering for musicians — but no *regular sched-ule*, no *money*, not for anything other than food or bills or minimum credit card payments or purely medicinal rations of alcohol. I had Gregor, and my uneasy truce with Andrew, and the affection of a handful of school pals, but most of them had fucked off for the summer months. I missed Halifax and my friends — my something like a *community*, the people who would flop over to watch me do my dishes, drag me out of my house when I was mired in misery like this. I missed Matilda. I would have even watched *Pulp Fiction* again.

The best friend I had was Abdul. He had learned to sit upright, but then had been slow to adopt crawling, preferring to scoot about on his behind, dragging himself this way and that in a sitting position using the power of one of his legs. Then, he'd dragged himself onto his feet, to stand, and skipped over crawling altogether to walk, assisted by the furniture, around the apartment. He knew a few words, but communicated mostly with his eyes and his fingers. Once, I made him angry — probably by not letting him play in the garbage — and he scooted over to my purse. He shoved it in my direction, and then pointed at the door, pouting. I burst out laughing.

"Boss," I said, through peals of laughter. "Did you just tell me to get the *heck* out of your house?"

Begrudgingly, he let me wash him and change him and put him to bed. He was quiet through our storytime, longing for garbage — his ultimate, forbidden plaything. He was pretty mad. He only really softened when I sang him his song — "I Want You Back" by the Jackson 5. When I turned off his light and closed his door, he was quiet. Then his voice came from inside his crib, inside his room — so quiet, a private little concert, just for himself, singing the *ooh*s and *yeah*s and *baby*.

Abdul's sweetness was my medicine. After a few hours of caring for him, I would leave, feeling almost normal. It would be days, sometimes, before the darkness crept back in.

Sandy's work schedule was five days of work, one day off. I tracked the days on my phone calendar, even though I wasn't so sure about *us*. The days he was going to call I barely got up, at all — waiting for his annoyingly short fifteen-minute call from a pay phone in some part of Ontario so remote and northern there was no cell service. As I waited around, one call day, I went to the washroom without my phone. When I came back, I had a missed call from an Ontario number I didn't recognize.

In a sudden panic, I called it back. It rang, but nobody answered. *Oh god, no*, I thought, with an explosiveness I didn't know was in me. *No, no, no.*

I rang the pay phone in Ontario three more times before I gave up. I sank to my knees, next to my bed, with my elbows on my mattress. I clasped my hands together, as if in prayer.

"Please," I whimpered — to Sandy, or God. "Please. I need you."

I cried, and I cried, and then I felt the bed vibrate. I looked up at my phone, and there was the number.

"Hello?" I gasped, obviously weeping.

"Hi, baby!" Sandy said. He sounded low, metallic, far away. I lit up with joy.

"Oh God, I'm so happy," I said, tears running down my face. "I'm so happy to hear your voice."

"I thought I missed you," he said.

"Me, too," I said. Then I said, "I love you," and I meant it with every part of my body that glowed and hummed with the sound of him.

I went to Kafein a few times in the spring and summer and Andrew wasn't there. When I finally got in touch with him, he told me that he and Dorian had broken up, and that he was too sad and crazy to do his normal things.

I saw a few good poets a couple times, but on average the scene had become younger and more heavily saturated. It was packed every night. I could never find a place to sit. I didn't feel moved by the work. I wondered if I was too old, now, to really get it — if I had missed the train, like had I missed the train for being a smartphone expert or a *Twilight* fan.

I was twenty-two. I was getting the second wave of inappropriate aging anxiety I had felt when I was nineteen. I had this sense that everything that was really great or cool or fun, which was ever going to happen to me in all of my life, had already happened to me. *I've really blown it now*, thought twenty-two-year-old me. All my friends from high school were graduating. I had at least two more years of school left to do before I could graduate. Dread spoke to me from somewhere primal and it told me there was something wrong with me. I stopped going to Poetry Nite at Kafein.

"The Best Ever Death Metal Band in Denton" by the Mountain Goats.

Late August 2014. Montreal Central Bus Station.

When he stepped off the bus, I hardly recognized him: brown as a paper bag, beard and hair both long, his blue eyes bright from all the way across the station. Sandy had been doughy with love and academia when he left three months earlier, but now his arms were rail-thin under the sleeves of his beaten white button-up, save for elevator cables of muscle. He grabbed his overburdened canvas backpack with one of those strong arms and effortlessly hoisted it over his shoulder. I could see that his back had been straightened by work. He wasn't walking with that bewildered look. He stepped with a confidence I didn't know was in him. He was *hard*. He finally looked his age.

He saw me, and softened. His stride faltered, before he gathered himself and continued back to me. I thought of Tim, standing in our kitchen on Birmingham Street, the moment I knew I really wanted him — the moment I started to understand that he was really pulling away from me. Sandy didn't pull away; Sandy walked forward, nervous and brave. I saw glimmers of the man he had been, and it struck me, then, that I'd already seen him become different people. The mild-mannered veteran animator with a nervous stutter who had quietly slipped me his virginity before I knew what was going on had been a different man. So had the first-year art student, who had seemed so much younger — immortalizing my aggregating curves on paper, desperate to preserve the beauty he saw in all the parts of me I hated the most.

This man — strapping, weather-beaten, accomplished, mature — was someone else, entirely. I wondered how many new skins he would age into, or shed. I felt some wall I'd built after Tim start to break. I hoped wherever Tim was, he was good.

We didn't speak, when Sandy reached me. He set his bag down, so softly it didn't even shake the ground. I pressed myself against his chest, and he put his arms around me and kissed me, and all was well.

Abdul could say new words whenever I arrived. *Remote. Lapin. Milk.*

I would come depleted and sad to Abdul's house, and then get to work doing his bidding. *Collation. Peppa Pig. Hug.* I followed him around the house while he asked for things, naming them, learning. He only listened to my *no* when I said it in Arabic: *la*. I followed him into the bathroom, where there was still a tub full of water.

"*Ma'an*," he said, but I didn't understand. He put his hands into it, splashing. "*Ma'an*," he said again.

"I don't know what that means, Abdul," I said, adoring him.

He looked at me, feeling bad for me, looking like a tiny old man. He came over, and took my hand, and then put it in the water. "*Ma'an*," he said, and I understood. The bathwater.

"Ma'an," I repeated, amazed. He nodded, relieved, like there was hope for me yet.

The sadness descended over me and weighed me down onto the floor. I called Kate, and she came to visit me, all the way from Halifax. She slept on the couch in the apartment in the Gay Village. I was happy to see her but I felt embarrassed. I didn't want her to see me messy and slow and stinking of misery. She fed me wine and Thai food, and tried to snap me out of it.

We went out dancing. We climbed the mountain. We went out for dinner, lunch, breakfast — ordered Caesars with our eggs and toast. When that didn't work, all out of ideas, we gathered the equipment for the heavy medicine. Kate boiled a sewing needle and a shot glass in water, stuck the eye of the needle firmly into the eraser of a pencil, dabbed a midnight blot of ink into the glass, and got to work. My jobs were these: to not move too much, and to feed her sips of beer so she could drink without sullying her gloved hands. I did my first job poorly and my second job better.

Matilda couldn't come for the trip, so we inked her into my leg. We deposited her in there, by way of the same pain, over and over again, meticulously opening me up, until the dots joined together, made little black words that spelled *NOTHING WILL BE DIFFERENT.*

"The Modern Leper"
by Frightened Rabbit.

September 2014. Montreal.

In the fall of 2014, I tried to cure myself with academics. I felt old and insecure and like I needed to make up for it.

At first, it really did work. I started the year on an impossible high. Everything was too easy. I had the answers to every question. I walked from school to study space, to work, to party, music blasting into my headphones, feeling exactly like a character in a TV show about my life. Then, one day, without much fanfare or much of an antecedent, that high hit some kind of solid and invisible wall. *That's funny*, I thought, as the feeling changed direction like a snake in a video game. *Huh*, I thought, as the feeling curled tightly into itself. *Uh* ... I thought, as it took several huge and painful bites out of itself, confused. Huge tumours bloomed from its mouth and out of the wounds. Its belly swelled. Its tumours started to pulsate and drop off, eight more hydra tumours growing in its place. It was thrashing, eating itself and its cancer, and growing. It was all around me. I couldn't get out. I lost my mind, completely.

In November of 2014, I texted my dad and told him I couldn't stop crying and I was scared of everything. I told him I felt like nothing was real and I was so sad and I couldn't get out of bed. I was sick: there was an infection in my mouth that wouldn't go away. My muscles felt paralyzed and thick with some embodiment of my misery. When I walked down the street, the street looked at me — it was unchanged, except that every aspect of it was sinister and cruel. The cars were sinister, cruel cars. The sky was a sinister, cruel sky.

That is depression, Tara. It runs in your family.

I told Gregor, a sweet man who loved me, that I had to move out. I didn't know why I had to move out, but I did. I had to get away. I broke his heart.

Sandy and I moved out just before Christmas. I called in sick to my family Christmas, and I didn't head back east with Sandy. I ran a bath, and drank an entire bottle of wine in it, alone, in my new apartment. Sandy and I chose it specifically for its distance from downtown. I didn't want to be close to any people, or parties. I didn't want anyone to have access to me. I wanted to be anonymous and separate and far away. The new year passed with little fanfare. I drank and I was quiet. I saw a therapist who couldn't prescribe me anything, but who referred me to the bipolar study centre at the Douglas Mental Health University Institute.

"I'm calling to confirm that you're on the waiting list," said the receptionist, or the nurse, or whatever, from the Douglas. "We will call you when you have an appointment. It might take a long time."

"Some Unholy War"
by Amy Winehouse.

January–May 2015. Montreal.

When the depression got so bad I couldn't get out of bed, sometimes I could trick myself. One of my best tricks was bothering
Sandy until he brought coffee into our bed, which I would drink
until I was sick with anxiety. The anxiety would light a dull fire
under the hot blanket of nothing that was my depression, make
me so scared I would need to leave the bed. I was still burdened,
heavy — gravity schemed with wretchedness, nagged at me like a
guilty conscience, tried to pull me down to the earth. From the effort of staying upright, I would sweat the foul, sweet vinegar
sweat of a sick mammal. I imagined it was what hell smelled
like. I only had enough gumption to care about a few, select things, so I walked around, letting the world smell the sin
on me. I did only what was necessary, and then I went back to
bed.

My other trick was Antoine. *Antoine.* We had a few of the same classes, and when I woke in the morning and knew I'd see him, my depression dropped straight down into a gnawing pit of want. I painted my face and carefully chose my clothing, pulled forward like a starving person toward nourishment. It was night and day: the desperate scramble toward him, the languishing hours of nothing.

Sometimes, when I got to class early, I'd sit a little farther away from the rest of our friends — not far enough that it was any kind of big sacrifice, just far enough he'd have to make a choice, if he wanted to be with me. When he arrived, he always came to me.

"Hi, handsome," I said. He blushed, taking his seat. We drew swirling doodles and penises on each other's school books while our lecturers talked about epistemology and political theory. We smoked cigarettes together on every break, huddled together in a private universe. I figured it was as good a reason as any to start smoking for real. I sent my prayers up to heaven with my smoke: *Give me what I want.*

When I started craving the cigarettes without him, I was angry. *If I get a tumour, I'll name it after you,* I wrote in a poem. Like it was his fault.

Sandy wasn't really non-monogamous. He could handle my not being sexually exclusive, but he could see me pining and felt threatened. He would ask me, "What do you want?" I'd say, "I don't know." Now I thought about Antoine every time I walked past a depanneur, or smelled a cigarette. I started writing the Jenny Holzer truism next to my notes, in class, over and over again: *PROTECT ME FROM WHAT I WANT.*

What I wanted, unfortunately, was dating *her,* again — the same girl he had talked about at the bar. They were monogamous, of course. *Typical.*

I hated that he was dating her, but I didn't actually hate *her*. I felt a sort of loyalty to her. I wouldn't kiss her boyfriend — I couldn't. I would get no pleasure from it. I would just *pine* for her boyfriend — let the thought of her boyfriend fill me up so full I couldn't eat and my pants got loose. I would just watch her boyfriend's eyes linger on me the smaller I got. This chaste betrayal felt like the fight for my life — when I didn't see him, the heaviness piled on to me. The agony was so vast it wasn't even interesting, boring me straight to the doors of death. There, I would consider crossing over, and then turn on my heels, to run back to another girl's boyfriend. I lived for the little slices I got of him — the way he looked breathless when he told me *Hello, Beautiful* instead of *Good morning*.

When we got together outside of school, it was always to drink. One night, we met up to study, and snuck beers into an empty room in the philosophy department. I was impaired by the drink, but mostly I was high on him. I didn't want to leave. I was afraid that if I broke the spell the heaviness would pin me down again — and what if I couldn't get up this time?

The night gathered — study hours turned into drinking hours turned into carousing hours, and by the time I checked the clock it was past 3:00 a.m.

"Shit," I said. "We have to leave. It's almost morning."

I called us a cab to drive us, one after another, back to our lives. When it arrived, I was suddenly terrified at the idea of being in the back seat with him. I could not be trusted, back there, with another woman's boyfriend, his body so hot and so close. I basically ran for the front seat, face burning, and felt him crawl in behind me. We rode in silence, for a while, and it was almost fine. I had remained chaste, and loyal, to the girl I didn't love. He shifted in the back seat. I could feel him staring hard into the back of my head. Then he reached forward, between the headrest and the passenger side window, and tangled a longing, probing, searching hand into my mess of black hair.

"I like you," I told Antoine. I was wearing my black American Apparel party dress. We were outside, on the street. He had class in a minute. I had to leave. A school magazine I was editing was having a launch party downtown, and I had to go set up — the stuff I'd done with Andrew and Hannah had been good training, after all, and I was starting to grow into an identity as *a writer.* The launch party would have cool local indie bands, hip hop groups, a live DJ. It would be very well-attended. We were going to stuff the cash box with donations for a local LGBTQ youth organization. All the hip young queers would be holding a copy of the magazine that I had *actually finished,* with my team, while they bopped and swayed in the black box theatre we'd rented on Sainte-Catherine Street. I didn't know I'd been doing a good job — I'd been studying hard, saying the right things in class, turning in my papers despite the crushing force of *the depression* that left me alone.

He blinked, confused. He seemed speechless, for once.

"Like, I *like*-like you," I said. "And I know you're with some-body, and so nothing has to happen — like, I don't expect anything to happen — I just ..." I thought, *Every time I see you I am lying. I'm allowing this relationship to continue under false pretenses, and while I know that telling you can only serve to make your life harder and my life easier, I want to believe that this is the right thing to do. This levels the playing field. This tells you where I'm at. This makes it less hot — but it does make it right.* Instead, I said, "I was going crazy not telling you."

He looked at me with his sad blue eyes, hiding under his floppy hair with his neck craned forward, his hands fumbling with his leather briefcase. He looked, suddenly, less like the handsome young man I'd fallen in love with, and more like a tall boy playing dress-up. After much thought he said, "Okay."

"Come to my show tonight," I said, and I sounded calm, but it was a plea.

"Okay," he said, but he didn't.

"Not the Same" by Ben Folds.

May 2015. Sudbury, Ontario.

I was checking my list. It was cold in the parking lot outside the Foodland on the outskirts of Sudbury, and my fingers were numbing where they were sticking out from under my hoodie, running over our list. We had everything, I think. Very importantly, I had the new antipsychotics I'd been prescribed at the Douglas Mental Health University Centre. Tents, check. Bug spray, sunscreen, check and check. I could probably use more socks, but couldn't we all?

"Water bottles," I said.

"Huh?" Sandy punctuated his question by throwing down the hockey bag he had been carrying all the way from the motel, hunched over and sweating, an overburdened squire. It hit the ground with a muffled thump and sent a radius of tiny rocks around us jumping into the air.

"We don't have any water bottles," I answered, and I was suddenly panicking. Pickup time was at one in the afternoon, and it was twelve thirty. Down to the wire, much? What, did I not think that water was important? *Stupid.* Sandy could see me getting anxious. Of the two of us, he was usually the anxious one: his anxiety radiated off him, filled up a room, got on to other people. In this situation, he was surprisingly calm. Suave, even.

"I got it, babe," he said, knowingly. "Be right back."

He left. I waited in the parking lot, which was sunny and bright and cold. The brightness got in my eyes, and the cold wind blew my black hair into my eyes, and I had to squint so hard to see anything, and there was nothing to see. Everything looked blue and white and washed out, like a movie poster that has been left in a sunny window for too long.

It was the middle of spring: the very tail end of April 2015. In two days, I would be twenty-three. The year that had started with a mental breakdown had ended up preparing for a common last-ditch option for the depressed and the downtrodden and the out-of-options: my very first season of professional tree planting in Canada's boreal forests, a great northern rite of passage.

At 12:45 p.m., Sandy returned with two grocery bags. I had grown impatient in his absence, and I was relieved and a little angry when I saw him. What's more, I was confused: so far I could see only four or five other planters, scattered about the parking lot. We were supposed to get picked up in fifteen minutes. I had insisted we show up early.

"We don't have to," Sandy had said.

"We absolutely do," I'd said, before launching into a sanctimonious diatribe about the importance of making a good first impression and how that may not be important to him but it was to me, and on like this.

"Okay, babe," said Sandy, not pressing the matter. At least we were still technically early, and finally with all of our stuff. Sandy put the bags down and reached inside. He pulled out two four-litre milk jugs and a Diet Coke.

"Here you go," he said, handing me the Diet Coke.

"Babe," I said. "Is this my water bottle?" I asked, motioning to the Coke bottle.

"No, babe," he said, meaningfully. "*This* is your water bottle." He was holding one of the milk jugs aloft. He had purchased eight litres of whole milk.

"Babe," I said. "Babe, I'm lactose intolerant."

"I know," he said, and took a long, slow swig of milk. When he was done, the moustache of his full beard was cloudy with dairy. He sat down on the hockey bag. He was wearing a death metal T-shirt, ill-fitting jeans, a jean jacket. His reddish-brown hair was growing out of the bad haircut I'd given him myself at home a few weeks earlier. He sat back, relaxed.

"Are you going to drink eight litres of milk in" — I checked my phone — "fifteen minutes?"

"No," he said, and did not elaborate. He stared out into the parking lot. I looked at what he was staring at, but it was nothing. I sat down on the concrete in an empty parking spot, next to the hockey bag. I cracked the Diet Coke.

"So," he started. "What are the top five most meaningful parking lots in your life, so far?"

The clock was approaching two, a full hour later than I was told was the very strict, no-exceptions pickup time. Sandy had disposed of most of the first gallon of milk, at least. A bird cawed. The wind ran through the budding leaves on some tree that I could hear but I couldn't see. The sun had made it to our side of the strip mall, and I'd unzipped my hoodie, tied my hair up, relaxed a little.

A red car pulled into the parking lot and parked in a space a few over from where we were sitting. We had finished ranking parking lots and we were now ranking dirt roads. A tall man with a face like a French nobleman in a period movie stepped out of the car. He had delicate facial hair and skin that was sun-leathered and ruddy where it wasn't hidden by clothes, but I could see that he was young. He looked like an angel but was dressed like a cowboy: chisel-toe leather boots, blue jeans, an appropriately weathered vintage bomber jacket. He was grinning. He was looking at my boyfriend.

"Sandy!" he called out. "Buddy!"

Sandy looked up and smiled a smile reserved for his friends — his real ones. His decade-or-more ones. This kid was closer to my age: in his midtwenties, at the oldest. I realized that he must have been another veteran planter, a *vet* like Sandy as opposed to a *rookie* like me, someone Sandy had met last year. Sandy smiled his relaxed, lopsided smile. Sandy stood up.

"Cookie!" he called. "Dude!"

They walked toward each other, arms out. *Cookie?* I mouthed to myself, silently. I stood, sheepish and shy. I shuffled over to the car, which was now being unloaded with more human beings than it looked capable of carrying. There was a very tall man and a very short one, and three girls. One of the girls shrieked with satisfaction to be out of the car, reached her toned arms up into the air, and then immediately launched into a handstand, her legs pawing at the sky as effortlessly as a dog turning over at rest. I continued to shuffle over to the car, very aware of my body. My thighs rubbed together as I walked.

At the car, Sandy introduced all of the car people he knew. Some of them had strange and symbolic names. They were absurd things like Squeebus, or Pepsi, or Slutty Dave.

"I'm Tara," I said. "So, I'm assuming these must all be like, family names?"

They all laughed. Thank God.

"They're bush names," explained a six-foot-tall white girl with an ass-length blond braid, tiny circular glasses, and a wool sweater on under a pair of work overalls. "They usually start out as a joke or a stupid story ..."

"And then they just stick," said Slutty Dave with a sigh. Everyone laughed, knowingly. I did not laugh. I did not understand.

The group dispersed. Sandy and I returned to our spot.

"How come you don't have a bush name?" I asked.

"Be grateful," said Sandy, and I watched Slutty Dave disappear into the Foodland.

It was half past four. It had gotten cold again and I had my hoodie zipped up. The parking lot, which had been steadily filling, was spilling over with cars and trucks of every make, model, and size. Some were hitched to trailers, or piled up with camper extensions. Someone had set up a speaker. They keep playing "X Gon' Give It to Ya," and then "Call Me Maybe," and then a mashup of "X Gon' Give It to Ya" and "Call Me Maybe." Squeebus did, in fact, return to help us drink our milk.

"She's your girlfriend?" Squeebus asked Sandy, when he found out. I was annoyed to be spoken about like I was not there. He looked at me, genuinely concerned, and then back to Sandy. "You brought your girlfriend tree planting?" He took a long, slow, sad sip of milk. "Don't you like her?"

"Do you have any advice for a rookie?" I asked Squeebus.

"Don't quit."

Carly Rae Jepsen was drowned out by the company car speakers before they even got into the parking lot, blasting "(Don't Fear) the

Reaper." There were four pickup trucks and five Chevy Suburbans in a long convoy, going too fast. The first truck to pull in was Mike's: a towering white Ford F-350, beaten by a few years of heavy use, baptized in mud, both windows down.

"That's Mike," said Sandy, clocking him. "Camp supervisor. Our boss."

The wind blew Mike's blond hair back just enough to show the halo of pale skin hugging his hairline. It was one of the few places the sun had not gilded him gold. His golden arm was bent casually out the window. The other golden hand was sketched with lines of oil and dirt, which was sealed in with callus where it pressed on to the steering wheel like an afterthought, two fingers pinching a cigarette. If his face was not as beautiful as any film star's, it was only because it was more so: a firm brow and a jaw ready to cast long shadows in low light, a beard that looked perfectly coiffed completely by accident. His face was serious and playful, devilish and mature. His eyes were a blue so clear and pale and severe that they hit me like two bullets, even from the road.

My problem with would-be cult situations is that the circumstances aren't appealing enough to warrant their severity, and also that the so-called *charismatic leader* of a cult usually strikes me as a dumpy, ugly idiot. Since that spring in northern Ontario, I've thought a lot about how tree planting has a lot in common with a cult, with the important missing piece of a leader able to manage on unreasonable good looks, charm, and personality. Nobody, in my four seasons in the bush, ever pulled it off. Except Mike.

Mike was *too* handsome. When he stopped the truck, he opened the door, reached his generously muscled golden arm up, and stood in the passageway of the open cab. His tattered white shirt was torn in a way that just made me look at his body — obliques like tree roots headed down toward the belt on his work-painted slacks. I felt embarrassed — too warm, suddenly confused, looking at him. This was my boss? He surveyed us for a second, as a murmur struck up. Then he leapt, effortless, to the ground, like a superhero, kicking up a dust cloud under his Blundstones.

"All right," he said, wickedly, as the music was cut, and a hush fell over us. "Fresh meat!"

"Oh God," sighed a rookie girl, staring, from where she stood a few feet to my left.

We arrived so late we had to assemble the tent in the dark. Confused, stumbling, and bickering, Sandy and I put our rain fly on sideways. When we woke up in the morning, I refused to fix it. I didn't want to be late for work. On our first training day, I planted 450 trees while thunderclouds rolled in, a trickster on a chariot. It started raining just after lunch. When we got back to our tent, everything was sitting in a puddle of water. While Sandy dried our sleeping bags as best he could by the fire, I fixed the rain fly and bailed the water out of our temporary home. I tried to cry quietly, the rain washing the tears down my face.

At dinner, sensing I was upset, Mike clapped me on the back. "Cheer up, rookie," he said, smiling. "The rain will break soon, don't you worry. You'll be able to dry all your shit out and wipe that bummer look off your face."

It rained for a week straight, without a single break.

On my first real planting day, after training, which was the second day of the shift, I planted 450 trees. On the third and fourth day, exhausted, I planted 200. On the last day of our first shift, I really pushed, and I planted 350 trees. I thought about ladening myself down with more trees, packing my back bag even though I wasn't very strong yet, and wondered if that would save me time. That same day, a vet used this method to plant a thousand trees in a few hours, before he took one wrong step, slightly twisted, all burdened as he was, and slipped a disc in his back. He was sent home immediately. I kept to my tiny, pathetic bag-ups.

By the time I got to my first night off, I was so extraordinarily sleepy I didn't see how I was supposed to stay up for the party that was manically brewing around the campfire. I carried a single beer back to my tent, and as I walked I watched as the clouds broke above the tree line.

The sun burst through the clouds in time to set over the Algoma Forest. I thought about staying at the fire, but my body screamed out for rest. The sun was splitting into prisms of rainbow, in all the colours of God's laughter, to touch down onto the lush expanses of residual forest.

Sandy and I were on different crews. My crew was bad. We were all rookies, so we had no perspective on what was good, how to become good. We knew that good was an abstract number: two thousand trees every day. We picked up the planter lingo within a couple of days. "Two thousand trees," the concept, was "two-K:" a verb, as well as a noun. *I need to two-K. Have you two-K'd yet?*

We were planting seedlings: usually no longer than the length of your palm and fingers, plus a root and soil pod sticking out of the bottom. We were paid per tree: each tree was eight point three cents. We planted in twenty- to fifty-year-old clear-cuts, still-healing wounds in the lungs of the earth. We wandered the wilderness, looking for appropriate spaces. Then, we would throw our D-handled spades into the exposed mineral soil, deposit our imperfect offering — our tiny, pesticide-soaked clone of a tree — punch the hole closed, and move on.

The clear-cut blocks were more like war ruins than a field — replete with the sharp and scratching limbs of undeserving arboreal casualties, piles of abandoned timber stacked like ruined buildings two or three storeys high, rotting animal corpses, and the shit of whatever killed them. Sometimes, we'd find glens, lush and green, with small mounds of exposed mineral soil reaching up to take our trees and it would feel like flying. Sometimes every step twisted my ankles, ripped holes in my clothing and the skin underneath, sent my muscles screaming, *No, turn back*, as I fought my way through the swamps and the sandy hill banks, up the ridges of Canadian Shield, sharp and solid as the back of a great turtle.

It didn't matter that our crew was bad because the season had just started and everyone was bad. People talked about how the body was not yet prepared, how if we went too hard too fast we would overdo it and hurt ourselves. Politely, some sacrificial lambs stepped up and overdid it, as if to demonstrate — some hotshot or another planted an insane number, tore a ligament or triggered his old tendonitis, and he was gone forever.

Slowly, around us, everyone started to get better. The vets put in a few days of a thousand trees. Twelve hundred. Fifteen, fifteen, fifteen. Then two thousand for most of a shift, then twenty-five, heading into the third shift averaging three thousand trees. I was still planting a few hundred trees a day when we got to the Swamp.

The Swamp, a gift from Mike, was supposed to be our coming of age. The Swamp looked like it was some nice road access blocks. It was the last section of the contract before we were all supposed to move. The rest of the camp would be joining us as they finished their own pieces. *Make sure you don't get creamed out.*

I held onto my planting bags, stuffed full of my things, as the wind whipped around me. We needed four-wheel drive to get to the Swamp. We were short on trucks with four-wheel drive. We bounced and shuffled behind the cab of the truck, one hand gripping the metal sides, the other trying to hold down our planting bags and block packs and shovels, scrambling and rearranging every time the truck hit a boulder or a ridge on the abandoned dirt road and set the load — our bodies included — flying several inches into the air.

I liked the flatbed ride because it was long and because it was exciting and because it wasn't planting. I was still bad at planting, and I hated every second I spent doing it. I liked the long ride in the Chevy Suburban to the abandoned road. I liked standing around, laughing, with my crew, while we transferred our gear and heaved our bodies onto the exposed wooden planks and the way the early morning air whipped past me, how Harry passed me his cigarette to take steady drags on smooth stretches of road. It felt peaceful, to be heading somewhere — on the truck rides to work, I had not yet had the opportunity to fail. On the truck rides home, it was too late to do anything about my failure. Might as well relax.

About three-quarters of the way through the ride, we had to dismount the flatbed to get through the washout. The washout was a place where some new winding stream had started to run over the road so much that it had eroded it completely. We all had to get off the truck, pull our stuff off, watch the driver gun it over the water. We'd hike our stuff high over our heads, and ford the washout on foot — the dirt road reduced to smooth clean pebbles under the steel shanks of our boots, water running cold and almost to our knees, small fish flicking their tails against our shins. We'd get back on the truck, cursing the cold, on the other side. That's when I'd really wake up — see the starkness of the dusty road and the eternal brown and green of the forest around us, the way the bushes on the roadside were pushing to take over, craning their skinny fingers toward us, knotty with verdant buds. These buds were the reminder that this green we saw was nothing, really — an overture of the green to come. It was fewer than three weeks into May, and I already felt like I'd lived a whole other lifetime. I couldn't believe how quickly the world was changing: the thaw creeping deeper into the ground, the birds screaming out their announcements of the way the forest was coming alive, complex and perverse as any ocean. The ground seemed to hum as the fungi began its political negotiations with the roots of the many trees. In the shadows, everywhere, I could feel the black bears — as plentiful as the lice that used to colonize my scalp and twice as hungry.

I didn't think of any of that. I didn't think about the danger of our commuting strategy, or the profundity of the natural wonder I was witnessing. I felt anxiety close around my throat, a choking fist. I didn't want to go to work.

I had been trying to work out *the secret of planting*. I tried a shorter shovel, not eating, eating more, and all of those had failed. If I had worked out any secret at all, it was only this one: if I started thinking about deadlines in chunks that were too large ("I have to have one thousand trees planted by noon"), then I was already behind. I was not naturally gifted as a planter, so I did not have the luxury of checking out for that long. I worked out that if I planted about fifteen trees every five minutes, I would be okay. When I thought about the day in five-minute increments, I did well and I stayed focused. When I did not, I had an *extremely* bad time. My impossible task was made up of a series of very small, maddeningly possible tasks — if I simply did them, in the right order, then I would be fine. *Break up the big task into smaller ones.* Basic stuff. I, of course, considered myself too tragic and unique and exceptional for the standard advice. Yet, here was the standard advice working. I hated it.

I had not yet discovered the other secret of planting, which is this: everything that can go wrong is manageable, unless what is going wrong is that everyone is being incredibly cruel to each other, so don't be cruel. Cruelty is stupid. Cruelty runs counter to survival. In the forest, I was just an animal — and not a very good one. I had no claws, no fur, no good hunting teeth. All I had were my friends. My friends were my defence, my offence, my only hope for survival.

We had to stay together. We had to make it work. The truth of being a human animal is that there is no other option.

Our nice road access had been a lie: the map had not accounted for the flooding that had caused the washouts and generally taken over the area. Our path to the block was a long corridor of clear-cut, which had two travel options: a mad scramble over two-storey-high mounds of abandoned lumber at either edge of the residual tree line, or a slog through the waist-high muck that lay between them. Since tree delivery was difficult, we had to do this with our day packs, water, and as many trees as we could physically carry — about a fifty-pound load. I'd tried to scramble over the lumber, first, and had sprained my ankle. One of my crew mates had slipped and fallen four feet, face-first, onto more lumber, and broken his nose. I resigned myself to the swamp slog, which was slower, but less dangerous. I was the last one across, by a wide margin, every single day.

On a day off, I called my dad. Shakily, I explained just how bad it was, just how terrible I was at it, how fucked up my ankles were. "Welp," he said, simply. "Just think about how much character you're building!"

It was probably the most traditionally fatherly advice I'd ever gotten from him, and I was extremely grumpy about it. I understood the subtle intonation: *Don't quit*. My fantasies of getting to retreat back to his place to wait out the summer disappeared. The next morning, at work, was the very last frozen morning. I forded the Swamp, having to smash my feet through a layer of ice and lower my leg thigh-deep into the loose, watery mud. It took me two hours to get from the truck to my piece and make my first eight cents.

The cold backed off. Us rookies celebrated the simple pleasure of not having to put our boots on frozen in the morning. Nights that only crept below freezing for an hour or two, usually when we were unconscious enough not to care, didn't seem that bad. I didn't have to sleep in all my clothes and my jacket, mummied into my sleeping bag, with my hat on and my scarf wound around my face so tightly that only my frozen nose stuck out enough to breathe out big plumes of condensing moisture. The coming warmth felt like mercy. The rookies rejoiced. The vets didn't, which was always a bad sign.

"Enjoy it while it lasts," they said, with a sense of far-eyed foreboding that I didn't like.

One day while planting, I heard a tiny buzzing noise in my ear, reached in, and squashed something. My finger came away smeared with more blood than seemed possible for the tiny creature responsible: its body was crushed, but I could see it was very small — the six legs still stuck in a rhythmic death spasm were so tiny I could barely see them. "Did you get one?" asked Harry.

"What is it?" I asked.

"It's a blackfly," he replied. "When you kill one, you release a smell, and then more come. Get ready, because his friends are coming, and they're going to be mad."

Mosquitoes, in the concentration they exist in northern Ontario, are their own special kind of hell, but the season is different than blackfly season. Mosquitoes can be avoided. Mosquitoes are larger than blackflies, which means they're slower. They can bite through thin clothing, but they can be outrun and confused. They can be held back by the right attire.

Blackflies can't bite through your clothing. They will, however, find any fold, rip, or crevice in your clothing, and bite you there. I kept tearing open a way for them to get inside. When I slid my mud-soaked tights off at the end of the day, my legs would be patterned with a bloody daguerreotype of every hole and rip in my clothing, an impression of the landscape.

I bought containers of cream that was 30 percent DEET, unambiguously carcinogenic, which was covered in warnings to apply it *on top of clothing only*. We would slather our naked bodies in it like it was a moisturizer and then layer on clothing too thick for the mosquitoes to bite through. It was the only way I found to remain sane. If I didn't plant fast enough, sometimes the bugs still found the places where I couldn't put the cream — they crawled, biting, into my ear canals. They swarmed the wet insides of my lips.

Finished my piece, barely behind my set schedule, and desperate for more land, I thundered down the drying mud road that emerged out of the Swamp. I saw one crewmate struggling to work her shovel into the ground. The halo of blackflies around her was visible from the road. She grew more and more desperate, wiggling her shovel. She started smacking her legs with one hand, and then let her shovel fall and smacked with both hands. The blows travelled up her body, until she was knocking her head back and forth, hitting herself full force across her own face. She let out a deep, guttural scream, kicked her shovel, and started running. She was running away from the truck, and the rest of the crew. She wasn't trying to get help, or shelter. She was just trying to get away.

Farther down the road, I found Billie. She had been planting hard that day, also trying to hit her two-K.

"How's it going, Billie?" I called.

She looked up at me. "Tara?" She was disoriented from dehydration. She took a few stumbling steps. She rubbed her eyes and I could see her hands come away bloody. "The bugs are biting my eyes."

Gross. "You've got it. Don't stop," I said. I kept walking toward the closing sections of open clear-cut. She nodded, picked up her shovel, threw it into the ground.

I ran out of land somewhere around 1860 trees. It was still way more than I'd ever planted before. Satisfied, I headed back and I found Harry, dirty and smoking. He saw me and smiled — big, and wild. "You hit it?" he said, meaning two thousand.

"No," I said, sheepishly. "But close. Anyway, dinner tonight should be ..."

I trailed off. Harry wasn't smiling. "You go back in and you hit it," he said.

I stopped. "Dude, there's no more land."

"Get back in the fucking land and plant your trees," he spat, with a darkness in his eyes I had never seen.

I did as I was told. I entered the first piece immediately off of the road, which was already planted, and started putting my shovel in absolutely anywhere I thought I could even conceivably get away with the tight spacing. I pushed the boundaries of what constituted a double plant the way Mr. Kim pushed the boundaries of renovation. *Best of luck*, I thought to my trees, abandoned in extremely questionable planting areas. *Really. You will need it.*

I did this all the way back to a tree line, then I dipped into the tree line, planting the babies in gaps between the existing stands of black spruce. *This is not technically theft*, I justified. *There is a reasonable chance that they will grow! I think! Maybe!*

"How many do you need?" Harry screamed from inside the stolen piece. "A hundred and forty!" I screamed back. It was an impossibly high number. I was never going to make it. I couldn't go on. Suddenly, I felt my bags labour down with trees again. Harry had dashed back to the cache to grab me more bundles so I could hit my goal. He was so nice! I hated him for it. I didn't want to plant anymore.

I stumbled on my always-aching ankles. *YOU CANNOT GO ON*, they shrieked at me. *I MUST GO ON*, I shrieked back, as I pushed and I pushed. I was angry. I was angry at Harry, and trees, and the earth, and God. I pushed, angry, stumbling, failing, up against an edge that said, *YOU CANNOT GO ON*. I was *so much angrier* to discover that the edge was instead a false wall, and that if

I pressed it hard enough it moved. *I'll go on*, I thought, horrified. I planted 2,100 trees.

I didn't fall down and stay there and never move again, like I wanted to, when it was over. I threw my shovel over my shoulder and rested my arms on it. My muscles went soft from effort underneath my skin. I found Harry, first, and he hugged me so tight I thought I'd break in half. We walked back on the drying mud road with a devastation of clear-cuts all around us to find our friends.

When we found the rest of the crew, on the dusty road, Billie was swaying and tired. "Did you get it?" I screamed. "Yes!" She screamed back, but something was wrong. Something with her eyes. I got closer and closer and she turned toward me and lurched her body forward in a weary shuffle. The whites of her eyes were a deep maroon. Her eyelids were swollen into cysts and lumps where the bugs had bitten, streaks of blood and their small bodies — crushed and writhing and still biting — running down her cheeks like tears.

"Always Be My Baby"
by Mariah Carey.

Anwar finished his training and got a permanent position in Boston. He, Maryam, and Abdul were all leaving. At work, I watched Abdul pace happily from his living room to his bedroom and back again, babbling, talking about his toys in English and French and Arabic.

"What do you think you'll do, when you're finished school?" asked Anwar, kindly.

"I don't really know," I said, because I didn't. I watched Abdul and my heart ached. "I think I'll apply to law school?"

"Is that what you want?"

I looked at Anwar and his kind, round face, which was just like Abdul's.

"I don't know."

"You know," said Anwar, "I always thought I had to go on to the next thing, right away, every time. I wanted to prove that I could achieve things. I don't regret anything, my life is good, but sometimes I wonder what would be different if I'd taken a bit of time, you know …" He was looking at me kindly, but carefully. He wanted me to understand. "If I'd taken a bit of time, to get to know who I am. There really isn't any pressure. You don't have to figure it out, right now."

He was a smart man. A healer. I kept his advice after they packed their lives into boxes and emptied the apartment where the baby had taken care of me.

"Melodies from Heaven" by Kirk Franklin.

November 2016. Concordia University, Montreal.

I was stumbling through the streets near Concordia, my eyes filling with tears. I didn't know why, but after what had just happened — the horrible, horrible thing that had just happened to me — I had to be back somewhere familiar.

I ran up the stairs to the philosophy department. Mercifully, it was empty, except for Rohan — sweet, brilliant Rohan, the department administrator, shuffling papers at the front desk.

"Tara!" he said, happily, then saw my face as my lower lip trembled. I burst into tears. "Oh, honey," he said. "What is it?"

"It's so awful," I wailed.

"What?"

"I …" I could barely say it. "I *graduated.*"

Rohan was quiet for a second, and then he laughed at me. He

laughed at me so hard. "I'm late," I explained, through tears. "Like, I graduated late ..."

"What does that even *mean*?" Rohan laugh-asked.

"I'm twenty-four!"

"Oh my God, you're hilarious! You're a baby, that doesn't matter."

"And then I just didn't do the paperwork to graduate, for like ever, and I just did it, and people usually graduate when they're *twenty-two*, Rohan."

"Sweetheart," he said, with palpable affection in his voice. "Nobody, in the whole world, gives a single shit or fuck. Oh, you're so funny. This is so funny."

I gave a watery smile. "I feel like a failure."

"Oh, honey," he repeated, putting an arm around my shoulder. "You're in the right place. We're all failures, here."

February 2017. Notre-Dame-de-Grâce, Montreal.

"I'm going to apply to law school," I told people, and then I worked nanny jobs, and tree planted, and produced poetry readings and cabarets, and didn't apply to law school. This happened for years.

I went to a yoga class at a studio in my neighbourhood, and it was being taught by a hippie lady with the same name as my mother. When I arrived, we did a short sequence, warming our muscles up and stretching them out like taffy, before she told us to lie down on our backs.

She told me to picture falling through space, my body slowly filling up with light, and then emptying out. I was as relaxed as a puddle of goo on my mat.

"Imagine a place you feel safe," she said. "Where is it?"

I've been having this dream. There's a house that used to be a church. Somewhere is a room, and in the room is a cupboard. If I pull really hard, I can get up inside and I can close the cupboard door behind me, be all closed in there, in the safety of the darkness. I push the back of the cupboard, and it clicks in my hands. A false wall. A door opens up. A hallway.

The teacher might have been saying something, but I didn't hear her. I didn't feel the mat, or the air, or my breath coming in and out. I just crawled down this narrow little hallway to what I knew was on the other side.

A space behind the Gothic windows of the church — Catherine windows, like a rose, or a breaking wheel. Twenty feet high and filling the space — a space, really, not a room — with prismatic light.

"What's in there?"

One of those old swooning couches. Victorian, carved wood and faded silk. I lay down on it, dappled by the light beaming down from the shapes in the windows in straight shafts, like the long fingers of God reaching down from heaven.

"Is anyone there with you?"

I look to my left, and it's her, on another matching couch. Her hair is long, dark blond, and straight — not short, curly, and blond like it was after the chemo. She's on one side, curled up, wearing a brown dress, with her head in her hand. She looks exhausted. Like she's travelled a long way.

"Hi, Mom," I say, and she looks at me. I'm not surprised, but it still hurts when I see her expression. She's disappointed. I don't have to ask her what she came here to tell me. I don't doubt for a second that she loves me — the disappointment on her face is like when you're invested in something that isn't going the way you planned. She's tired. I'm old enough to understand this. She shouldn't have to explain it.

The lights came back on and I was ripped, gasping, from the room, and the light, and my mother. I woke up sweating under the fluorescents of the studio.

"I'm *sooo* sorry," vocal fried the college kid in the Lululemons, here to mop the floor. "You must have fallen asleep."

Shaking, I gathered my things. I locked myself in a bathroom stall, peeled my yoga clothes off, and got changed, while I hacked up deep sobbing tears from somewhere foundational, primal, animalistic. The tears came from somewhere as buried as my childhood and as physical as my relationship with my mother. I cried straight from that cavernous, yearning void of longing that had been ripped in me one day, in the sunshine. I didn't even know there was anything left in there to cry about. *I'm so sorry, Mom.*

I could have seen her body, if I wanted. I didn't want to. I wanted to remember her alive. I wanted to remember her watching movies. I remember her curled up under my father's arm, losing her breath in peals of laughter as we watched *The Princess Bride.* Her laugh was unencumbered and foolish — almost operatic in its drama. Tears of joy in her eyes.

Her friend was up from Toronto to visit her in Cannington. They were sitting under a blanket, side by side, in the living room. I could see them, just for a moment, as I descended the stairs in search of a snack or water or something. They were sitting close enough they could balance a bowl of popcorn on their knees where they pressed together, each in their cotton pyjamas with their toes sticking out of the bottom of the blanket, wide-eyed as little girls as their faces were illuminated, in waves of blue and grey, by the television screen playing *Jurassic Park.* My mom, slack-jawed, slowly bringing a popcorn kernel to her mouth. Then, the abrupt musical shift of a jump scare, and the two women flew backward in terror, shrieking, throwing their arms around each other, their eyes fixed to the screen, the popcorn flying away from them in a long, fluffy arc.

The dining room felt so alive, with light. Our crappy upright grand piano, perpetually in what my dad called "church basement tuning"; the low buffet table spread with a white tablecloth, stained glass hung up in the windows to filter in the light. She was wandering around, humming, in her brown dress — the one I called *her Cinderella dress*, because of its network of patches in complimentary shades of brown and orange. She was arranging cut flowers and hanging older flowers up to dry. On the table were a series of dark-brown wooden boxes, and I opened and closed them, dreamily. She wasn't sick yet. I was probably five or six.

Inside one box, the hospital bracelet from when my brother was delivered and a long braid of his blond hair — from his first haircut, on his twelfth birthday. A line of photo booth portraits of the two of them — my brother drooling and cooing, a fat toddler. My mother, beaming — mischievous, magical, and not yet twenty-five. I closed that box, and moved on to another. Inside that one, a worn deck of tarot cards. Slips of dried herbs.

"Mummy," I said. "Mummy, are you a witch?"

"All women are, kind of," she said, wrapping a line of ribbon around a bouquet of flowers.

"Will you teach me a love spell?"

She looked at me, serious. "No, honey. That isn't how love works. People fall in love, or they don't. That's why it's important."

I could handle the ashes. They were sufficiently abstracted. The small shards of bone seemed perverse, but they were human remains, after all. More perverse was that they came vacuum packed in a plastic bag from the crematorium. We were all seated on the floor in front of the altar, and I watched my father and the priest divvy up what was left of her. I was relieved to see her leave the bag. They shook her into an urn in a long, steady stream. Parts of her stuck to the frayed edges of the plastic, where the bag had been torn open. This angered me. I wanted all of her out of there — free of something common and destined for the trash.

"There we go," said my dad. "Almost done." I could hear the emotion in his voice, his task nearly completed. Then, something went wrong — his hand slipped, or the priest's did, holding the urn. The last two teaspoons or so of my mother fell flatly to the ugly maroon of the church carpet.

"Oops."

We all sat around for a while, staring at it. Then my dad reached down with his hands, and picked up what had been his wife with his fingers. When he was done, there was still a dusty grey smattering on the floor, in the carpet. There was more silence.

Then, suddenly, giggling. I looked up, and my dad was laughing. I looked over at the priest in his cassock, and he was also laughing. The priest reached over and put his hand on my dad's shoulder, and the two men collapsed for a moment. Then my dad reached out and ran his hands over the last whisper of the ashes, evenly distributed them into the carpet.

"She'd understand," he said. "She wouldn't mind."

At home, I threw my bag on the floor. Sandy was already asleep. It was late. I wasn't tired. In the foyer closet of our Notre-Dame-de-Grâce apartment — in the neighbourhood where my mother was a little girl — I had stored a large blank canvas, and now I took it out, with my acrylic paints and a Joni Mitchell record. In one sitting, I painted a portrait in three-quarter profile in shades of blue — a boy with sad eyes.

When it was done, I looked around the living room, at Hex flicking her tail and staring off intently at nothing. There was a tension in the room. She had to know I understood. "A lawyer," I muttered, and then scoffed. "I'm going to be an artist, Mom. I promise."

Nothing changed, but I felt different — like something inside me was filling back up.

"We Belong Together" by Rickie Lee Jones.

September 2017. Notre-Dame-de-Grâce, Montreal.

I was trying not to drink. Drinking was like the dog park: it didn't matter how well you could conduct yourself, you couldn't trust the other people. I was doing okay, a few weeks in — after all, I could still smoke weed all the time. Unfortunately, while stoned out of my gourd, flat on my back, in the old Associated Screen News building, I came to an upsetting realization about my new life as a teetotalling stoner, which was that I did not actually like being high very much. *Oh no*, I thought. *Whoops.*

The utter enormity of *life on earth* — and *my life* specifically — felt altogether too much to bear. I was terrified, and sure there was something *wrong with my body*. I was thinking about breathing — thinking about it so much I was becoming afraid I was about to forget how to do it at all, even as my chest continued to rise and fall.

Everything felt wrong and too much — how was I supposed to keep doing things, with my sister out there, living her life, vulnerable to threat? Knowing my father was out there, somewhere? Knowing that one day, he was going to die? Was I just supposed to *keep going*, as someone who *had* a mother, once, and a brother — and *did not*, anymore? It all just felt wrong, and too much. My mouth and legs — also wrong. Also too much.

This was how Sandy found me when he walked into our new apartment — the one we'd just moved into, in the Associated Screen News building, with our new roommate Layla. Layla was a pot-smoking stripper, Sunday school teacher, and religious scholar. She had smoked me up and then flounced off to the Early Islam class where she was a teacher's assistant, leaving me swimming through another dimension on the floor.

"Babe," said Sandy. "You okay?"

"Grief is a cruel guide," I moaned.

"What?"

"Marijuana."

"Oh," he said. "Let's go for a walk."

In Westmount Park, he was calm while I took him through my itemized list of neuroses.

"I think I'm an alien," I explained. "I don't think I'm built to survive on this planet."

He just nodded. "Mm."

"I always feel so sick, you know? I always feel like I'm fucking dying."

Again, a nod. "That's too bad."

I was looking around at the sinister grass and the sinister sky, wet and grey with the first snap thaw of late winter. A warm breeze blew and it was all wrong. Too early. *The world is ending.*

"Sandy, none of this is right. Like, just ... *now*, you know? It's too heavy. I'm never free of what's already happened."

He didn't ask for clarification. He just nodded again. Then, he said, "The present is a runaway train that drags the past behind it."

I stopped walking.

He turned, looked directly at me. He was straight-backed, confident. A whole different man than the one who got off the bus from North Bay, or the one who arrived holding the cat crate on a train from out east, or the one who was so afraid of me on our first date. His big blue eyes behind his tortoiseshell frames and his wild brown hair under his black hat. The structured maturity of his beard. His elbows making harsh angles out from the black of his double-breasted peacoat, his slim waist. His midthirties, looking good on him. I could feel our past, dragged behind us — thousands of days spent drifting in pleasure so ubiquitous it was commonplace, almost not worth mentioning. Thousands of crises neutralized, efforts left unwasted, mistakes softened into synapses so I could learn again. In front of me, he was precious and required and the other part of me. The way he made every necessary thing beautiful. The unrivalled bravery of his notleaving.

I was so fucking high.

"It's like ..." He sniffed, looked around, scuffed the ground with his foot. "You know, like, crashing into us. And shit." He looked back at me. "Babe? Are you okay?"

I had no idea he was the kind of person who could say, *The present is a runaway train that drags the past behind it*, like I had no idea he was the kind of person who would take a train to me with a suitcase in one hand and a drugged cat in the other and give up a regular paycheque for a life of sacrifice in every area except the exquisite and voluminous glory of love. I knew I was fucked, then. I knew I was fucked worse than I knew I was fucked when he left for planting and I didn't stand up for two months, unable to carry the weight of his absence.

"I want to marry you," I blurted out.

He smiled. He didn't look surprised. "Good."

"Anywhere I Lay My Head" by Tom Waits.

August 2018. The woods near Mackenzie, British Columbia.

I shuffled my tarot cards like I was playing blackjack. I held two halves of the deck in each hand, taut between my thumb and my middle finger. I let them cascade toward each other, one after another after another, reorienting.

I was leaving in the morning. The light of the thick full moon was filtering eerily through the green fabric of my tent, making the whole thing glow like a Nalgene bottle with a flashlight underneath. I had strung up dollar store Christmas lights from the few straps that hung from the top of the tent: the battery pack smacked my head whenever I came in, but I didn't mind. For my birthday — May 1, the first day of the season — my sister had given me a medallion with a Buddhist goddess on it. She was sitting cross-legged, one foot on the ground and one palm turned forward, beaming at the viewer calmly and serenely, naked from the waist up except for jewelled adornments and strings of prayer beads. The Mother of Liberation — Green Tara — one of my namesakes. She was dangling down among the lights. I had a Mexican blanket on the floor of my tent. My bed mat, foam roll, and sleeping bag were all clean and made up. I had been reading — I brought Nietzsche with me, to read in private in my tent, so no one would tease me. "I want to learn more and more to see as beautiful what is necessary in things," Nietzsche wrote in *The Gay Science.* "Then I shall be one of those who makes things beautiful." I fancied myself one of those who made things beautiful, so I liked that. *Why do people always hate on Nietzsche?*

"*Amor fati:* let that be my love henceforth! I do not want to wage war against what is ugly. I do not want to accuse; I do not even want to accuse those who accuse ..."

My eyelids drooped. I was way too tired to read philosophy. I settled instead into novels — *Kiss of the Fur Queen, Bridget Jones's Diary.*

I was good in that tent. I didn't wear my boots inside. I didn't eat or drink inside. It was not the tent of a *crusty vet,* to use planter lingo: a grumpy, work-worn veteran of many years of work, too jaded by bad days and injuries and the demands of capitalism to care that much about something *soft* like keeping your tent looking nice. But it was nice: it even smelled nice. My friends and I had essential oils mixed in our tangled, ratty hair: spruce and pine and eucalyptus, lavender and tea tree. We had become as sentimental and ephemeral as middle-aged neopagans. You start a British Columbia tree planting season an ironic, city-slicking hipster, and you end it with flowers behind your ears, talking about the energy of the forest and the magic of friendship, with a bouquet of herbal oils keeping the bugs off your neck.

We were all cross-legged on my Mexican blanket, drawing tarot cards. It was a night off — nobody worked in the morning. The air was alive with the possibility that comes after days and days of hard work. My tent was in the tree line. The tree line kept the noises out. Somewhere, a drum — but we could barely hear it. Every once in a while, we heard laughter, blending in with the ever-present chorus of the forest: the caw of birds startled in their nests, the yipping and howling of rival gangs of coyotes, the rumble of wind through the vast expanse of trees. Every so often, there was a deep moan as a tree creaked over, and then cracked: eaten out from the inside by beetles or disease, to be knocked over, finally, by a stiff breeze or the persistent rubbing of some beast. It was Tse'Khene territory. It still is.

Every hour or so you might pass someone's hunting cabin. The closest colonial outpost was barely a settlement: a thrown-together assemblage of the relations, lovers, and children of the small bands of labourers busy rendering these lands profitable enough for settlers — loggers, mill workers, and other enemies of trees.

My friends had already pulled their own cards. According to the cards, Sophie would overcome her recent period of unease about her career future by way of healthy competition leading to a meaningful mentorship. Amy was going to achieve a state of temperance by reflecting on her past instances of strength and learning how to ask for the help of her community. I shuffled the cards.

"I just had a birthday," I said. "I just turned twenty-six. What do I need to know about this year?" I cut my deck into three smaller stacks and rearranged them. I splayed them open. "Past," I said, and I pulled my past card. The tower. A sudden, unexpected change. A calamity. On the card, lightning strikes the top of a tall tower, dislodging a huge symbolic crown, which was, until recently, perched on top. Two figures, their safe place full of fire, fall to the rocks below. Or did they jump?

"So, a disaster in your past," said Amy. Sophie nodded, knowingly, then said, "A dis-past-er."

"Yes," I said, mock serious. "Flamey, flamey." This could have referred to anything. We all collect calamities when we've been around for long enough. Who among us is not a pastiche of the commonplace tragedies that make up a childhood?

I drew another card, for the present. The lovers. Two beautiful, naked people, beaming at each other despite the mountain between them, being drawn together by an angel reaching down from the heaven, which is cracking open to ensure the victory of their union.

I looked up, delighted. "Well, that's good!"

"A sexy one!" said Sophie. "Is it you and Sandy?"

"Probably," I said, laughing. I thought about going on the *but we are not strictly monogamous, so you know anything could happen* rant but, honestly, I had gone on it so many times this season, and nobody had kissed me, so I was starting to wonder as to the point.

I still had the future left. I splayed the cards out wider on the red Mexican carpet, which was glowing green from my tent, which was glowing a mishmash of festive colours from the dollar store lights. My left hand, which I used to put trees in the ground, was permanently dirty — dirt had gotten onto my skin and callus had sealed it in. I was in the habit of wearing a glove on my left hand, but it only did so much. It kept the sun out, though: my hand was as pale as my white stomach. My right hand — my shovel hand — went ungloved: it sat on top of my shovel, its back to the sun day in and day out. It was the deep, golden brown of my face and shoulders and the one part of my left leg where my bags rubbed against my quadricep to make a hole in all of my work tights.

I played my future card, flipped it over. On the card there was a Reaper-like figure on a horse, approaching a crowd of cowering people. Under the horse's hooves is the fallen king, his crown at his feet. On his knees in front of the horse, a man of God with a tall hat, praying. A beautiful woman. A child. At the top of the card, in roman numerals, is the number thirteen. At the bottom of the card: *Death*.

"Uh-oh," said Amy.

"It's okay," I said. "It doesn't always mean *literal* death." This was true, but I was not doing a great job convincing myself. "It also means the death of an ideology, the slow ending of something. Inevitability." I looked up. They did not look convinced. Stupid, stressful card game.

"It's about how endings come for everyone, you know? It's not, like, your fault. These people have money, power, beauty. Piety. Innocence. Things end all the time." In the background of the card, a new day is dawning. "Life goes on."

The other girls pursed their lips, eyed my spread. I took a long, pensive sip out of my water bottle. Gatorade and tequila. It was all I had.

"Do you guys wanna go again?" I asked, still staring at my cards. My great-grandmother read tea leaves and the tarot for money to the white folks in Halifax. The Rider-Waite tarot deck was published in 1909, and now the past was here to tell me my future. I wanted to memorize my cards. I wanted to hold them close to me, like a bad habit, or a rationalization.

Sophie shook her head vigorously, and then reached into the pocket of her vest for another can of beer. "Absolutely not," she said.

We joined the party instead. Outside my tent, the ground was somewhat even. There was a fallen tree we had to step over right outside, but there were relatively few boulders, most of the earth pillowy with mosses and liverworts. We all turned our flashlights on, illuminating the closest of the trees that stood up like pillars between us and our comrades. I called the area *danger tree grove*, because there was no way these trees were all sturdy: they loomed with the promise of a crush injury, swaying even when the air felt still. One night, in a thunderstorm, I had woken up to the crash of the spruce trees falling so hard and so close they shook the ground. I grabbed my wolf blanket and my teddy bear and booked it to a truck to sleep the rest of the night, half-wet and crumpled in an odd shape in the back seat. My tent was still standing when, blushing, I retreated the next morning past the burly silviculture workmen and the busy cooks, crossing the gravel pit in my socked feet.

To get to the main part of camp, we had to scale a pile of earth and gravel that had been piled around in an immense half moon: it was a hard scramble, with few footholds, and I was grateful we were not yet too drunk. We moved slowly, in the dark, helping each other — by which I mean, mostly, that Amy and Sophie helped me. At the top, we could see the gravel pit that held our camp, the logging road beyond it, the rim of tents and trailers and personal vehicles: cars, trucks, converted minivans with the back seats taken out to make room for shelving units and cots and propane stoves. Beyond that, the tree line: the jagged edge of the known world, sticking up into astronomical twilight like a line of broken bones.

Our company structures consisted of a half-cylinder mess tent, as tall as a beached whale, taut beige waxed canvas over huge steel ribs. There was the converted school bus, painted grey, off limits to everyone except management, the back four feet sectioned off with plywood as our first aid station. I liked going to the first aid station. Since Sandy had retired from planting, first aid was one of the only ways I got my body touched in a way that wasn't painful. Having my twisted ankles stabilized with physio tape, or bits of twig picked out of a fresh wound I couldn't reach, was physical contact that wasn't falling down a gully, or being smacked in the face by a branch, having the log or the pile of boulders under me give way so I came in sudden and brutal contact with the ground. There was a trailer that held the gas stoves and counters and the walk-in fridge where the cooks worked, and another trailer with three shower stalls. Off in the distance, as far away from the main camp as possible, were five tall canvas structures called only *the shitters*.

A safe distance from the mess tent and the management bus, a crowd of dark figures were gathered. The thud of the bass emanated from a huge Bluetooth speaker. There were chairs, but people mostly stood in small circles, and bigger ones, laughing or yelling or dancing. There was a loose assemblage of flammable waste products: cardboard and small wooden boxes that had once held food, supplies, or equipment. There was a tree stump two feet across, a long-handled axe sticking out of it, the constantly diminishing stack of wood, the smattering of wood chips around it, all of it rimming the heart of camp, the centre of our universe: our bonfire, licking its many long tongues into the summer air, spitting sparks to catch all the corners with little bursts of light. From the distance, I saw the flash of our teeth, the many colours of our skin, the whites of our eyes.

Tree planters came from the art schools of Montreal and the intentional living communities of Berlin. We came from the shores of California Bay and the political district of Dakar, from Bhutan and the Beaches and Barcelona. We came to clean up the mess made by the tree crushers and the sawmills, to put back the forests — or some agricultural approximation — one hand-dug hole and six-inch seedling at a time. We were the architects of the future of the great northern forests. We were the best idea yet set into motion: a workforce that caused diner cooks to duck outside for a quick cigarette, or several, who tore through the grocery and liquor stores like locusts, caused the locals to spit on the ground with disgust.

Sophie, Amy, and I braced our hiking boots against the gravel embankment, stored our flashlights, and downed the last of our open cans. And then we half-ran, half-jumped into the pit, stumbling on our twisted joints and our tired muscles toward our friends.

When are you coming home? read the message from Antoine, the next day. I was folded tightly into the back of Britney's sedan. My knees were forced up because my dusty day pack, loaded up with the endings of my rushed packing job, was under my feet. My phone was almost to my nose. It was hot out: the dry, subarctic British Columbia weather had really bloomed into summer since August had started. My knees: one tanned, one white, already sweating in the small, packed car, sweat even more furiously as I read the message. He barely talked to me these days, and he *never* talked to me first.

It had been a long season: I'd stayed for the summer plant for the first time. Three months is a long time to live in a tent. I'd bought my ticket back to Montreal on one of those last-minute websites: *lowest price guaranteed* for the tiny catch of several paragraphs of fine print. One of them was that I couldn't change my ticket. When the season ran long, I decided to leave on my departure date, instead of sticking it out until the end. I didn't want to take the financial hit, even though I technically could have — planting is a lucrative business, after all, even when your numbers remain stubbornly *not very good* despite years of experience, like mine had. The facts were these: I *wanted* to bail before the end of the season. Britney, Elliott, and I made a plan — Britney had to go through Vancouver before she met her boyfriend on the coast. She offered to drive me to Prince George, or right on to Vancouver.

My flight was leaving from Prince George, connecting through Vancouver, and then on to Montreal. Right before we left, I decided I was supposed to get off one plane in Vancouver and get on another to head to Montreal. There was no reason I couldn't just ... get on in Vancouver?

Yes. Yes, this sounded right, to me. Britney and the other planters who were driving with her were all delighted. A road trip! We *deserved* this.

This is how we ended up weaving our way through alpine highways, with the little car tracing the curve of the mountains like a finger along a shoulder. Above us, some of the peaks reached high enough for snow to reappear, the trees getting stumpy and more determined the closer they grew to God. Climates circled the mountains like the rings of a cut log: snowy caps abruptly became coniferous forests, which blended into lush deciduous ones somewhere below us. Our car would skid, just slightly, every so often, on the rocks and gravel that fell off of the sheer rock face on one side of the highway, and Britney would calmly correct us away from the guardrail that was the only thing holding us back from the abrupt drop down into the forests below and the long snaking rivers that ran through them.

I'll be home in four days, I wrote back to Antoine, smiling, something effervescent sparkling behind my soft palate. *Why?*

Get here faster, Antoine wrote back immediately. I knew there was no guarantee we'd have cell service for much longer. The sparkling in my face bubbled big into a giggle, and I wrote back, *Why are you obsessed with me?*

I got dumped. I want to hang out.

His heartbreak was the best news I'd gotten in *years*. I thought of him home, alone — maybe crying — and I was overjoyed. I had never known him single. I wrote back a standard reply: *Shit, dude, I'm sorry!* and hit send. No cell service. Message not delivered.

I tried to read more of my philosophy books, but I was too worked up. I made it only a couple of sentences. "My formula for greatness in a human being," wrote Nietzsche, in an essay called "Why I Am So Clever," "is *amor fati*: that one wants nothing to be different, not forward, not backward, not in all eternity. Not merely bear what is necessary, still less conceal it … but love it." Blah blah blah. What does that even mean? Antoine, Antoine, Antoine …

"Woah," said Elliott, from the seat next to me.

I looked over at him, my head still full of bubbles, ready to start an argument. Elliott was dating Kate — my Kate, from Halifax. He and I had a friendly, mutually antagonistic relationship. We got drunk and wrestled on nights off. I would say, "I am leaving this conversation forever, because I hate you," at dinner, and come back with dessert for him on a little piece of brown paper towel. He left notes that said stuff like, *You are the worst. I cannot stand you!!!! Do you need a ride into town tomorrow? Britney is driving and we're going out for brunch.* We pitched our tents next to each other. I called him *Yelliott* because *Smelliott* was too mainstream, and he called me *Traa!*, like the call of a bird.

Elliott wasn't looking at me. He was wide-eyed, folded into the back seat. Elliott was six foot two, and clearly extremely uncomfortable with his huge day pack between us and more sweaters and wallets and bookbags under his feet. He was folded like a thick blanket shoved into a small shelf. He was clutching a cigarette in his huge hand like it was his only hope for safety. He was looking straight past me, his mouth slightly agape.

I turned around quickly and looked out the window. Across the expanse of nothing between the highway and the ridges beyond, up past where the eagles circled in their tight hunting circuits, a single mountain rose as thin and imposing as a tower. It was the hot, dry season on the Pacific coast — a season of grizzly bear tracks as wide as a forearm, a season when the parched blue air conjured skinny sticks of lightning even without the mercy of rain. It was a season of mushrooms blooming in blackened burn sites, where feral horses still wandered, retracing steps that didn't lead home anymore. A season of fire.

At the top of the mountain, which was a tower, smoke billowed high into the cheery blue sky. The very beginning of a burn was crowning the tip of the mountain, the trees flashing as they were engulfed in flames, the branches waving in ecstasy or reaching out for help and then exploding into fire.

"The King of Carrot Flowers, Pts. 2 & 3" by Neutral Milk Hotel.

August 2018. Vancouver, British Columbia.

"I don't understand," said the horrified person in the line ahead of me, waving her plane ticket in the face of the Major Canadian Airways customer service representative. "Isn't there anything you can do?"

The customer service guy's eyes went temporarily distant and out of focus. Above him, on the departure screens, dozens of flights out of the Vancouver airport were flashing *DELAYED* or *CANCELLED*.

"Like I said," said the customer service agent to the angry traveller, "there is a massive thunderstorm over Toronto. Unfortunately, I do not control the weather."

My flight connected Prince George to Vancouver, and Vancouver on to Montreal. I had paid my fare for the guarantee of seats on two separate airplanes. Surely, it would be no big deal to get on just the second one.

"Actually, yes, it is," said the woman on the Major Canadian Airways customer service line, when Britney got us into cell service in the suburbs above Vancouver. "You bought a ticket from Prince George to Montreal, not Vancouver to Montreal."

"But the flight connects through Vancouver," I said, confused.

"Yes, but when you don't get on in Prince George, your ticket in Vancouver will be cancelled."

"Can't you ..." I made a sweeping hand gesture, as if she could see me. "You know, like ... call someone and let them know?"

There was a silence, on the line. Then: "No."

Apparently it would cost *nine hundred dollars* to buy a *last-minute ticket* from Vancouver to Montreal. I explained this, incredulous, to Elliott, as we unloaded the car, kissed Britney goodbye, wished her luck with the rest of her trip.

"Despite the fact that I *already have a ticket from Vancouver to Montreal*," I scoffed, as we dragged our bags into the nearest bar. We had ratty hair and dirty calluses that betrayed our profession, in spite of our clean town clothes, wearing our weird tan lines like an ID maker. People turned their noses up slightly. I threw my bag down in a corner. "It's ridiculous, Elliott — I'm still *taking the flight* to Montreal, I'm just not getting on *some other, separate flight.*"

"I guess you're out nine hundred bucks, then," Elliott said, ordering me a beer.

"If anything, I am *saving them money!*" I yelled, two hours later, handing him another beer, after determining none of the local hotels had last-minute accommodation. We ran through our phones to find the names of people whose couches we could crash on for the night. I picked at a mole on my tanned knee so aggressively that it came off in my fingernail, bleeding. "They'll have a whole other empty seat they can sell!"

"Tara, what I'm saying is your actions have consequences," Elliott slurred as we arrived, wasted, at the house of the fool who agreed to host us, threw our bags down, and crashed onto the soft furniture of their living room.

I woke, hungover, at six the next morning, and called customer service again. My flight left Prince George at 1:00 p.m. That meant I still had time, before I was declared a no-show.

"I just don't see any *actual reason* why I can't just get on the second airplane," I said to the customer service guy while I put a stolen Band-Aid over my knee-mole injury. "I understand that it's a policy reason, but there isn't, like, a *physical reason* ..."

"I can offer you a new ticket, or I can advance declare you a no-show," he said, clearly losing his patience. We had been talking about this for a while. I was not letting it go.

"That doesn't work for me," I said. "Is there, like, a manager I can speak to, or ..."

"Look, *lady*," he said, exasperated. "I'm looking at a *computer screen*. I only have *so many options*. There is no *change the ticket for no price* option. I *do not have this power*."

"Oh!" I said. "Okay, well, *that* I understand! Who does have that power?"

He sighed. "Go to the airport. Plead your case."

"I love you," I blurted, and I hung up. I grabbed my bag, and called a cab, and made a run for it without saying goodbye to Elliott or the person whose couch I'd just been sleeping on.

I wasn't nervous, at all. I had a feeling it was going to work out. I was fresh from three months of forest work and fully *bush crazy* — strong, and brave, and confident, and fairly certain that the rules and conventions most people lived by had just been made up by someone who was strong and brave and confident enough. What made those people any different than me?

"Hi," I said, dripping with sweetness, at the customer service desk, at the Vancouver airport. "I have a problem."

This customer service guy raised his eyebrows. Behind him, the screen flashed *CANCELLED! DELAYED!* Flights to Montreal remained unaffected.

"First of all, I am *not* going to Toronto, so you can relax! Ha, ha ... ahem, anyway, uh, I was supposed to get dropped off by my planting company near Prince George, but the season ran long, and we actually got dropped of in Kelowna ..." Only this last part was a lie — the season *had* run long, due to a particularly good summer raspberry season that had left the planters foraging in their pieces more than actually reforesting them. Our crew bosses kept finding us *sitting down*, pink-teethed and sticky-fingered, alone and eating. Later, when all the shame was gone, they even found us in groups, shameless.

"Get back in the land!" they'd shout. "And plant your fucking trees!" When we'd run, giggling or swearing or both, out of eyesight, they'd bend over the bushes themselves, slipping fat pink husks of sugar off the bushes to bring them to burst in their thirsty mouths.

"Anyway, now I'm here, and my flight is connecting out of here at three, but my first flight ..." I batted my eyelashes. "... leaves from Prince George at one p.m., and I don't want to be listed as a no-show."

The customer service guy looked at me, then looked at the small screen in front of him, then looked behind him at the departures screen with its DELAYED and CANCELLED signs, and then behind me at the long line of fuming people who were all going to ask him to reach up into the sky and rearrange the heavens themselves. Then, he looked back at me — a person he *could help*. He leaned in, very serious.

"I am supposed to charge you for a whole new ticket," he said. Then, there was a twinkle of mischief in his eyes. Maybe it was chivalry. "But, since you're here ..." and he charged me seventy dollars for a ticket change and sent me onward to freedom.

What I've learned from this experience, I texted Elliott from the airport bar, *is that there are no consequences to my actions ever.*

At home, things had changed. While I was planting, Hex had been diagnosed with mammary cancer. Her condition was terminal. She had a few weeks left. She was heavily sedated when I arrived, tossed my bags on the floor, and fell into Sandy's arms. Hex still patrolled the house, but now she left vinegar-smelling wet spots on the furniture where her tumour protruded, veiny, ever-larger, above her belly. That summer was so hot as many as seventy people died from the heat in Quebec alone — human meat, cooked alive inside their homes. If I was too slow to spray and wipe down one of Hex's tumour spots, I'd know. Within an hour, the bacteria on it would bloom, filling the apartment with the sweet smell of death approaching.

Antoine had changed, too. He was three weeks sober when I picked him up from his fry cook job to go get him drunk. He told me that things had gotten bad when she'd left — that the drinking had gotten sinister, and dark, and weird. Things had never been sinister, dark, or weird between us, though. I figured that he and I didn't have the same kind of baggage as he did with her. He, after all, would always be my light — my beacon, my reason, my escape.

I wrote theatre reviews. I invited him to come see a play called *The History of Sexuality* at Place des Arts — the show was set in contemporary Montreal and loosely based around the Foucault work of the same name. As the characters mimed BDSM scenes onstage, I watched him sink into his seat, uncomfortable. I felt bad, and I took him after to a bar nearby to ease his discomfort.

He let his sobriety go like a handful of balloons. I saw him open up again. I started asking him questions.

"What do you think of Nietzsche?"

"One of the most profoundly misunderstood thinkers — unfairly misconstrued, especially by people who have never read him! I do, however, prefer Deleuze writing *on* Nietzsche to Nietzsche himself."

"When did you know it was over with her?"

"When she came over and we were screaming at each other in the kitchen." He got quiet. He looked out at nothing. "It's like ... when did it get that bad, you know?"

I imagined it was that night four years before. I leaned into him whenever I could. What if things had been different, that night at the Cock and Bull? Sandy and I had been going through another monogamous episode, and I'd spent the years after kicking myself, sure that that night had been my only chance — Antoine's last low point, in his relationship with *her*. Could I have saved him from the heartbreak he was feeling now?

He was taller than me, and warm, in a linen button-up, smelling like sandalwood and sweet vinegar, still sturdy even though his nervousness in sobriety had whittled his slim figure down into the eerie depths of thinness. I brushed my hands over his chest, his face, his arms. I threw my head back in laughter and then nestled it into his shoulder. Manual labour had made me broad and stocky and brown, and I would never be small again, or I would have worn the black party dress from that night — the one where I had the show, and it had felt right, and I'd been brave and told him how I felt, and he said he'd come to my show but he didn't. I felt haunted by that dress, by the Cock and Bull, by his sad blue eyes. We had unfinished business.

Nothing happened. He laughed at my jokes, made his own, finished the pitcher, ordered another. It was getting late.

"I guess I should, you know ..." I made a dramatic show of yawning. "Head to bed." I struck what I hoped was some kind of sexy pose.

He nodded. "Sounds good!"

We paid for our drinks, wandered to the metro. I struck another pose, my arms over my head, weirdly, half yawning. "Mmm, yes, can't wait ..." I said, meaningfully. "You know, for *bed*."

"Night!" he said cheerfully, gave me a quick hug, clapped me on the back, and then headed for the metro turnstiles.

"Text me when you get home," I slurred. He didn't even turn.

"Okay!" he called back, but he didn't.

Kate arrived the next morning to visit. She was staying with Elliott and his parents in the suburbs, but first she and I went out for brunch — small plates of eggs and toast and hollandaise and many enormous tall glasses of vodka flavoured with tomatoes and the seeping vinegars of dead sea creatures.

"I don't understand," I told her. "I was so obvious."

"He didn't notice," she said, simply.

"How could he *not notice*?" I asked, incredulous. "I was like, hanging off of his arm."

"Here is what you do," she said, frankly, like she was explaining subtraction or addition to a sweet, slow child. "You text him, 'Sorry I flirted with you so much last night. I am a drunk bitch.'"

I thought about it for a second, then punched the text message into my phone, verbatim, and hit send. Within seconds, it buzzed with a reply: *Oh, I didn't notice,* read Antoine's text message. *Fuck, I am really clueless.*

"Told ya," said Kate.

My face was burning. "I'm so embarrassed."

"You have plausible deniability," she said, putting her Caesar straw in her mouth. "You *did* say, 'I am a drunk bitch.'"

My phone buzzed again. Antoine asked, *Do you want to hang out tonight?*

I squealed, showed Kate, strategized. *Come to Casa del Popolo at 8,* I wrote back. *Kate is in town.*

We were having a proper party. Elliott, Sandy, Kate, and a smattering of other friends were crowded around a table on the back patio at Casa del Popolo — all people we knew from the great Young Person Exchange that exists between Montreal and Halifax.

I got up to go get another drink from the bar.

"Hey!" someone said, behind me, as I was waiting. I turned, and looked — Antoine, wearing a shirt that fit better than the linen one he'd worn before. He was obviously coiffed, in a way I'd never seen him — his hair in pomade, his short beard carefully trimmed.

I smiled, overjoyed. He kept my eyes, and smiled back. He'd never looked at me like that, before.

He and I sat together, and drank, and laughed. In a daze, I noticed that the rest of the party drifted away — to catch the last metro, or to go hook up, or to go to another party. By one in the morning, Antoine and I were standing at the bar talking only to each other. Several pints after that, I noticed the barmaids starting to put things away.

"Oh," I said. "They're closing."

"There are more drinks at my place," Antoine said, and I knew what he meant. On the walk from Casa to his Mile End apartment, I snaked my arm through his while we talked, our laughter pealing up into the milky summer sky. We walked quickly, urgently, leaning into each other. Like a couple who had been together this whole time.

We didn't kiss until we were already in bed. I suddenly clammed up again, at his place. Not making a move with him, out of some intra-girl solidarity that I shared with his now-ex-girlfriend, was so thoroughly second nature by this point that I didn't know how to snap out of it. I was very aware of the social contract as we sat in his living room, close together, taking turns at his sound system playing songs for each other. We were going to fuck, this much was obvious. I realized, suddenly, that I'd spent the last four years negotiating with my sexuality around him. I would feel it swell up, often — I'd get overwhelmed, holding his gaze for too long or pressing my leg into his or leaning into him while we smoked. Declaring my love in a party dress in front of the philosophy department. Channelling my frustration into love poems and cloying covers of Quebecois indie ballads.

Mostly, though, I pushed my desire down. I denied my desire. I tried to kill it. I punished myself for my desire by trying to act sexless and ugly. I had wanted to be a *home wrecker*, and then I had hated myself for what I wanted so badly and for so long that now I couldn't figure out how to exist as a sexual creature in a home he'd wrecked on his own.

I couldn't break through. I didn't.

"You can sleep here, if you want," he had to say.

"Sure, great, thanks," I muttered, nervously, and then headed to his office with its pullout couch.

"You can sleep in my bed, if you want," he said, exasperated. *Aaaaah!* I thought. "Ha ha, okay, yeah, cool, sure," I said, but he didn't hear me. He went to brush his teeth.

I wandered into his bedroom, feeling like a soldier behind enemy lines. I suddenly felt very stupid for what I was wearing: a sleeveless purple maxi dress and probably a solid pound of copper jewellery. I took off my necklace, and put it on his bedside table, and thought about how I wasn't wearing a bra, and he was too thin for me to cheekily sneak one of his T-shirts. I took off my huge clanging copper earrings, and I started to panic. Surely, even given the fact that *we both knew we were about to fuck,* getting into a bed with my kitties fully out was a *little on the nose,* right? My forearms were totally covered in bangles. I took them off and clattered them down onto the rest of my jewellery and started to freak, because I could hear him finishing up in the bathroom. The magnitude of the situation climbed up in me. Maybe I could still get out of this, and we could wake up, still friends. I heard him moving around, and acted quickly, without thinking. I slipped off the remainder of my jewellery — five rings, or so, and an *anklet,* for fuck's sake — abandoned them, lifted his sheets, and leapt into his bed fully clothed. *Aaaaaah!* I thought. *Aaaaaah!*

When he came back, in socks and underwear, and got into bed, I was flat on my back, stiff as a board. My hands were holding the sheets chastely under my chin. I still had a full face of makeup on. I was not even looking at him.

The bed sunk where he got in. He was quick, cavalier, confident. "Good night!" he said, cheerfully, and then shut off the only light — a lamp on his bedside table.

"Night," I squeaked, from where I was huddled, terrified, into his white cotton sheets like a bedwetter at a first sleepover. We were plunged into mostly darkness. My eyes slowly adjusted, making out shapes in the navy-blue light granted by the slip of the moon beaming in from his bedroom window.

We lay there for what felt like a very long time.

"Do you want to cuddle?" he said.

I genuinely had to think about it. The dark made me a little more comfortable. I inched over, on my shoulders and hips, until I found where he was waiting with his arms open. Everywhere our skin touched, my skin shimmered with a wave of pleasure. There was overwhelming relief as I felt my body relax. I folded into him, relieved. He was hot and sturdy all along his thin limbs as I curved myself around him, snaking my hands around his rib cage, burrowing my face in the crook between his neck and his shoulder.

Gently, he grazed the work-roughened pads of his long fingers over me, flattened his palms on the backs of my shoulders, the arch of my lower back. I'd been humming for four years with the effort it took to stop myself from closing the space between the two of us. With the gap finally closed, it was like, *of course*. I swelled against him, arched into him, exploring. When he snaked his hands down my thighs and pulled the long skirt of my dress up around my waist, I was walking through a dream I used to have all the time and had only just remembered. I turned my head to find his neck and shoulders. He curled into me, familiar. He ran his hands up my back, under my dress, like he was telling me something I already knew. He lifted the dress up and over my head. He buried his hands in the tangles of my black hair. The kiss hit with the velocity of the last four years.

You're so beautiful, I was gasping. *I have wanted you since the moment I saw you*, I said, breathless. Not thinking. Then, really not thinking: *I love you*.

"The King of Carrot Flowers, Pts. 2 & 3" by Neutral Milk Hotel.

The next morning, 2019. Mile End.

We did it again in the morning, but something was wrong. Instead of pleasure, orgasm pulled the trigger of a migraine that I hadn't noticed was loaded in my head. With my head pounding, I tried resting it on his chest. I may as well have tried to cuddle with a writing desk. He was shut down, his eyes already miles away. He had retreated. He was already gone.

Later that day, he texted to name the inevitable: *I'm sorry. I thought I was over her. I'm not.*

I understand, I wrote back and I did. My eyes full of tears, I texted him, *Will you still be my friend?*

Of course, he said. But he wasn't.

"Do you remember your brother's father?" my dad asked me, eight years after he died.

"I remember some things," I said.

My dad was mad about something. "Your mother had terrible taste in men in her early twenties," said my father, who raised my brother. My brother called my dad *our dad*, because it was true. *Our dad is my real father*, my brother had told me, during those sixteen shimmering months of sobriety before the heroin took him. Biologically, we had different fathers, but I knew what he meant. He meant: *we are what loves us.*

August is a brutal month. A time of fear. Antoine's messages abruptly slowed to a monosyllabic trickle. This made me anxious, and desperate. I flung more messages at him — jokes, suggestions, requests, pleas that were all some approximation of *Have you gone? Were you*

ever here? Sometimes he'd give me an excuse — *I'm just really busy,* he would say. *Something came up. Something major. I'll tell you later.* Eventually, the messages stopped completely.

I was horrified to see our years-long friendship die so violently. I constructed elaborate fuck-you monologues that I would definitely scream at him, if I ever saw him again.

"You!" I fantasized about screaming, when I saw him again. "You shithead! We studied fucking feminist philosophy together, you asshole! You *went off* about how *pissed* you were when dudes would *pump and dump* your friends! Where is your *high and mighty equality discourse now,* you *dick*? This had *stakes*! My body is *important*! I don't just sleep with *anybody*! You don't get to just *dispose* of me! How *dare* you!"

I was still pulled toward him like eyes toward a car accident. I knew I couldn't have him. I couldn't go, literally, to his apartment, as much as I thought about it. I endlessly paced the streets of Montreal, instead, fuming. "Is that all our friendship is worth, to you? Four years for two shitty drunk rebound lays? Fuckhead. Asshole!"

I fantasized about buying a carton of eggs and whipping every last one at his front door, screaming, "Misogynist! Fuckboy! Liar, liar, liar!" I fantasized about charging into his work to make a scene. I fantasized about slandering him, wheat pasting his face and his full name all over town with the words, "Liar! Misogynist! Abuser!" He'd told me who he was, in plain language, enough times. I could have taken him at his word — but who was I, an idiot? I searched our interactions, looking for something I could construe as violence. Violence was just the only word to describe the way I felt blasted open on the inside. I reread my Habermas — *all language is violence.* I wanted to call what happened violence, even though that wasn't what happened.

"Liar! Asshole!" I looked for the violence, and I couldn't find it. I just found my broken heart. I paced my city until my legs knotted up with tight balls of swollen muscle.

"There were *stakes*. You *broke my heart*. At least act like *there were stakes*, act like I had a *heart to break*, act like that *mattered*. I love you. Asshole!"

I lay on our bed and had Sandy knead the wretchedness out of the parts of me I had walked into knots. "Harder," I said, my voice cracking, until I was wailing and crying on the bed with Sandy's fingers knuckle-deep in the flesh of my thighs, the dying cat watching with her swishing tail, her cancer weighing her sticky and wet and vinegar sweat onto the sheets of my bed.

In October, we needed money for the cat's euthanasia. My planting money had gone toward my debts and the decisions I'd made over the summer. Now that I was writing criticism, I could get some work writing for money. If I kept moving — kept pacing the streets, kept looking for work — I wouldn't think about Antoine.

I thought about him, anyway. His birthday was approaching, and while he did not respond to my pathetic little girlish pleas for attention anymore, on one of my breathless walks I dipped into a wool store and bought a ball of grey yarn. I took it home, to *knit, purl, chain* a silly little grey hat. I tied knot after knot, trying to bind him to me. I played the entirety of *In the Aeroplane Over the Sea* so I didn't think about how I'd learned to knit in a hospital waiting room while my mom was sick.

I finished both assignments in the nick of time — the writing for money and the hat for love. The cat wasn't eating much, anymore. Her tumour was almost as long as her legs and it hurt her to walk — she caught it on things, nicked it open, stopped in a daze to try to lick up what oozed out of it. Sandy made the appointment. We cleaned the house, set a sage bundle and some throw blankets on the balcony. I rushed to the Mile End on Antoine's birthday, with the hat inside of an old tobacco tin, a card that said *Saturday* in case *happy birthday* was too obvious. I came home and put on Neutral Milk Hotel. Two women in white coats arrived, on a beautiful fall day, to kill the cat.

Hex knew something was up. When Sandy reached for her, she swiped at him — dug her fingernail deep into his finger, ripped blood and a flap of skin free, and darted into the bedroom to save herself. I followed her in and into a corner. She curled into herself, eyes downcast. She looked small, and young, and scared. I put my hand out to her, and she sniffed me, trusting.

"It's okay," I lied. She lifted her chin to sniff my extended fingers, her tiny white canines pointing out daintily on the black fur of her mouth. I'd never felt so close to her, in all of our years together. We had so much in common — both negotiating for the affections of the same man.

"I love you, you asshole," I said. I put my hand around her neck, and scratched her there, and she leaned into me. I didn't want to miss my opportunity. This was the only real chance I'd ever had to take care of her. I quickly gathered the skin at the scruff of her neck. She stiffened, but didn't move.

The women came and slid Valium into her veins.

"That's right," I said. "Good girl."

She melted into my hands. I carried the cat who never liked me onto the balcony to die.

I tried to soothe my sadness with tattoos, again. I got bold capital letters on each of my arms: *AUTONOMIE*, freedom from external control or influence; *ALTÉRITÉ*, the state of being other, or different. I love this word, *alterity*. Philosophers in the Frankfurt school wrote about it like this: *The Other is always radically other*. What is outside of us cannot ever really get in. We are all fundamentally alone, but this is what makes real empathy possible. Searching for the Other, I fall and I fall, and I never land. The futility of it doesn't make it less valuable — we're all alive, on earth, after all.

When they healed, I still felt empty. I didn't know what to do. I called Kate, and she took the train to come see me. I packed up my writing assignment, and she and I headed back east to Halifax for Christmas. In my parents' kitchen, on St. Margarets Bay, the Atlantic wind whipping their rented house, I tried to work on my assignments, or at least get into the holiday spirit. I made dinner for my parents, and ate the dinner they made for me. I partied at Kate's punk house. I tried to hold my drink, as best I could. I wrote bland web copy for landscaping companies. I took the dogs out. I tried not to think about how desperately I wanted to be adored, how desperately I wanted to care for what adored me.

I got a message from Antoine. It said: *I owe you an explanation.* His explanation was that *they* had gotten back together, for a time — and then split again, with such force that it had driven him hard into the bottle, all the way to a rehab centre.

I'm better now, he said — but, you know.

I missed Antoine. I missed my brother. I missed Adbul. I missed Gertie and Pip, my childhood dogs. I missed Hexadecimal, who never liked me. I wanted to take care of something so I could stop thinking about everyone I couldn't take care of, because they were already gone, or they wouldn't let me.

"Brookie!" I yelled out to my stepmother. She poked her strawberry-blond head out from where she was playing tug-of-war with her Mexican rescue mutt.

"What?" she said, jostling as the beast pulled her happily back and forth.

"I think I need a dog, or something."

"A Case of You"
by Joni Mitchell.

February 2019. Mile End.

When I got back to Montreal, I got a therapist again. She was at a well-respected clinic. She was affordable — new, under supervision, only a few years older than me at the absolute oldest.

"Tell me about your childhood," she said.

I didn't want to talk about my childhood. Instead of telling her about my childhood I talked about cancer, and God, and the economy. I talked about wanting a dog and how I had weaned myself off of the antipsychotics.

"I was having insane side effects," I muttered. "I couldn't get my fucking psychiatrist on the phone." Her eyes went wide, and she made a note. I tried to explain myself.

"You're really not supposed to drink on them, you know? And I couldn't stop drinking. I know you're not supposed to."

"I believe you, when you say you have good reasons," said my new therapist. I relaxed, a little. I talked about Antoine. My friends were so sick of hearing about him that nobody let me talk about him anymore. My therapist's silence, while I waxed poetic about my stupid crush, felt well worth the eighty dollars I paid her at the end of the session.

Antoine texted me late at night, when I was already in bed. On a whim, I had applied for an office job at a non-profit at Concordia. To my genuine shock, I had been offered the position. I had to be at work for training at 8:00 a.m. I was a few weeks sober, again, in my pyjamas, looking wistfully at pictures of rescue dogs on the internet, imagining some tranquil future with Sandy, who was still here.

Antoine's message relayed that his stint in rehab hadn't stuck. He told me, *I can't believe how little anything in my life ever changes.* He said, *I can't believe how hard I fight to keep everything exactly the same.*

"Nothing's going to happen," I told Sandy, as I put on a shirt and my coat and my boots. "My friend needs me." I don't think he believed me.

It was going on 11:00 p.m. — approaching the longest, most desperate hours of the night, and moments before the depanneurs stopped selling liquor. I had been attempting sobriety again, but I knew the price of being with him. I walked into the dep across from Vendôme metro. I knew if he made it until morning, everything would be okay, at least until the next round of midnight hours. He had sounded so desperate. I told myself I needed ambassadors, as I loaded the counter up with cans of his chosen poison. I would make a martyr of my sobriety. I was only doing it, I rationalized, because I cared about his safety.

A friend of mine told me once, *We humans, we're not logic-al creatures, we're rational ones.* I'd come to this city to study philosophy — to learn how to persuade — but mostly, what I found out was that if you give a person a few hours and twelve hundred words, they can provide you with a defence or a condem-nation of anything. You can't change anyone's mind about any-thing if they don't already want to change it. If you try anyway, they will only push you further away. I can't be mad about this because it's also how I operate. I can make such convincing argu-ments for almost anything I want. I start with my feelings, my biases, my conclusion — *I am getting drunk tonight* — and I work my way backward, to righteousness. I will do what I want and then project a reason that it is good, in retrospect. I will project a story backward, like the clever liar that is anyone giving an account of one's self. I will fight so hard to make it look like I'm changing. I will fight so hard to keep things exactly the same.

A theory: night becomes day, or vice versa, at a time just after the count of four. I hate 4:00 p.m., which is exactly like Sunday, or August — the last few middling moments of light before the dark-ness. Anything before 4:00 a.m. is nighttime, but at some point between 4:00 a.m. and 5:00 a.m., night turns into morning. I had to get Antione across the precipice of 4:00 a.m.

I genuinely did not mean to sleep with him. I was going to go over, talk him down, prop his computer open, tell him to pick a song. We'd go back and forth like this, until the clock read 4:00 a.m. or he fell asleep — whichever came first.

As soon as I cracked the first can, I knew I was in trouble. The drink shot to my head, filled me up, swept me off my feet. The drink took the world in both its hands, cracked it right open, and held it out to me — pink and raw and living and full of magic.

"Can I play this?" I said, standing up on my knees on the couch in his office, reaching for where his guitar hung from a hook off the wall.

"Sure," he said.

I played the first few chords of "A Case of You," but I fumbled on the fretting. I could smell his sandalwood and vinegar smell, feel the warmth of him when he leaned in. He slid the guitar out of my hands, without speaking. He knew the song.

He strummed the chords, better than I could. I sang to him. I was sure I'd known him all my life. I collapsed before the song was even over, folding into him, finding the crook of his shoulder. He put the guitar down and we went to his bed.

When I woke up, I curled into myself. The argument for why I simply had to be here, in this bed, with this man — so compelling the night before — fell apart in the light of day. I cursed myself for being so easily persuaded, as my hangover migraine rang out like a shot inside my skull. I'm always so convinced by my rationalizations until my own bad behaviour is over, and I'm just sitting in my life.

Antoine and I woke up in his bed and we were sick and nothing was different. I think I figured that if I was the one to help him like this — if I came to him when he needed someone, just like this, if I lay down just like this, if I made him feel wanted or needed or *something* just like this, I'd change something. But I woke up, and I had to leave. I left his apartment and the winter light was too bright in my eyes. I cast them down to the ground, still tucked into that February cold. The snow had been loosened just enough by the longer days to snap into a treacherous sheet of ice. It coated every-thing like plastic wrap. I left him for the last time, walking out into the snow-sharpened daylight, blinking my eyes against the impos-sibly pale blue of it all, the little pieces of cloud turned so bright and full of light that they drove pain sharp as ice crystals into my eyes and into my temples. I raised my hands to the sky above my head to try to blot it out. I cast my eyes to the ground, and then to the smoking table on his front porch.

The tin I'd left on his birthday was still there — opened, examined, with the hat on the table next to it, wrapped in the tight icy grip of winter. I walked away from him — over the Rosemont overpass, where the industrial building still reads *THE ST. LAWRENCE WAREHOUSE COMPANY*, where the churches are still the highest thing in the sky. Copper evergreens. It was February 17, 2019. I did the math, really quickly: two months, or so, frozen to the table. I felt, in the very sinews of my body, my ancestors, blood and adopted and ancestors in spirit. I was my father, a holy man departing the faith. I was my grandmothers and grandfathers, drawn to Montreal like a beacon in the deep darkness of their youth. I remembered Thomas, who said, *We're supposed to make everything to rot away. We inherit nothing but our stories.*

That's how I get back to the beginning of the story — the story I started, before I had to go back. I ran my hands over myself. I found something stirring in me. I went to my doctor. Are you following? Do you understand what I mean?

"Dress Sexy at My Funeral" by Smog.

September 2019. Concordia University, Montreal.

I called security to unlock the door from the student-run café across the street from my office. I was on the Concordia campus, where I worked. It was the day after my Pap test and breast exam. It was 8:00 a.m. I like to be early for the same reason I like being sober. When I fail, and I often do, I don't like to fail because of something I can control.

The student-run café had been put in by one of the on-campus sustainability groups a few years earlier, in a bid to replace chain restaurants with local co-operatives. I was a big fan of the student-run café on principle: their coffee was awful, and the management was a never-ending drama cycle driven by eighteen-to-twenty-five-year-olds who thought the peak of activism was being mean to each other on Instagram. But it was cheap, and it was social-ism. There were resilient little potted plants, and cute people. I loved it there, for these reasons, and because it reminded me of Antoine.

I liked working at Concordia. It really did seem, sometimes, like I still went to school there — like I could pop over to Kafein for Poetry Nite, even though Kafein had been closed for years. It seemed like I could walk into Stephanie's class like it was nothing, meet up with Gregor. I could march up the steps to the philosophy department to shoot the shit with Rohan, who didn't work here anymore. It seemed like Antoine could turn one of the street corners, with his silly leather briefcase in his hand and a cigarette perched in his mouth, to ask me what I thought of the Spinoza reading. Much of the same was still going on — in the student-run café, I saw serious Gregor-types, with their cartilage piercings and their stack of modernist poetry, their phones *ding*ing Grindr notifications on top.

In the back, a tall boy with blond hair and sad eyes was leaning into a wall and toward a girl, swinging his briefcase like a little boy would swing a toy. My heart caught in my throat, until he turned — it wasn't Antoine. It was just another tall, freaky blond. Another kid playing dress-up.

Finished with calling security, I decided to try my psychiatrist, even though I knew it wasn't going to work.

You have reached the Douglas Hospital, a division of the McGill University Teaching Hospital Network. Please enter the extension number of the person you wish to reach, or dial one for the reception —

I pressed one, watching the barista with the shaved head pull my double espresso shot.

"Douglas, *bonjour*," said the receptionist, or the nurse, or whatever.

"*Bonjour!* Hi, I'm a patient of Dr. Lavoie, is it possible to —"

"Dr. Lavoie isn't in today."

Of course, she never is. "Okay, sure, can I leave a message?"

"I can patch you through to her line."

"Okay, cool, but you see, the line leads to —"

Too late. There was a dead tenor tone, and then a series of beeps like a phone number being dialed, three busy tones, and then a clunk as the line went dead. At that point, I could have sung the whole thing off by heart, like a choral piece. I had made this same fruitless phone call, every few days, for months.

"Double shot in the dark?" said the barista with the shaved head, emptying my espresso shot into my small coffee. This barista was a new one. They had a septum ring, like all the other baristas, and a big cute smile, and they looked about eighteen.

"Thanks, sweetie," I said, maternally, before I could stop myself, and then I took my coffee to the self-serve cream-and-sugar counter to dump a few shakes of cinnamon inside and take a big sip. *Aah. Awful.*

I walked toward my office and checked the time on my phone: 8:23 a.m. Still too early for the sustainability crowd, who tended to herd in around two or three on Monday, if they showed up at all. It had become a joke between me and my colleagues: *Concordia's sustainability organizations: available any time! Except on Fridays. And most Mondays. Especially in the morning. And the afternoon, too, honestly. Monday's out, actually. And Tuesdays are basically Monday, then, so make that like 2:00 p.m. earliest. And then Thursday is basically Friday, so I'll probably be leaving early. So come over any time between 2:00 p.m. on Tuesday and like elevenish on Thursday, I guess. But then, any time! Unless I'm in a meeting. Or I don't want to.*

The sustainability organizations mostly occupied the second floor of a converted apartment building on Mackay Street. There was the Concordia Food Coalition, who founded projects like the student-run café. There is the Sustainability Action Fund, a quarter-million-dollar annual fund for projects that promote environmental and social activist causes. There is also my organization, Sustainable

Concordia. We had spent the last six months in very long meetings, full of very full flip-chart papers and whiteboards, because we didn't know what we did, and we were trying to figure it out.

At my job, I handed out Antifa stickers to impressionable young freshmen. At my job, I put on thrifted three-piece suits and my clacky heels, and I firmly but politely argued with the university's investment magnates about the virtues of divesting the university's investment stock from fossil fuels. At my job, I advertised the school's composting program, holding a hand-drawn sign that said *COMPOST RICH PEOPLE*. I had never intended to get the job, and so I was never really stressed out. I always felt like I was trolling, like I was getting away with something. It was insane that this was a job, and even more insane that they'd wanted me to do it, and even *more* insane that they wanted me *so much* that when I left for tree planting that spring they had responded by giving me a raise and upping my hours, nervous I was going to leave. I put my bag down on my desk and took out the requisition forms, and I was nervous that I was going to leave.

I went upstairs, to the kitchen, and I put on another pot of coffee. I made the rounds and watered the plants that dotted the office. I went back to my desk, and my bag, and my requisition forms, and I stared at them for a long time while I drank my coffee. I went back upstairs and poured myself another cup. With it warm and reassuring in my hands, I opened the door at the back of the office that led onto the black metal scaffolding of the fire escape, and I pulled out my phone. *Radiology Montreal*, I searched on my browser, and I called the first clinic that came up.

"Because Dreaming Costs Money, My Dear" by Mitski.

September 2019. The Queen Elizabeth Health Complex, Montreal.

I was the youngest woman in the radiology department.

It smelled awful. Hospitals always smell awful. It's how death actually smells: some lingering heart-note, the blunt, wet rot of decay. A hospital smells like what it means to remember that you're an animal and you rot like everything else. Nobody can get that smell out, it's always there: the low notes of sweat and misery on the lanyard strings of an overworked nurse. The nervous acridity on the neck of a doctor ready to deliver bad news. It bruises into blooming while you're trying to cope with whatever new information the doctors have given you or have been unable to give you.

The fluorescent bulbs flicker in their stained white containers and fill the air with light that never truly illuminates. This light renders even the healthiest among us sallow and yellowed from the inside out. That day in the radiology department, this light swelled wanly into its white rooms. My boots squeaked on the ground — the cream colour mottled with random-looking TV static brown and grey and black. I wondered if they came like that. Are hospital floors printed all over to camouflage the inevitable slide and smear of a tiny layer of boot rubber? Do they just accumulate these pieces of the people who have walked over them before? How many of those people are dead now?

There were posters on the wall to remind us to sneeze into our elbows and get thirty minutes of daily exercise. Flyers promoted health studies paid in Amazon gift cards, grief counselling services, group therapy, weight-loss centres. The waiting room had plastic chairs in uniform maroon. I walked close to the wall with the flyers and passed the waiting room. I went deep into the belly of the department to speak to the nurse at the reception desk.

I leaned my body into the desk, expectant. The nurse was not there. I craned my neck over, but I saw only piles of paperwork, and a few staplers, and a coffee cup. Hand sanitizer. A computer still booting up.

"Hello?" I called out.

I heard a shuffle of movement, and saw a beleaguered nurse emerge from behind another florescent-lit corner. She was holding another pile of papers and another coffee cup. She looked surprised and annoyed to see me.

"Yes?" she asked, putting down whatever important papers she was holding.

Hi," I started, smiling as sweetly as I could. "Mammogram?"

She furrowed her brows and pointed to the counter in front of me. I looked down at it and saw there were plastic baskets, waiting, bearing signs. One said *Incoming* and one said *Appointment*, each of them in many layers of packing tape, greyed, approximating a lamination job. In big letters, on a plastic stand above them, were the words *CLIP YOUR MEDICARE CARD TO YOUR*

REQUISITION FORM. "Oh," I said, surprised. I looked back at her. *I am very appreciative of the hard work you are doing*, I thought, and tried to beam the sentiment out at her through my eyeballs. "Thank you so much," I said, all syrup.

"Sure, honey," she said, picking up her papers, sipping her coffee, her frustration softened — a little, and only at the edges.

I rummaged around in my purse and found my crumpled requisition forms and my medicare card. I took one of the provided paper clips and paper-clipped them together. I put it in the file labelled *Appointment* and I went back to the waiting room.

As I went into the waiting room, I had a sense of entering a space where the rules of time and space worked differently. I think hospitals are like airports. All hospitals are really one place. Every hospital, one flat ontological field. This is what I mean when I tell people I was *in the hospital*, explaining that I passed into some compound space defined by the smell of astringent-death and lighting that makes even the well look ill.

In the hospital, even the waiting rooms that look different also look the same. In the radiology department, which was every radiology department, I thought about how privatized medical systems *charge money* for hospital waiting rooms that smell and look the same — a grift compounding a greater grift. I adjusted myself on the waiting room chairs, which were all waiting room chairs — reasonably comfortable, in the grand scheme of things. I sat in the sallowness of the lighting, which is always blue in movies. It isn't actually blue, it's yellow — an anemic yellow, and somehow also grey. Both a colour and that which negates a colour. I breathed in the sour twinge of antiseptic: firm and high and ringing and trying to cover the bouquet of sorrow and death underneath and never quite succeeding.

I went through the same mantra I went through in every hospital waiting room, reading my lines dutifully: how long will it take, haven't got all day, there aren't even many people here. Then, calm yourself, woman, you're twenty-seven, not bleeding from a gushing head wound, not vomiting stomach acid. Have you fallen down a flight of stairs carrying a nail gun? No. Are you a teenager who went into renal failure in math class? No. You, Tara, are not a father of six celebrating eight months of sobriety with a liver transplant, and you are not a three-month-old pulled from a twelve-car pileup, and you have no gunshot wounds. The doctors were busy stitching people back together who would die if I didn't wait. In *Critique of the Gotha Program*, in 1875, Karl Marx wrote, "From each according to his ability, to each according to his need." I had no nursing degree, I could not do surgery. My ability, here, was to wait.

I looked around for something to do. I saw that the other people waiting in the radiology department were reading their very old magazines or looking at their phones. I saw that next to me, on a table, was a bright pink bin, full of yarn and knitting needles and small knitted squares.

All hospitals are, in spirit, the same hospital. I looked at the bin full of yarn and knitting needles and small knitted squares, and thought, *Isn't that interesting, now all radiology departments have bins, like this.* If I were in charge of hospitals, I'd make a few changes. Hospitals are where you go to do unpleasant things and be worried on behalf of yourself or others — a good thing to do when you are sick with worry is keep your hands busy. Hospitals all smell the same and they are all lit the same and they have the same activities — magazines from years ago, spotty cell connections, and lighting that is not good for selfies, unless you want to look sick, and no judgment, if that's your thing. The yarn is in all hospital radiology departments. At least, all the ones I've been in.

I don't remember what my mother was going in for on the day I learned how to knit.

Two ladies in the waiting room chairs offered to watch my sister and I. The waiting room chairs were goofy and well-worn in that waiting room, too, but everything was more brightly coloured. The lighting was not better, but it was brighter. Everyone still looked sallow, and still looked drawn-out, but the characteristic yellow of the hospital lights was orange at all the corners. I feel like most things in Toronto are more orange, on average — like someone is editing the light as it enters my eyes. Montreal is a stark red, except for at night — at night, in Montreal, everything is navy blue.

These two ladies seemed ancient to me, but I was eight. One of them had tufts of very pale white hair — the kind of pale white you do not get naturally, but instead by buying that purple shampoo and conditioner that was first developed for old people and then appropriated by children on the internet. She had an ice-white old lady perm, still with a touch of violet where it hadn't all blended yet. The lady was as pillowy and warm as the seats we were sitting in. She beamed at me. She was folding the yarn over in her fingers.

The lady was wearing a pink T-shirt, her puffy black parka splayed out into the seat around her, where she'd sat down with her coat still on and settled into the confines of the chair and its arms like a liquid filling a glass before she started to take off her layers of outerwear. There was another woman, too, but she is a black maw in my memory: a huge blank hole where my mind has snipped out everything unnecessary. I wonder if she had the same silk turban my mother wrapped around her head to hide her sparse buzz cut. My mother had developed a routine of cropping the hair close to her scalp so she didn't have to watch it fall out as she got deeper and deeper into the brutal country of her chemo treatments. It did fall out. She swept up what was left, smaller and smaller collections of hairs shorter than an eyelash gathered into the tiny bathroom trash bags. She wrapped lengths of silk around her head, diligent as a monk.

The first woman had hair and a warm smile. She was knitting strands of pink back and forth and around each other with long knitting needles. I asked her how she did it.

"It's easy," she said. She pet the seat next to her. "Come here, baby."

Knit, purl, chain.

Once she had explained, she set me up with my own set of equipment. I sat there for so long, weaving these strands together, realizing I had made a mistake and backtracking and starting again, too lost to remember why I was there, until my parents came to get me.

I wondered, in the radiology department in Montreal, at twenty-seven, if the plastic bins with the pink yarn inside were for some purpose, or just to occupy lonely children with how to knit while they waited for their mother to come back. I already knew how to knit. What else would I do while I waited — for her to return, or to go somewhere to meet her. I wondered, if I picked up the yarn and some of the provided needles, if I could weave together parts of my life until they made sense. If I could knit together all the disparate parts, stand up in this radiology department, walk through some gap in the space-time and put my knitted work down in a bin that looked the same, except for the light.

I'd be able to sit down next to the youngest people in the radiology department: two little girls, their hands full of yarn. I could tell them what was coming. I could tell them to hold on to each other. I could tell them to hold on to anything. I could tell them to prepare, because the worst thing is coming. Maybe most importantly, I could tell them about all those years in the bush: how the only time things really go wrong is when we all start being very cruel to each other. They're so young, though. Would they even understand?

Some other pattern, and I could put my knit work down, and pick up my two daughters and take them home, and maybe it would be early enough for me. Some other pattern, maybe, and I could find a woman with silk wrapped around her head coming back from the hallway, where only the patients go — a woman with my grandfather's strong jaw and handsome eyes. I could say something, maybe, with my knitting in my hands. I could say, *"Mom, I —"*

"McGowan-Ross, Tara," someone called, in the radiology department in Montreal. I was twenty-seven. I went to speak to the nurse.

Top 40 music was playing over the radio, a mishmash of French and English, most of it saccharine and terrible. Every tenth song or so was deeply moving, because pop music is fundamentally good, but then the drone of formulaic horror would begin again, and I was irritated. I was fiercely aware of how unattractive I looked under the lights. I had a headache from the smell of the hospital. I sat down to speak to the nurse.

"I'm here for a mammogram," I told her, before she asked.

"You're here to book a mammogram," the nurse corrected me, and sipped her coffee. I raised my eyebrows. *I am here to what a what?*

"Oh," I said. "I thought …"

"And you're too young for a mammogram, you're here to book an ultrasound," she said, making a note on my requisition request, which looked like crossing out the mammogram request, before she booted up her computer to start my file.

I should challenge her, I thought. My requisition request was for a mammogram, not an ultrasound. I knew from research that a mammogram was slightly more accurate. The nurse had been very firm, however, and she was the healer here. I couldn't get knitting rhythm out of my head: *knit, purl, chain two, knit …*

The nurse found my hospital file. I had been here before. She checked my details: address, name, phone number, all accurate. I needed her. *From each according to their ability.* She studied nursing and health care and not me, and I wanted to be polite, but I also wanted to live.

"I think the requisition request is for a mammogram, not an ultrasound," I said, finally. She stopped what she was doing, and slowly moved her eyes to look up at me. I could feel tears burning my eyes. *Please. I need you.*

"You're too young for a mammogram," she said, firmly, but with more kindness. "A mammogram is radiation. We can't, in good conscience, radiate the breasts of a woman in her twenties if we don't have cause."

"But there's something in there," I said.

"I understand," she said, calmly. "We will do the ultrasound, and if we find anything, we will get you a mammogram or an MRI right away. We need to make sure you need it." I nodded, somewhat reassured, but also giving up. *To each according to their needs.* She clicked on her computer a few more times and took another long swig on her coffee up. "Go take a seat," she said, handing me back my medicare card. The waiting room was very empty, and there were so many seats available, but I went back to the seat near those little scraps of yarn.

"They're to make little blankets for the NICU," said the lady with the pink T-shirt and the ice-blue old lady perm, in the radiology department waiting room, when I was eight years old.

"Nick-you?" I asked, confused.

"Neonatal Intensive Care Unit," she said, calmly, her hands not stopping. *Knit, purl, chain.* "It's where the sick babies go, to get better."

Materials provided by the generous donations from the Côte-Des-Neiges–Notre-Dame-De-Grâce community, read the sign on the bin in the radiology department in Montreal when I was twenty-seven. I read it, and I heard it in the voice of the lady in the other waiting room, nineteen years before. She had a backlit, smiling face and tufts of white hair. Everything was backlit, when I was a child. When people smiled, they were smiling down at me. All adults had big bellies and chins. I spent so much time addressing their knees and their hips.

I wanted to leave my childhood peaceful and undisturbed, in its final resting place, like we left my mother's ashes in the garden wall at St. George the Martyr Anglican Church. I wanted to leave it like a shot dog behind a shed. I wanted to leave it in the annals of time, where it belonged, but the hospital is a space outside of time, and I felt memories rise in my throat like sickness. I had pounded my childhood tightly into the dark corners of body — my stomach, my thighs, my hips. I had compacted it deeply enough I was sure it would never emerge. It would flare up, every once in a while, and send surges of pain along my nerves and muscles, but then I could just lay very still, praying that what was inside of me would stay there, would never emerge, would never charge into my bloodstream to make me feverish and sickly and aware.

It was a beautiful day. My dad was cracking jokes while my sister and I pulled at his hands and his arms, chased each other around, shrieked peals of laughter up into the bright joy of the sunny sky. The grass was so impossibly green. The air smelled like concrete and spilled gasoline. Sweet trees. Baking bread. I don't know where we were.

My dad on his knees, in front of us, like he was begging for forgiveness. He looked small. Frustrated with his own inability to fix this. Crushed by the weight of his burden. I felt overwhelmed by the urge to help him carry some of it. I decided to pick some of it up. I don't think I ever put it down.

Suddenly my memory goes dark, and I just hear my father's disembodied voice. *Unless there is some kind of miracle ...*

"Tara?" called the nurse, and I was back in that hospital that smelled like every hospital, and was illuminated like every hospital, and was full of bubblegum pop music that was trying to bullshit me in both official languages. I walked over to the desk and she motioned for me to sit down.

My sister's voice: *Miracles happen all the time.* She was six. My father, his hair still so long, his face so young, on one knee so he can look us both in the face where we sit on the park bench. The most merciful way to tell children something horrible is to do it in the sunshine. I thought about Hex, limp in my arms, headed out to the balcony for the injection that would stop her heart. It's good to have a nice view when something has to die.

232

"I've made you an appointment for two weeks from now," the nurse said, not looking at me.

My left breast throbbed where the lump was hiding. I wanted to throw up on her desk. I wanted to say, *Thank you*, but instead I said, "Are you sure the requisition isn't for a mammogram?"

She shook her head, no. "Cancer in women as young as you is so rare, you have to understand." Cancer in women in their thirties is rare, too, and my mom still died. "I know you have a family history." People reduced my mom down to things like this all the time: family history, her last name, statistics about life expectancy and recurrences. Her odds, which were horrible, right from the beginning. Maybe they would have been better if they had caught it earlier. "If we find anything, we'll do a mammogram right away."

I was absolutely positive they would find something. I'd already found something. There was something in my breast, throbbing and asking for attention. I was diseased. The cancer would just be another in a long line of issues with my body and spirit: I'd been an obese child, trying to fill that void that got ripped inside me with anything that would comfort me. I'd had aches and pains and diseases meant for the very old since I was a little girl: sciatica, acid reflux, kyphosis. My body already had a tendency to send calcium deposits to my salivary glands when I didn't drink enough water. These tiny stones would clog my mouth up, prevent it from sending in wet things, swell the space under my tongue until I leaked putrid muck to taste and to swallow. It tasted like *something is wrong with you*. I had already planted hundreds of thousands of trees, bending over every time, curling up on my side on the cold forest floor to sleep, my muscles and tendons shredded and stewing in the inflammation. I was ready to bloom with tumours all over. This nurse didn't understand that what we were talking about was a hair trigger. She didn't understand that what we were talking about was a birthright. The voice of dread, calm and certain, said this wasn't a normal statistical situation. I was an exception. I was a medical marvel. I was a miracle.

Some kind of miracle. Miracles happen all the time. When I was a kid, and my mom was sick, I didn't know if a miracle would happen but I kept on hoping it would. I think, when I saw my dad on his knees, and he looked small and lost and like he needed help, hope felt like the only thing I could do for him. Hope is so stupid. Hope is all we have.

"Thank you," I said to the nurse, as an adult in Montreal. She printed out information about my appointment onto some kind of sticker, peeled the back off, and stuck it to the bottom of my requisition form.

"Have a nice day," she said, and I thanked her. I left the hospital and I was back into the world — back into time and space. My childhood clung to me, dumb and loud and calling out for attention. I wished it would shut the fuck up. I wished it would leave me alone. I remembered my dad kneeling in the sunshine, looking at me with hope and horror and love and disappointment. I could hear his voice. For some reason, I could not put these two parts of my memory together. I couldn't see his face and hear his voice at the same time.

As I walked away from the cloying bullshit of the Top 40 music and the horrific perfume and the awful lighting of the hospital, a bitterly cold Montreal downpour started up. It was so dark on the sidewalk, there in the middle of the day. It was a short walk to my apartment. There was a bottle of wine and some whisky at the apartment. I didn't care about the rain. I was busy thinking, *Knit, purl, pass, tie, repeat,* and *There is a bottle of wine and some whisky at the apartment.* I tried to stay very busy, thinking these things, so I didn't feel the way my childhood clung like two little girls to each of my legs, wrapping their arms with their sticky fingers and their dirty feet around me to weigh me down and bring me back. If I did think about that day, I tried to think about my dad's face. I tried to think about the way he marvelled at his two good little girls, who didn't do anything wrong, and didn't deserve what he had to say — and he did have to say it. It was taking care of us. *Unless there is some kind of miracle, your mother is going to die.*

"There's a job opening up, you know," she was telling me.

I blinked. I hadn't even noticed that I had zoned out, completely. I was at a work event, standing next to a woman I knew from work, in the socialist café on campus. It was after-hours, and we were having some kind of sustainability-related event, with drinking, but I wasn't drinking. I wasn't sober, but I was trying this new thing where I wasn't drinking at work, or with people from work. When people asked me why I wasn't drinking around people I worked with, I told them, *I have a relationship with sobriety,* instead of the truth — which is that I couldn't stop drinking, and that when I did drink, I fell into a dark hole — a deep pit of sadness that felt altogether inappropriate for work.

Around me, at this work event, people drank normally. When people asked me if I wanted a drink, I said, "Not tonight" instead of the truth, which was that I was certain something was wrong with me. I was approaching the end — the last act in the great, foolish drama of my life. I couldn't rush the ending, as much as I wanted to — as much as I wanted to open my mouth and take in as much liquor as I could fit, and feel the rush of falling in love again, climb up onto the highest point at the fundraiser raffle or cabaret or whatever the fuck we were doing, and announce, "Please excuse me, I'm going to be dead soon" — and wait for the reaction, that delicious recoil, that exquisite moment of pity and regret. I would tell them that I was dying, in order to make up for any and all ways I had been unkind or irresponsible or unreasonable — the same way I told people, *I have a relationship with sobriety*, instead of, *I'm an alcoholic*, which is to apologize, in advance, for my eventual failure.

"Tara?"

Shit, fuck, right, still at work. "Sorry, Gabby, I'm so tired, there have been all these human resources things to deal with lately and I'm losing sleep ... you were saying there's a job opening? Where?"

"At the bookstore, where my boyfriend works!"

"Oh, yes. Right. Love the bookstore."

The first time I was sober, my first slip was champagne at my cousin's wedding, when I was handed a glass by a well-meaning party facilitator. I was in an echoing, cavernous room, in a bicycle-printed minidress. My hair was dyed pink. I was so happy. I had said no to drinks before we got to the reception, no to drinks in the days leading up to it, no to drinks for six months before. My sister was there with me. I was the only one not drinking.

"Do you want me to get you something else?" she asked — softly, discreetly, leaning in so it was only us. She would have gotten me something else. She was confident like that, a problem solver like that. She would have marched up to the bartender and asked for a Diet Coke or a ginger ale, would have gotten it in a champagne flute so I could toast without feeling left out.

I felt a strange pang of guilt. I wanted to be the one to solve this problem. I wanted to be a normal person. This wasn't one of those *dangerous drinks*, I decided. I wasn't drinking to escape a terrible day at my job, or a heartbreak, or a disappointment. This was a happy time — I was safe and surrounded by family. I was so happy. I wanted to drink the champagne. One drink wouldn't feel like a relapse.

The problem, of course, is that one drink inevitably leads to other drinks. This one drink was no exception. An alcoholic is never the exception and they always think that they are — this is probably the biggest barrier to recovery that exists. I thought I was an exception. I thought I was an exceptional person taking an exceptional drink — I thought I was far too smart, too interesting, too complicated, and too tragic to be a textbook case. Surely I wasn't one of the someones for whom simple solutions were written by people who knew what they were talking about — solutions like *quit drinking and never start again, not even once, not ever.* Solutions like *you can't control other people.*

A few months later, drunk out of my mind, Antoine and I fucked in his bedroom with my purple dress still crumpled up around one of my ankles. It all seemed so normal, like such an inevitable progression from point A to point B, but I wouldn't have done it if I hadn't been who I was when I was drinking. It's not that I drink until I end up in jail, or close to death. It's that I hate who I am when I drink, and who I am when I drink shows up after one drink — even if she is just somewhere on the horizon, running very slowly. She is hooting and hollering: *I'm coming, baby!*

Ugh, this bitch. I groan. *Who invited her?* I am asking my friends, my ancestors, the universe.

You did, says everyone and everything. She's not invited when I'm at work anymore.

"Tara?"

"Shit, Gabby, I'm so out of it. Sorry, what were you saying?"

"I said you should apply for it."

"The job at the bookstore, with your boyfriend?"

"It's full-time, with benefits. I think you'd be perfect."

"That's a good idea, Gabby. Thank you."

The man taking out my nipple ring was tall and handsome — thick and white and shiny, like a tattooed Mr. Clean. He had me down on his table, my shirt still balled up in one of my hands.

"Why do you want it taken out?" he asked, readying his materials. Everything smelled acrid with antiseptic. I waited until he was touching me, one gloved hand prodding the underside of my breast, before I spoke.

"I'm getting tested for breast cancer," I said, and there was something delicious about it. I watched his face for a reaction. His hands did not waver, but his brows furrowed just a little. He clamped one end of the barbell, then the other, and twisted it open in one smooth motion.

"I'm sorry to hear that," he said, pulling the foreign body out from inside of me. I tried to pay him, but he didn't let me. I walked out smiling.

I applied for the bookstore job without thinking about it. I didn't think about whether or not I was qualified. Convinced death had begun its slow march toward me, I mostly applied because I *wanted to see what would happen.* The stakes seemed to be completely drained out of everything. Faced with the approaching end of everything, everything I did felt like a bit, a laugh. A fun joke.

When I was offered the job, I laughed. Then, I had a difficult choice to make. There was nothing wrong with my job at Sustainable Concordia. I liked my colleagues, the work environment, the creative looseness of my job description — it was fun. The question ultimately came down to, if I was going to die, did I want to die trying to convinced nineteen-year-olds to compost or be surrounded by books?

I took the bookstore job.

Back in the hospital waiting room, I sat near the knitting bin, but I tried not to look. I didn't look back after my name was called, and I walked down the narrow hallway to the imaging rooms, had the soft cotton gown handed to me. I thought about the bad hospital smell and the bad hospital music. I wondered if there was not a single nurse or orderly or doctor in existence who had strong opinions about music and what music should be played in a hospital. I wondered if it would kill them to hire a DJ.

I walked out of the changing room with my street clothes balled up in my hands, and looked at the sad watercolour prints on the walls and the renal failure lighting and the bullshit music. Sage is antibacterial. I'm not saying burn it, but a little in a spray bottle.

The beautiful ultrasound technician leaned out of the dark room where she was working, a clipboard in her hands. "Tara?"

"Yes!" I said, too loud.

"Wait here," she said, pointing to a line of chairs in front of the door. I sat. I tried not to think of what was inside.

Instead, I thought about music. *If I were the hospital DJ,* I thought, *I would play something curated. Something to reassure people. There is an adult here — one with strong opinions. One who cares about the little things.* I would play soaring post-rock and singer-songwriters making sense of the horrors of the world. I would play inspirational nineties hip hop and reassuring Canadian indie folk. Music had raised me — it had kept me fed, kept me out of the deepest reaches of the darkness, been my companion when I got as deep as I did. Music had been my voice when I couldn't find my own. In the hospital, I clung to music — a kind of drug, another decoration for time — so I could hold myself away from what was walking up the long hall of my mind. I didn't want to remember. I wanted to listen to music.

At my mother's funeral, I looked at the belly and knees of a woman who had known her. She was dressed in dark things, like everyone was. She had dangling earrings and short, greying hair that spiked up around her head.

"Do you miss your mother?" she asked me.

At nine years old, I thought, *What a stupid fucking question.* I looked up at her large chin, her trembling mouth.

"Uh-huh," I said, confused. Looking back now, I see a grieving woman — someone who had also known my mother, and loved her. As a child, I thought adults knew things I didn't. I couldn't fathom that an entire adult would be genuinely lost for words at the sight of a little girl — prepubescent, abruptly unmothered. I didn't understand the concept of an adult, with grey hair and a laugh-lined face, not knowing what to say, which is why I was shocked to anger when she continued: "Does it make you sad to think that one day, you won't remember her?"

When we got back from the hospital, Mom was crying. We were in the house in Toronto. I was in the upper level of the bunk bed in the room I shared with my sister, and Mom was crying in the hallway.

She was pacing, up and down. Her sobs were deep and terrified —
like they are when you're confronting death, against every shred of
your will, and that death is still far enough away that it can creep
toward you, slowly. I pulled my blankets tighter around my chin.

I was used to my mom's tears, and her yelling — she was an
expressive woman. I liked that about her. She felt her feelings fully
and completely, pulled them out of herself, held them in her hands,
turned them over, wept at their magnitude, shrieked from the effort
of carrying them. She would scream, sometimes, while processing
one of her big feelings. Sometimes she would pick something up,
and throw it. She would make a metaphor for her misery from a
chipped Salvation Army mug. She would put all of her feeling into
it and then break it — exorcise it, let the feeling fly into the air and
be gone.

There was nothing menacing or cruel about the violence she
enacted on cheap china, my father sitting at the Ikea pressboard
kitchen table — listening, nodding, understanding. When she was
done, it was over. She swept the pieces of broken things into the
trash, put a record on, calmly started to cut an onion.

I always thought *orphan* meant someone who'd lost both of their
parents, but you only have to lose one. In animals, people only really
talk about the mother. I am, after all, an animal — seeking moments of comfort in the slow shamble toward death, hoping my
meat doesn't rot before my brain gives out.

What if the hospital DJ gig was some kind of public service? Like
jury duty. What if all of the best DJs in the city got served with
a summons and had to arrive at the hospital DJ booth for their

civic duty? At the back of the club, later, they could all swap stories about how they were on duty when that bridge collapsed, when the power plant melted down, when there was something in the air and an eighth of the oncology ward made inexplicable recoveries overnight? How would it change the nightlife, the drug supply? How would it change the way the disc jockeys spoke over the radio waves — their voices still crackling over the sound system as the paramedics and firefighters moved in on the fifteen-car pile-up burning so bright they could see it burning in the next town over?

The technician was beautiful and young and quick. Black, with a long straight wig and maroon scrubs. I took my top off and she gently moved my breasts from left to right with her gloved hands.

"Has your nipple always been inverted on this side?" she asked, about my problem breast.

"I don't know," I said, because I didn't. "It's been pierced since I was twenty."

She pursed her lips so minutely I barely saw it. She pulled out a long tube of imaging gel lubricant. "This is going to be cold."

There is the kind of crying that happens when you are very sad, or very disappointed. I had seen my mother cry like that. Then there's grief crying, which is something different — this was closer to how my mother was crying, in the hallway, in Toronto, except she wasn't grieving someone else, she was grieving herself.

She wandered the hallway, thinking of the life she expected to have and how she wasn't going to have it. She cried tears of bitter disappointment and most complete, resigned, horrifying fear. All I wanted was to tell her it was going to get better, you know? But it wasn't and it didn't.

The technician found the lumps in my breast easily. She wasn't gentle with them, forcing the ultrasound wand into the tender side of me, pressing up against the edges of the judas cells in my breast, forcing it until she found the edges, feeling them flop jellylike over the edge of the wand, hurting me. She needed to get good photos of them. She needed a lot of angles. She wasn't afraid of hurting me. She knew what needed to be done. It was care, ultimately. I closed my eyes and tried not to cry.

I think I said something like, "Are you crying because you're going to die?" from under my covers in the bunk bed, watching my mother grieve herself. This made her scream more, and louder. She said some things I don't remember. This was all a really long time ago, you know? I was probably still eight. She died a few weeks after my ninth birthday. Memory is stupid. I don't remember if she said, "Don't say that," or "Yes," or "I'm not going to die."

The technician told me to get up, and I pulled my gown back up around me and stood. I was all slick and sticky with the imaging fluid. The room smelled like astringents.

My mother suddenly walked over to me, a wild look in her eyes.

"If Mommy does die, if I do die, if Mommy dies, you have to promise me ..."

I was trembling slightly as I put my clothes back on, as I checked my bank balance. I'd passed through sadness and just felt a little ball of nothing inside me. I felt the nothing expanding, eating my sadness. I wasn't going to cry about it. I was going to get really drunk. I didn't want to be in this hospital anymore. I didn't want to remember being in this hospital anymore. I wanted to forget this hospital like I forgot the promise I made to my mom when she was dying. I promised her I wouldn't forget and I did. I remember everything stupid and I forget everything important. I'm so sorry, Mom.

"Me & My Dog"
by boygenius.

November 2019. Montreal.

"Guys," I said, approaching the front desk of the bookstore with an arm full of papers, in my clacky heels. My employees — a gangly undergraduate and an equally gangly master's student with slightly better hair — both stood bolt upright, where they had been slumped over the front desk. It was a slow day at the bookstore — one of the first slow days since I'd started, at the tail end of the rush we always got at the beginning of the school semester.

"What's up, boss?" asked the master's student, who was supposed to be training the undergrad.

I took a big breath, like I was about to say something important, and then deflated.

"I'm bored," I said, throwing my papers down. It was near the end of the day. We could goof off, for a bit. The undergrad turned the volume up on the sound system — something upbeat, but bitter, like the Mountain Goats, or Phoebe Bridgers.

The bookstore job was the first job I'd ever had where I could get away with not doing anything a lot of the time. This registered as deeply wrong to me. Planting trees and working in kitchens meant that one wrong move or one neglected task could result in the death of another person. While I was working as a nanny, I had to carefully choreograph my days: the urge of employers to spend as little as possible meant I often had a very small window of time in which I was expected to perform what was, at one point, the twelve-hour labour of an intergenerational workforce of women and girls. I was a lifter, a dancer, a therapist, and a gymnast, carting thirty-pound loads up and down flights of stairs while the stew simmered and the chemicals worked the shit free from the walls of all the toilets. I would have a series of alarms alerting me to the narrow slices of time I had to change over armfuls of laundry, babies on my hips and at my ankles, careful to stay cheery lest the children forget to be joyful, careful to get the tissue-dissolving solvents only into my lungs and never into theirs.

I thought that the more you got paid, the more you were expected to accomplish things. I found, as I transitioned to office jobs from manual labour, that actually the opposite was true. I found a world of pencil-pushing and long coffee breaks, of people who always had *so much on the go* coming back and forth from days where a scant few tasks were accomplished. Not only was this normal, but I found there was an inertia I eventually reached if I completed *too many tasks*: I was met with confusion, or hostility cloaked in office culture niceties. I would see the delivery guys shuffle away from me as I entered the university loading docks to ask where the book packages were. People stopped returning my phone calls.

It had been nine years since I'd left high school and emerged onto a job market just fully adjusting to the after-effects of the

2008 financial crisis. It was my first full-time job since Uncommon Grounds, and a decade in the gig economy made it feel like an impossible luxury, especially since the management position paid eighteen dollars an hour, had benefits, and included paid time off. I got up in the morning and traced the same long line to one single place of work — on one of the city bikes, before it got too cold, and then on the metro or in my booted feet. I did my work well enough that I wouldn't freak myself out, but not so well that I bothered other people. I went home. I watched television, kissed my boyfriend, ate until I fell asleep, and started all over again.

After a few weeks, I was already feeling boredom creep in. The years of desperately cobbling together thirty-to-eighty-hour work weeks made of three-hour babysitting shifts, admin work for bored lawyers, tree-planting, busking, grave-digging, sex work — the years of never being able to plan very far into the future, of having to run ragged from minimum wage to minimum wage — this had had a perverse kind of rhythm to it. *What will today bring?* I would think, as I strapped my guitar to my chest to ward off poverty with the power of song. *There's always tomorrow,* I would think, on days I failed to keep my account from overdrafting, which was most of them. As I settled into my circuit of up, work, home, TV, sleep, up, work, I thought to myself, *This full-time-job way of living one's life could be one I eventually find profoundly alienating.* But then, I would think, relaxing, *You know, if I wasn't dying.*

Dying, I asked my employees, "What is your most controversial music take?" and sat on a pile of donation books, crossing my leg over my knee in the one nice skirt I'd bought with my new full-time wages.

"That depends," said the master's student, eyes fiery with mischief. "First, I need to know how many good Strokes albums you think there are."

Deadpan, I said, "I don't know enough about the Strokes to have an opinion."

The master's student opened their eyes wide, impressed. "Thank you for your candour."

I had nothing to hide. I was dying. This was my superpower. This was genuinely how I felt about it. I was sure, deep in my core, that there was something wrong with me. Every morning, I woke up and greeted the day a dying woman, with nothing to lose. I did my work confidently, with the morbid determination of someone justifying the last motions of life on earth.

None of it depressed me. It gave everything a kind of magic. I dealt with each customer with all of the grace and joy of a guilty woman who hadn't yet been sentenced to life in prison, but knew it was coming — every interaction might be the last one I made, free from the information on its way from a blocked number on my cellphone. The call was due any day. When I got it, everything would change. When it changed, I would be ready. The ugly, dead stock zines were so beautiful — who carried zines anymore? What was this, 1998? I loved this place. I vacuumed, alphabetized, ran off restock orders, followed up with our artisans, snooped through the email inbox for evidence of old workplace drama. I revelled in the humanity, the utter aliveness of it all.

I was dying, sure, but mostly I was grateful — grateful for the dust in the air and how it made my eyes water and my skin erupt in violent little itchy pinpricks. I was grateful to be at the front of the store, goofing off, doing what I called *relationship building* when I spoke to my superiors, but was just talking about the Strokes. My favourite film is *High Fidelity*, with John Cusack, based on the Nick Hornby book of the same name. The book is also excellent, but I think it may be one of the few examples (*Fight Club*, *Bridget Jones's Diary*, *The Silence of the Lambs*) of the film actually being better than the book. The book is ultimately about music culture, and the film gets to have a soundtrack — hard to compete with that, you know? I fancied myself something of a Rob: charming,

self-absorbed, self-destructive, and too vulnerable to stop rationalizing my own behaviour long enough to notice I was acting like
an idiot. That was the point of the film, by the way. Rob is, like, a
villain. When people are all like, *"High Fidelity* is good, but does it
stand up now that we're all feminists?" or whatever, and I'm like,
"Yeah? We were always supposed to think that guy was an asshole,
watch him come to understand why he was an asshole, and then see
him actually try to get better. That's the plot. Were we watching the
same movie?"

I was Rob, walking up the brownstone steps in the morning,
counting the cash, cataloguing things. My previous job had been
free-form jazz — whatever I wanted to make of it. This one had
expectations as clear as the alphabet. I was a reader, and a writer —
I liked books. I liked books so much that it made me physically
excited to be around so many. I ran my hands over them, and I got
jumpy with excitement, with joy, with possibility. I would make lists
of books we had that I wanted to read — commitments hundreds of
thousands of hours long. Each book opened up into a private universe, a world of information and insight and escape, both serious
and completely frivolous. This was my last chapter. I was happy it
was happening among the stacks of books. The first few months at
the bookstore, I thought that if I could remember earth after I died,
then this was how I wanted to remember being alive — talking
about the Strokes, as the sun went down over Montreal, with the
cool people I worked with.

The people I worked with were cool, and young — *extremely*
young. I was, of course, also cool, and also extremely young. I was
not, however, *quite* as *extremely young* as the people I was working
with. I started there a few months after I turned twenty-seven — the
rest of management were people in their late twenties, like me. We
had one part-time bookseller in his early thirties, but everyone else
was in their late teens or early twenties. This, I figured, would be
absolutely no problem, as we were comparable ages. Right?

This was, in fact, very wrong. Within a few weeks, I became aware that to these freshly minted, dewy-faced young bucks, I was *an old person*. I laughed it off, for a minute, because it was ridiculous — but then it didn't stop. To my absolute horror, it then proceeded to *hurt my feelings*.

I became acutely aware of my back problems. I would tell people about things that happened in 2012, when I was twenty — and they would giggle, because in 2012, they had only been, like, eleven. I tried to explain that that's because twenty is not very much older than eleven, in the grand scheme of things, and they looked at me like I was insane. I had been dating Sandy, now, for *over seven years*. I tried to explain that I had been *very, very young* when he and I had gotten together — only nineteen! But that was the age that they were now, so to them this was not very young, but a kind of normal average-person age. It did not help my case that I was no longer able to stay awake past 9:00 p.m., except under very special circumstances. I had to get a standing desk put in, because if I sat for too long, my butt would start to hurt. I was, of course, waiting for more information about the tests I'd had done on my unidentified breast mass. *Oh shit*, I started to think. *What if I am old?*

I had not felt old in a while. There was that weird period after Tim dumped me, when I was nineteen. There was the Great Depressive Episode of 2014, when I was twenty-two, in which I felt old *again* — but that had been because of depression. That was only, what? Five years ago? Five and a half? That's not … that's not so long, right? Right?

The kids I worked with knew how to do things on their iPhones that I did not understand. I did work things in old, clunky, inefficient ways. They corrected me on things. I had to ask their help with newfangled contraptions, applications I couldn't decipher. When more than one of them were in the same room, I had to ask them to speak slower, to explain their dialect — a pastiche of references, a patois of English and meme. Meanwhile, in my first hierarchical management role, I was fiercely aware of the fact that I had a certain responsibility to *allow* for a chasm of space between us, between which they could understandably vent about the annoying specifics of their job, or even — God forbid — make fun of me. I was, after all, the store manager, and their boss. It was their right.

I tried to be cool. Cool guy. Supercool. I'm not like, a normal boss, I'm a cool boss. But not so cool! Not like, cool as in I do not have workplace boundaries cool. Cool like I understand your need to hold me at arm's length, or talk shit, or whatever! I am above all that, after all. I am *an adult*: a real one, with an older-than-twenty-five brain, complete prefrontal cortex and everything. You'll understand when you're older, kids! I looked hard at my face in the mirror — discovering tiny folds I'd never seen before. Were they wrinkles, or just what my face looked like? I thought about panic-dying my hair pink, or green, or something.

My mom died when I was nine, and I hit puberty pretty much immediately after. I was already fat, when this happened — I ate for comfort, and I always had, and I still do — and puberty sent hormones in to really shake the game up. I am grateful, really, that I was a weird-looking kid. I think it was good for me. I have one friend who, despite being a relatively competent and interesting person, has almost *negative* social skills — he seems to actually *pull* charm *out* of any room he is in, making other people more awkward and weird by social osmosis. I blame this almost entirely on his being altogether too beautiful for his own good. I have known him since he was a child, and it has been a straight shot from angelic-looking young teen to ruggedly handsome adult man. He has recently started losing his hair. This may, in fact, be a blessing from God. In his late twenties, I can only pray it is not too late for him to become normal — exceptionally beautiful people are at a disadvantage. I'm not kidding, and mean this genuinely. I absolutely had to do other things — learn skills, figure out how to talk to people, work out how to at least appear to be a *nice person* — because by the time I was thirteen, I had the body of a forty-seven-year-old mother of three, complete with a patch of grey hair.

When I told people my age in my teens and my very early twenties, they would look at me, aghast. "Oh my God," they would say. "You are a baby," they would say. "You're like, still a fetus. Your umbilical cord has yet to be removed. I thought you were *old*. Does your mother know where you are? Did you track amniotic fluid into my living room, on the bottom of your tiny baby shoes, you old-looking baby?" I wore these shocked and appalled moments as a point of pride. All of this seemed to disappear somewhere around the age of — *hmmm* — twenty-seven. When I told people my age, people older than me would look at me knowingly, like, *Yes, that is also the age that I began to die*. People younger than me would look sad, like they were sorry for my loss.

"I think it's weird that you don't know the Strokes," said the undergrad.

"Oh yeah?" I said.

"Yeah, like, I think I'd expect it in people our age, but like ..."

Our age? *Our age?* I grimaced while they shared their opinions on the Strokes, which I don't remember. I excused myself back to my office to do work.

My office was in the back of the store. When I'd first started work, the fire escape was blocked by a mountain of books to be returned to their publishers. Hastily hand-assembled shelves buckled under the weight of years-old math textbooks, each of them heavy enough to crush a skull. The air was thick with dust: toxic mould and bits of old bugs and the hundreds of billions of microscopic skin cells of people who hadn't worked there in years. Microfibres dusted off from the pages of all of the old books, turning the air itself into a potential chain reaction, ready to catch at a single spark, ready to send the store into a fireball in a matter of seconds, escape packed full of deadly plugs of trash nobody could be bothered to throw away. I learned, quickly, that at my job, safety and fire code were brushed off as an efficiency-interrupting inconvenience. I'd gotten to work trying to reduce the health and safety hazards immediately, but the threat of a quick and violent death still surrounded me when my phone rang on my standing desk. No caller ID. It was the call I was waiting for.

"Hi, Tara." Eve's voice was kind and reassuring. "How are you doing?"

"I'm fine," I said, and my breast throbbed.

"We have your tests back."

I slammed the door to my office shut. I turned around, my back to my door, and took in the beautiful and chaotic mess of the room, the dirty floor, the filthy air, the standing desk and a wooden stool. The divine evidence of human existence. My last safe haven.

"Give it to me," I said.

"It's not cancer."

"Oh," I said. I sat down on the wooden stool. "So what, is it like, a cyst?"

"No," she said. She explained that there was an abnormality scale, and I had scored almost nothing on it. "Like, two out of fifty," she said. "It's probably inflammation. There are no masses, either hollow or solid."

My breast throbbed again. Something knotted in my stomach.

"Oh," I said, again. "What a relief!" I said, weakly.

She explained that my nerves had pockets of inflammation. They were full of fluid. I was in pain. I thought about the hours spent twisting toward low wages at odd angles. I thought of the insecure, procrastinated assignments — slammed out in caffein-ated fits and rages and always at the last minute. I thought about the lifting, and the pulling — hundreds of thousands of hardwood trees slammed into the ground in the Canadian wilderness, my fingers bending backward, catching on things, shedding their nails. I thought, too, about the long hours spent curled around myself, tight as a potato bug, wondering how still I'd have to sit to never feel the pain in my heart and stomach and mind. I thought of the way I'd spent years in heavy oscillation, running between stillness and frantic movement, constantly swapping out one thing for another I thought would make me feel better.

"Do you still do lots of things that would make you collapse into your pectorals — put strain on your arms, fingers, neck, chest?"

Office job. Writing. Playing the guitar. Reading. Everything I loved bent me over. I felt safe coiled up like that. My safety was breaking me.

"Yeah, some things," I said, flatly.

"I think what you need is physiotherapy, and massage — some people have a lot of success with acupuncture, too."

All of those things cost money. So much money. Savings-draining money. Eighteen dollars an hour suddenly didn't seem like a whole lot.

"Thank you, Eve."

"You can also get an occupational therapist."

More money.

"Yeah, I'll look into it."

I would have to if I was going to keep writing, and working, and not be in pain. I needed to figure out how to do it and not destroy myself. I thought about my dad, the guitarist, his arms knotted with tendonitis. The drafting table he kept as a desk, when Napster hit and his income tanked to almost nothing, and his hours had to get so much longer to compensate. That was the year after my mom died. I thought about his long hours. I thought about his genius arms, with their long ropes of pain. His genius fingers, tucking my hair behind my ears.

"You really have to watch your posture," said Eve, on the phone. I was always doubled over. I did not want to stand up straight. I found facing the day dead-on unbearable. I wanted to tuck into myself. I just wanted to be small enough I'd never be seen.

"Please come back if there's anything else."

"Thanks, Eve, really."

I hung up the phone and I was sitting at my desk.

I looked around at the death-trap office with its abandoned return piles and its drifts of trash. My sinuses puckered with the *ohshit* response of the same immune system sending fluid into my breast. The dinginess of the office, which had seemed poetic or lovely a moment before, was now aggressive and depressing and miserable. *Pathetic*, I thought, as I was filled up with hatefulness and disappointment.

The future that had been ready to stand, inoculated with meaning, lay bare. Full of that bitch, potential. If I had been dying, I would have been trapped into making something out of the time I had left. Desperation would have rendered me capable. I would have a response to the people I'd disappointed, screwed over, hurt, and rejected: *You can't be mad at me. Look at how I am suffering.*

I didn't want to look after the details of my life. I didn't want to work. I didn't want to go through the banal rituals of managing my surroundings. I didn't want to have to open my mouth and let out the repetitive incantations that tethered me to other people. Even less so did I want to hear them — my time felt finite, precious, pregnant, and always allocated for *the Other*. What about *my* time? What about my time, to be spent curling ever deeper into myself? To be spent twisting myself up so tightly, and against the screaming of my own nerves and tissues? What about my time, to be spent following every impulse toward relief, and ending up only with sticky hands and a floor covered in mess again? I didn't want to clean up the messes I made. I wanted to make things, and only sometimes, and never with any expectations, and always for a cacophony of praise. I did not want to live. I wanted to die, and I didn't even want to be responsible for *that*. Cancer, the cruel creeping crab of blight, was going to be my out. This is the ultimate hostility of depression: it makes you sick, and then responsible, and then your responsibility feeds your sickness.

I think there are people who say that *their depression has rendered them responsible*, and they mean that they hated themselves for things that were never that bad to begin with. When they show their hands, the cards are full of flowers and candies and love, cast with the sinister sheen of depression's distorted vision. I don't trust these people, because my depression has rendered me genuinely judgmental and cruel. I don't trust these people for the same reason I don't trust people in job interviews who say their greatest weaknesses are, in fact, *being too good at the job for which you are hiring*. I am not interested in those for whom depression rendered them falsely accused. If you were left thinking you were guilty of things when all you really needed was to talk about it and be reassured you were still one of the good ones, I am happy for you, but you are not one of my people. I am disinterested not because innocence makes someone undeserving of my attention, but specifically because of that deservedness.

I am interested in those for whom depression rendered them cruel, for whom depression rendered them unfeeling and irresponsible and unkind. These are my people. I wanted to be dying of cancer because I thought it would be good PR for a life depression and tragedy had already fucked up. I wanted to be subjected to the trials of cancer as a kind of restitution for what I believed was my profound and fundamental badness: this secret, bitter, judgmental, cruel self — she who I kept hidden from the public eye for practical reasons, not moral ones. She who was a fine ethical actor, but was not of good moral character. Ethics teaches us how to act, after all. Not how to *be*. Not how to have a soul.

I read as much of the data as I could stomach regarding the likelihoods of cancer occurring in either me or my sister. It seemed pretty high. I decided, because I was a writer, and not a scientist, that if one of us got it, the other one wouldn't. I decided that if I got it, it would make up for all of the profoundly cruel things that had happened to her, from which I could not shield her — something I took very seriously as *my job* as her elder sister and then failed at again and again and again. If I got the cancer, Maya wouldn't. I would make a redeemer of my tumour — a writer, I would make, even, a *metaphor* out of it. I would make it stand in for all of my failures, and then I would have it cut out. I would succeed, and walk away purified. Or I would not, and I would die, and I would deserve it. I'd felt meaning come into my hands like a blessing, and then it was gone. I sat in my office and nothing was different. My metaphor wasn't landing. It didn't mean anything. It was just a bunch of sad stuff that happened.

I went out for lunch to destress. Going out for lunch was my favourite way to destress. I still wonder if alcohol was its own addiction, or just a particularly destructive variant of my general impulse to put things in my mouth. I felt the hurt in my stomach like a rumble. My stomach is a rueful organ.

My misery fires like a nerve from my throat and into my stomach. It winds its way around the base of my spine. I can open my mouth really wide. I don't have much of a gag reflex. Anything big enough will scrape against all my grievances as it goes all the way down from my lips to the ends of me, but I was never naturally talented in the field of beauty, and never had the money to keep it up as any kind of a charade. Good fucks with anonymous people who didn't like me that much knocked some sense into me, as well. Food will comfort you, bodily, no matter what you look like. Food has always been there for me. Food is my drug of choice.

There is an old joke — *you are only a junkie if you can't afford it.* I wonder, then, if I would be a food addict, technically, if I could afford it. Friends of friends remark on the merits of the dollar-per-calorie ratio, and how this is how they eat for cheap. I have never eaten for cheap. I imagine that if I was rich as all hell I would spend the day eating bag after bag of something very expensive, which was designed to mimic the *sensation* of nutrition when in reality it is just puffed air and gelatin hybrid, or something. My ideal food is one I could be comforted by, all day, which was designed to dissolve into nothing as it touches my mouth.

My grief nags me, constantly, like a child. The child who is my grief is as tall and as thin as my vagus nerve. She doesn't know how generous my body is — how much my untrusting, unhappy body has already stored away for something long and horrible. She is so thin and so hungry and she begs me for things she does not need. One of the most mature things about me is that I don't have any delusions about being able to achieve perfection in motherhood, if I were to have a child of my own. I know a happy mother is good enough, and that children normalize what is demonstrated as normal. My will is in no way ironclad. I can only say *no* for so long.

I wandered through the Bulk Barn and thought about what I could buy to stash at work to eat so I didn't go broke at the Yunnan noodle place across the street. The noodle place sold food that was healthy enough for me to justify eating it in exuberant surplus. Soup is mostly water! They sold me water and fat and piles of chewy white rice noodle that snapped against my teeth.

My body did not understand that this food was supposed to stop something, or hold it at bay. Instead of satisfying me, the Yunnan noodle place seemed to unlock secret parts of my stomach that had instead been closed off. The little girl who was my grief said, *Is there more? I am hungry.* It was not the fault of the noodle proprietors. I could be the only person going into the Yunnan noodle place who has this problem. I ordered whitefish soup in an unctuous chili pepper broth. The broth steamed mung bean sprouts that burst in my mouth, mash sweetly with fat and little slivers of flesh.

I took my spoon and sunk it into the pool of rich broth, watched the peppers fall in. I put them all in my mouth. The steam filled my sinuses and they released, slick and gummy, down my upper lip. I wiped my face with my napkin and I mashed the chili peppers in my teeth. The liquid seared the roof of my mouth just to the edge of burning, and the back of my tongue went numb. I love this.

I mashed the peppers more in my teeth and hard things inside my head softened and fell down my throat. I felt a network of pores all spring to life at the base of my skull, behind my shoulders, the small of my back. They discharged sweat and something else onto my skin — something scared and diseased leaking out from deep inside of me. The peppers sent this something coursing down the back of me and soaking through my clothing. The soup was thick with peppers, crowding the surface of the bowl, around the drifts of flaking fish skin, oozing their sanguine oils into the water like the bloodied bodies of injured sea creatures. I ate every one.

"That one is very spicy," the waiter always warned me.

"I love spicy things," I replied, and I meant that *I love to purify and mutilate and nourish, all at once.*

At the Bulk Barn, I bought dried mangoes and nuts and vegan chicken broth and medium chain triglyceride powder. I bought these groceries because I hoped it would be the combination that would allow me to sit in my office all day, with the Yunnan noodle place staring me down from across the street, and not go spend money I did not have on another office lunch. What's more, I hoped that this would be the combination that would cause me to never have to eat again. I was always looking for what would cause me to never have to eat again — some magic potion to cure me of longing.

To congratulate myself for my smart and budget-friendly purchases, and also for not having breast cancer, I went to a sushi restaurant.

It was a celebratory sort of early afternoon. I decided that I would be a fool if I did not buy more sushi than one person should eat at once. Once that was ordered, I felt a bit better about not having cancer. I was happy — not so happy, but happy enough. I ordered a beer, as well.

The restaurant was too nice and I couldn't really afford to go out to eat. It was late 2019, and I was still carrying credit card debt from when I had blasted off to Europe in another timeline. I was holding my reusable tote bag, full of budget groceries, full of things I hoped would help me achieve my goal of being able to eat as little as possible for as long as it took. As a binge eater, I was mostly a begrudgingly reformed bulimic. As a bulimic, I was always a begrudgingly failed anorexic. As a twenty-seven-year-old in 2019, I was back to being just another twentysomething who had missed the hand of sister Death, this time. I was not yet facing the firing squad of eternity. I was just nestled somewhere along a line of choices that could've been better.

The server, who was not Japanese, brought me my beer. I took a sip and my throat instantly opened up. When I drink, my throat creates a vacuum — it's involuntary and I cannot fight it. As a chugger of fermented liquids, I have put frat boys and tree planters to shame. It's a talent and I never had to learn it. My natural state is excess.

Drinking like this soothes the little grief in me. In the restaurant, she felt the way the liquid blossomed inside me. The bubbles popped to tickle and scratch the yawning aching itch of my grief, and it wanted more. Now my grief was in control, a skinny little girl operating the heavy machinery of my adult woman body, coordinating a series of choking pulls on the beer that were deep and desperate like a sob. I pulled away with the drink nearly finished.

The alcohol hit my brain almost immediately: a giddy sort of slant upward, the opening chords to some big Broadway tune. The whole restaurant got a hazy kind of glimmer, like I was seeing it through a warm breath cloud on the lens of a camera. I felt a tightness, a satisfaction, a sense of wonder and possibility and relief, in my chest. It felt like *maybe this time.* It felt like *everything is going to be okay.* It felt like falling in love.

I was no longer a woman with posture so fucked up she had built a pocket of delirium in her breast as hard and tight as any tumour. I was a romantic hero. I was a modern woman. I was teetering on the shoulders of my beloved giants, adorned in the jewels of career and art and all my loves from great to tiny. I was on the brink of oblivion but I was not yet falling in.

I ordered another beer and drank it almost as quickly. It was one fifteen in the afternoon. I had to work until six at night, and drinking during work hours wasn't registering as a transgression but like a hilarious story I was already preparing to tell later. I sunk back into the comfortable booth and sighed, cradling my glass to my chest like the cold head of a lover.

I looked at my phone and saw that I'd missed a call from a number with no caller ID. I looked at my voice mails and it was my dermatologist. I called him back.

He told me the mole was cancerous.

"What?"

It was like the last step before it's like full-blown bad-news melanoma, he told me.

What?

He explained I would need to see a plastic surgeon and be seen by the dermatologist every six months for follow-ups, and he meant for the rest of my life, as someone with *a history of melanoma.*

"What?"

They probably cut it all out at the biopsy, but they have to be sure, he said.

"What?"

He told me, finishing, that it was pretty worrying to see it on somebody so young, which is also what doctors had been saying about my visceral fat score, and what they said about my dowager's hump and the disc degeneration there when I was sixteen, and what they said about the arthritis markers making themselves known in my hands and my elbows and my knees. The voice of dread speaks to me, but softer this time. It sounds like *act now*. It sounds like *get to safety. It's not too late.*

I said, "Thank you, Doctor." I always call doctors *Doctor*, at least when they can hear me. Out of respect.

I ordered a third beer. The drink was a celebration and the drink was a balm. I filled a bathtub all the way up with my drink. I forced my drink down and forced the waterline up. Maybe if I filled it up enough, it would be deep enough to hide my grief. I am so sick of her persistent demands. Maybe if I filled it up deep enough my grief would leave me be. *I am a good enough mother. I deserve a little rest. I deserve a moment of silence, a moment to hold her head under the waterline for long enough. Leave your poor mother alone for a moment.*

When I got home from work that day, Layla was in the living room.

"I don't have breast cancer," I told her.

"I knew you didn't. You're such a hypochondriac."

"I had skin cancer."

"What?"

What I meant was, *Do you feel bad yet?* I explained: My knee, the mole. Probably taken care of. Need to see a plastic surgeon. Layla's eyes were wide. She was quiet for a while.

"I'm sorry to hear that," she said, softly, eyes still wide, and retreated back to her room, closed the door. I heard her bong bubbling. I felt a sick satisfaction. I wanted to hurt people with this news. *Take that, you bitches. You didn't love me like I needed. What if I had died.* I didn't want to fact-check my own story. The entire ordeal had barely been one — the struggle that was true had been so overshadowed by the illusion of another struggle. I found myself wondering if I had *been sick,* in any meaningful way. I told my story in several different ways, trying to work out which one was the truth. *I had skin cancer. I had a malignant precancerous growth removed. I have a history of melanoma.* You only need to shift language a tiny bit, in different directions, to have enormously different consequences.

I hurled my news at people. Nobody knew what to say. Some people fretted over me, but mostly people were just quiet. I had gotten what I wanted — a growth to call my own, something to use to hurt the people around me. I still didn't feel any better. Any time I felt even slightly frustrated, affronted, bothered, I would sink into myself, run my finger over my scar. *None of you know true suffering,* I thought, comparing my suffering to the suffering of others like shiny stones, for clarity and colour and depth. *You don't know suffering until you have experienced this!*

This was a tiny mottled scar on my knee. It was almost invisible: just a hyper-pigmented spot. I had wanted a grand justification. I had wanted a reason to disappear for a long time. *This* was not it. *This* was devoid of drama, or flare.

In private, I tried editing my story. I experimented, silently, with a diatribe about my body's betrayal and the deep well of my fear and anger and my hurt. I thought about my vulnerability and my unmet needs, which were for every person who surrounded me to rise up in care whether they were willing or not. I could have said these things, but I would have only had to look at my tiny scar to know it was a lie — or, at least, an exaggeration so far removed from the truth that it may as well be a lie.

I was coming to the slow realization that I really had wanted to be sick, and that I had wanted to be sick in order to control people. I tried to look at it from different angles. Surely, it couldn't be that bad. I called myself a masochistic epistemologist — but the truth didn't hurt, really. The truth was that I was tired, and that I was lonely, and that I had needed to care for myself in ways that were not fair too early, and now I was sick of it, and I wanted to go back — this didn't hurt, as much as it made me pause with moments of compassion for my younger self. I thought of the kid who wanted to save her mother, who wanted to protect her father, who wanted to help her siblings, and didn't understand that none of that was her job — and it definitely wasn't her job as a child. I thought of the little girl playing dress-up. Acting big when she wasn't ready.

Thinking that I wanted to be sick, realizing it was true, mourning the illness I wasn't going to get — this did not hurt more than some of the other things I could have let myself believe. *I was abandoned in times of great need by people who were bad, because I am fundamentally broken and I cannot recover. To suggest that I can recover makes you, also, a person who is bad. Now my fundamental brokenness has threatened to rise up and devour me, and still I have been forsaken, but I will pray for all of you sinners like a holy mother now, and in the hour of your death, as it was in the beginning is now ever shall be world without end.* I could have believed I was right — I could have edited my own reality, projected my story backward, given a lying account of myself in order to argue that I was, in fact, the last small bastion of goodness in a sea of corruption and evil. In this idea, I remained correct. This idea actually hurt more.

The truth left room for *things were a lot more complicated than that* and *I have so much time left.* The truth left room for *sometimes your hurt is also a shield.* The truth set my defences down, like a bag that I had been carrying, which felt full of things that were all so necessary and ultimately too heavy for my shoulders. The network of snaking nerves in my breasts reached up into my tired shoulders, meandered into my neck, whispered into my ear, *Honey, I think it might be time to let some of this go.*

Somewhere inside of me began a great rearrangement. It didn't happen all at once. I drank and I sulked and I ate, and repeat. I didn't even go to see the plastic surgeon. *We probably took care of it at the biopsy.* I didn't want to do any more work. I just wanted to rest.

I kept drinking. I made vague plans to fix the way I was eating, but mostly I held the leathery dried mango to my mouth with one hand and typed very inefficient emails with the other, until the mango was gone, and I left the chicken broth and the nuts on my desk. I slunk back to the noodle joint like I was folding myself into an opium den.

I was packing for my Christmas vacation that year when I got a call from my stepmother.

"I found your dog," she said.

"What?"

"A dog. You still want adopt a dog, right? I found the perfect dog for you. He's your dog. Really."

I was informed he was a sixty-pound Lab cross who was mild-mannered, well-trained, and obedient. He was approximately four years old. Like all shelter dogs, he had a few quirks, but they would easily be trained out of him. I ran the idea over with Sandy and my roommate. We had a cat in the house, and nobody was totally confident about it. I struck up a deal: that we would have the dog in the house on a provisional one-month trial basis, at which point we could reassess. With absolutely no plans of honouring this agreement, I went to Nova Scotia for Christmas to get what I was already referring to as *my dog.*

The dog's foster parent dropped him off at my parents' place in rural Nova Scotia. He was not, in fact, a sixty-pound Lab, but a ninety-five-pound pit bull.

"He's mixed with Lab, maybe," said my stepmother as the enormous black beast cased out the basement of their rented house, sniffed the door where his old family had just walked out weeping, and whined like a baby. "Mastiff, maybe. Or a Great Dane." He was Molosser stock — a war dog, a cart puller. He had webbed, saucer-width feet, a hulking neck — his jowls hung loose from his massive jaws, bred to hold a whole ox still as it was branded. When he had finished assessing the basement, he sat down on his haunches in front of me, perked up his big triangle ears, and tilted his enormous head to one side.

Six hours into our relationship, I learned that he could jump at least five feet in the air without really trying, break out of his travel crate, and bite rocks in half. Our first walk indicated that he had both a passion and a natural talent for the chasing of small rodents — something he exhibited by pulling me clean off my feet to chase a squirrel. The squirrel escaped, unscathed. I decided his name was Goose, which I chose to honour the fearsomeness of the Canada geese I'd grown up trying to avoid in rural Ontario — and because when one animal has the name of another animal, that's funny.

Goose had been surrendered at the Weatherford Parker County Animal Shelter in Texas, some time in 2018 as a three-year-old adult dog. Assuming he had only been with his mother, and one other family before the shelter, we were his sixth home. People were struggling to handle him. I was informed, as he was dropped off, that while he had once had a jumping habit, this was now gone. This was a lie, and Goose jumps on people to this day. I also found out very quickly that, while Goose had many behaviours that seemed worrying, or even aggressive — the jumping, tearing at my clothes while I was still wearing them, a deep and demonic bark that sounded like it had some kind of reverb effect put on it in post-production — the aggressiveness was an illusion. He wasn't aggressive at all, he was just poorly trained and enthusiastic — his playfulness rendered fearsome by his bowling ball head and scissor bite, the natural consequences of his enormous size.

I eventually exhausted Goose with a game of tug-of-war, in which he displayed so much athletic skill that I was genuinely concerned that I would lose. Goose passed out belly-up in front of the gas fireplace. His floppy jowls folded around his big, curved canine teeth. His bright-pink gums stood out against his short black fur. His big (and admittedly Lab-like) ears were inside-out, their insides pale and exposed and curving away from his face like a pair of horns. His eyes were closed, but his heavy eyelids drooped with gravity and showed the red beneath. His eyes were too far apart from each other — like a cow or a hammerhead shark. His paws, which were as big as the palms of my hands, pawed at the sky as he stretched out the ropes of muscle that crossed each other under his skin. I thought about *Ghostbusters*, and Zuul.

"You're pretty cute," I said, scratching his big stomach. He writhed in pleasure, pawing at the sky. "For a demon."

I sat down on the cold slate floor, cross-legged, scratching his stomach. Then I shifted and lay down, tucking my head right next to his ribs. He flopped over, immediately, sandwiching my hair to the ground, and curled up around my head in a half-moon shape. He smacked his lips happily and then settled them against one shoulder and tucked his back paws under the other. We stayed like that for a long time — because I could not get up, with him on my hair like that, and because I already loved him so much.

I fought the January weather all the way to the Concordia Co-Op Bookstore, still wearing exactly what I had been wearing when I left work the day before. I had not showered or changed my underwear, and I had finger-brushed my teeth. Kate was in town, and we had been out on the town getting shit-faced the night before. It was the busy season at work, and I was going to work off my alcohol-induced misery. I just wanted to drink coffee until the rush started. I knew it would get too busy for me to be able to think about anything.

At work, I turned the bare minimum of lights on and put some water on to boil. I was going to steal my colleague's instant coffee and drink it until I felt like a human being. Kate had followed me to work, but she was leaving to go work on her thesis. As she left, I heard someone ask when we were opening from outside the door. "Fucked if I know," said Kate, just as miserable as I was, and she threw herself out the front door and back into the snow.

I had twenty minutes until we opened. I swept up the trail of melted snow and salty ice melter that Kate and I had tracked in from outside. I counted the cash. I kept the blinds shut on the door and windows that lead to the hallway of the brownstone, and I could see some lanky man in a long grey wool coat turned away from me and looking at his phone. *Keener*, I thought, horrified, pouring boiling water into a dirty mug and taking out the instant coffee from my colleague's stash under the front desk. You couldn't pay me to be in university again: lining up outside the bookstore at nine fifty in the morning? With your ... I glanced up at the man again through the window ... leather briefcase? Hilarious. *God.*

I opened iTunes and looked around for good working-hours hangover music. I put on a mix of sad and angry things sung by women: Alanis and Fiona and Ani, patron saints of sad girls with hangovers whose employees think they are old. My phone buzzed. My employee was calling in sick. I felt nausea churn in my stomach, but instead of throwing up I walked around and turned the lights on. I stopped at the door on the way back and opened the blinds: I couldn't really see the man waiting, I just saw him pick up his brief-case and start shuffling the things around in his hands, so I went back the desk, with Fiona Apple singing to me.

I took my place behind the desk as the keener outside walked through the door. He looked up, and around, and then we looked at each other. He opened his mouth a little, and then closed it. It was Antoine.

In therapy, I had decided what I would say if I ever saw him again.

"I'm going to say, 'Oh — *you're* still alive!'" I had said, after blowing my nose. My therapist had made a note, and said nothing.

"Hi," Antoine said to me, when I saw him again.

"Hi," I said, my mouth dry. "Welcome to the Co-Op."

If I did actually have a rock bottom, it was February 17, 2019, which was a little shy of one year before Antoine walked into the bookstore.

If you will remember, I had gone to his place to comfort him, or whatever. I'd brought beer with me. *I can't believe how hard I work to make sure things stay the same*, and so on. Stupid love songs. We fucked, obviously.

When I woke up, I felt like such an idiot. I felt like an idiot the way I always did after doing something I was hyping myself up very specifically *not* to do. Rationalizing can feel like a high, until it wears off. I can make such a *compelling* argument. Then it's over, and I'm just sitting in my life, and nothing is different.

I'm a slow learner. It was the last time I saw him until the bookstore. I didn't say anything witty. He stumbled over his words. "Sorry," he said. "I have a hangover."

"Me, too," I said, and then I regretted it.

I sold him the books and he said, "I'll see you around?" like it was a question.

I said, "Goodbye, Antoine." I meant *you're still alive. I love you. You, you, you.*

I never drank again.

No, I'm totally kidding. I think I got shit-faced again like, that night. My last drink wasn't poetic or smart or even extremely fun. I don't know if I ever hit *rock bottom*. I just got so bored.

I spent the night at a nice work thing. It was really a very truly nice work thing: the kind of genuinely pleasant perk that comes from a genuinely good job. I was working at a not-for-profit socialist bookstore, and it was book fair season; a few times a year, representatives would come in to the city and present us with very good arguments for why we should buy *X, Y,* or *Z* book for our store. They gave us lots of advance reading copies — unedited, free proofs of books — to prove how totally good all the books were. As a kid, the Scholastic Book Fair was basically Coachella for me. I feel in bookstores the way I imagine people feel at *the club* — a space which has merits I recognize without personally believing they would bring value to my own life.

At the book fair, I was in nerd heaven. February of 2020 was a special kind of year: a ten-year anniversary. The organizers took us out for fancy dinner at a nice restaurant — a hip place, the kind that had designer cocktails and expensive wine and organ meat and an oil painting of Biggie Smalls on the wall. I made some crack about how I'd need to make a note of the address so I could come back and eat here on a date or something. One of the other bookstore proprietors shook her head and assured me she had come here only twice, for two major birthdays. "It's really expensive." *Sick,* I thought, ordering a second cocktail before mine was even gone. I had to get my perk's worth.

I got drunk, but it wasn't that bad. I might have said a few slightly uncouth things, but the atmosphere was laid back; uncouthness was acceptable, provided it remained slight. I may have been a bit too loud, but most people actually find my drunken loudness charming (I think). I didn't black out, and I only had one moment where I swooned and swayed on the way to the bathroom. When it happened, I excused myself, gathered my things, and headed to the metro. I was a mature, evolved drinker now, and I knew when to call it quits.

I was very tempted to take a cab home — the restaurant was on Saint-Laurent, and there were plenty, but my account was already overdrawn, and it was a week to payday, and I still had to buy groceries. I had a metro pass for a reason, I decided, as I fought my way through the ice and snow and more ice that lined the many meandering streets leading to the metro station. The metro station was not *close* to the restaurant, in any way. It probably would have been about a half-hour walk on a good day, and I was drunk. I was fighting with the weather and my cheap boots, which had already lost their treads in the utter crap of the Montreal winter. The winters had been getting steadily warmer in the eight years since I blew into the city, tanned and broke and fresh-faced. *But they're still a test of endurance!* I thought, pale, and still broke, but older now. My boots made contact with a patch of loose snow, hiding a slick sheet of ice that was glossing over the sidewalk. My leg went out from under me, and I went down hard, slamming my hip onto the cold concrete ground, blood vessels bursting from compression, the beginnings of a bruise efflorescing there.

I pushed myself back up on ungloved hands, shook them off, stuffed them wet and crystalline back into my pockets. This happened three or four more times before I got to the metro.

The walk was probably close to an hour, but it felt like an eternity. I arrived at Beaubien station cold and wet and world-weary, battered from my multiple falls. My phone was close to dead, as usual, and the frigid sub-zero temperatures were terrible for the phone battery — I'd kept it locked and in my bra so that I'd be able to use it if I really needed to. Which was good, because as I approached the turnstiles, I reached into my bag to find that my wallet was not there.

I looked in my pocket — some loose change (thirty-six cents, not enough for a metro ticket), dog poo bags, wet receipts, and an empty pack of cigarettes, but no wallet. I looked in my pants pockets — also nothing. I was wallet-less. Had I *had* the wallet when I *left* the restaurant? I *sure fucking hoped not*, because that meant it had been dislodged from my person somewhere in the many tumbles to the ground that had ensued along the way. I looked at my phone — still freezing, despite my efforts to keep it warm in my bosom — and saw that it was midnight. I didn't have time to walk all the way back, retracing my steps to the restaurant, and then check the restaurant for my wallet, and then make it back on time. I'd have to call a cab from the restaurant, I thought, as my phone immediately died in the cold. Okay, I'd have to hail one. Or call one on the phone at the restaurant. If they were even still open.

Again, I wasn't wasted — just too drunk for this shit. I was tired and grumpy and off my game and not thinking clearly. Losing things. Plan one: walk the whole way, diligently retrace my steps in minus-twenty weather, hopefully discover my wallet somewhere along the way, but then maybe not and discover it at the still-open restaurant, but then maybe discover the restaurant closed, but then maybe discover it on the walk back to the metro again. This all still had me arriving at the metro long after the last train headed west, toward my apartment in Notre-Dame-de-Grâce. I'd still have to take a cab home, which I couldn't really afford, and I had neither a wallet nor a working phone. I'd have to mash the buttons on the keypad until Sandy woke up, if he hadn't already set his phone on silent. Then I'd have to get him to put pants on and come down with *his* wallet, and pay for my cab, or else I would have to run upstairs, bothering the surely already bothered cab driver.

I could call it and cab back as soon as I got to the restaurant, cutting down my arrival time to closer to one in the morning — maybe Sandy was up watching a TV show? Maybe the dog had woken him up for a nighttime jaunt down from our fourth-floor walk-up to pee? Or I could get in a cab now, hope against hope my wallet was at the restaurant, and then maybe get back to the metro in time to —

"*'Scuse!*" said a voice to my right. I looked over, abruptly, to see the metro attendant looking at me with an expression of exacerbated inquisition. I was still standing with my legs mashed into the turnstiles, lost in thought, my hands deep in my red leather purse.

"*Pardon,*" I said, and I slunk away. My accent, at least, was better now.

I got in a cab and rode it to the restaurant, told the driver I forgot "something." On the way, I was embarrassed. There was no one there to witness my embarrassment. I witnessed myself, and I felt shame. How much of my life had I wasted like this? What else had I lost, not thinking clearly? There was a five-foot snow pile on the curb in front of the restaurant. I had to climb it to run in. There were still a few stragglers from the event, talking to each other. "Hey!" said one of them, eyes bright with recognition. "We tried to call you! You forgot your wallet!"

I got back in the cab, and I told the guy to drive me home. It cost seventy-five dollars. I paid for it on credit and overdraft.

The next morning I woke up and just sat in silence for a long time. I didn't ruin anything or make anything terrible, as far as I knew. I had a creeping sense of shame and dread and malaise, anyway. I went over every single event from the night before, starting when I started drinking — assessing and analyzing for anything that could have been stupid, unkind, or offensive. I took that assessment and compared it against what I could remember from the five years of ethics classes. Then I factored in the booze I drank, and the whole thing fell apart.

I didn't know where the alcohol came in to throw the switch on the trolley car of my behaviour. I was the agent who took the first drink. I had told myself I would not drink at the event and then I had opened my mouth to take it down, anyway. I'd decided — determined, I thought — that work things were too high-stakes, too precious, too potentially pregnant with opportunity or meaning. The malaise permeated everything. I looked out at my bedroom and I hated it. It was all so sinister and cruel and it was mocking me.

I was nauseous and needy and desperate. I would need to feed my exhausted body with garbage to soothe my anxious brain, when my body was already swollen and creaking and cracking from years of soothing my thoughts instead of giving it what it actually needed. I would need to spend the day watching television I didn't even like, sending out text messages asking for reassurance, compiling lists of things I should do instead of sitting around and stewing in my misery, and then I would sit around and stew in my misery. I would not do as I should. I wouldn't even do as I wanted.

It would be a different day from the dozens or hundreds I'd spent just like this, but also it would be exactly the same. This was how I crawled on my knees toward death. This was how I would spend my life: desperately shoving a problem bigger and heavier than I could possibly carry alone into small, reassuring places. I would tell myself it's what I had to do. My skin was crawling with fear and sadness and unkindness. Somewhere along the way I had become deeply bored of my life, because I had become bored of who I was.

Next to me, in bed, Goose the dog shifted his weight. I could hear Sandy out in the living room, giggling about something — a podcast, probably — and clinking his coffee cup down on the table, making the soft shuffling noises of folding laundry. It was Saturday. Neither of us had to work. When we adopted the dog, we were informed that crate training him to sleep would be difficult, as he had not spent a night alone since leaving the shelter. Goose preferred to sleep with people.

Bleary-eyed, my dog raised his great body from the bed next to me. Gravity pushed me and all the other soft things closer to the ground underneath his paws. He adjusted himself on his feet, sniffed my hip and then my arm, and settled down hips first: next to me in bed so tightly he pinned some of my excess to the firm mattress like a bag full of warm bricks. His length tucked into me from thigh to shoulder. He placed his head down on his crossed paws a few inches away from mine. I looked over and his eyes were closed. He smacked his lips a few times, white teeth flashing under his floppy black jowls. Then he casually threw his lower jaw softly onto my breast — his heavy head settling into me with the force of someone tossing a bowling ball.

"Ow," I said, as I felt relief well up inside of me, and I wrapped my arms around him, and he padded his paws and his joints again and again and settled even more tightly against my body, sighed heavily, surrendered. This dog didn't care what I'd done.

I returned to Montreal after planting the year I pulled the tower and then saw the mountain burning. The City of Mary welcomed me like I was a lonely, wandering child. I found Antoine clear-faced and three weeks sober. With my work-strong arms I dragged him straight down into hell with me the first chance I got, on the off chance he'd reach across the table to touch me. He did. At what cost? I got insecure and grandiose when he started pulling away, and he was Tim all over again. Maybe if I said enough dark, coded, cruel things, he would come crawling back. Maybe I would at least make myself feel better. What an idiot's bargain. The devil, speaking straight through me. *But I love him*, I told myself. As if we poison the people we love. So many excellent rationalizations. *Pray for us sinners — now, and in the hour of our death.*

I drank for a whole other year. There was one two-month sober reprieve fuelled by spite and nothing else: a bright-burning fuel that runs out too quick to sustain any real action. Bill W., one of the founders of Alcoholics Anonymous, writes that alcoholism is usually only cured by a profound spiritual experience. I hate February. The month breaks my heart.

Apparently, after February 1, the earliest waves of spring really start to emerge. It's still winter, but things are coming back to life. *I'll believe it when I see it*, I thought. This is Canada. It snows into April in Montreal. Everyone insists it doesn't, but they just forget. The Montreal rites of spring involve stuffing our coats into the closets and throwing open all of the windows, taking our sundresses and our good boots out of storage and moving our potted plants to the balcony. We leave our hearts unguarded for when the winter comes to throw one last wet party. All my countrymen fight the urge to die. We forget that the spring means snow, here. We forget to love where we are.

February 1 is the feast of St. Brigid, who was probably a Christianization of the Irish goddess of the same name. Brigid is a triple goddess: a mother, a maiden, and a crone. A blacksmith, a poet, and a healer. She is a scholar. She knows things I don't. On the morning after my last drink, in my darkest month, with the dog's great head on my breast, I found it in me to take a walk — not because I wanted to, but because I owed it to my animal. I walked along the icy, brutal streets. I looked at the cold, dead ground. I looked up into the sky with its spindly little tree-hands across it, and to my utter shock, some of them were coming in green. Impossible. I looked closer — buds. Life! The future, returning, from the past.

I wanted to scream. What an idiot I had been. Young people, am I right? Of course I was wrong, again. Of course the wild, holy world was coming back.

I never drank again — or rather I haven't, yet.

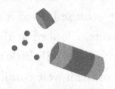

"What I Am"
by Edie Brickell and
New Bohemians.

March 12, 2020. Montreal.

I'm not kidding this time. One morning in March, I headed to work. I was coming up on a month sober — and what a difference a month had made. I was sharp. I wasn't wasting as much time anymore. I had this full, fluffy pink cloud hanging over me full of thrilling possibility.

Goose and I had taken to running every morning — this got his breed-specific yah-yahs out in a time-sensitive way, left him napping happily in my bed while I headed out to walk the forty minutes to work, to stand all day at my desk. My persistent grogginess was gone. The exercise had shifted my constant aches, rearranged them until my body was a vehicle of unbelievable pleasure. Where I'd had tight clusters of tension roped onto me like bondage, I now felt my body contort and move and sigh with relief. *Thank you for the blood*, it seemed to say, as I walked and I ran and I felt good. Breathing felt good. I felt no pain, no difficulty. I was so sure I never would, again.

Work occasionally piled up, but I fought back against it with longer hours and tougher grit. The house was getting a little messy. Goose's expenses were piling up. But I had reliable work, and so did Sandy, and it wasn't like we had to spend all day inside. Sobriety experts, my elders in abstinence, had informed me that this sense of imminent possibility would eventually rend itself from me, and my emotions might become volatile and difficult again. I didn't see how that was possible. If it happened I'd just make sure I spread my life out with *more* firmness and *more* determination. The secret to life is just to move back and forth from work to home to writing jobs at the local bars and festivals and bookstores. I could not believe I hadn't seen it before! I just had to do it: to physically get up and move my body outside of my little cocoon of my misery and enter physical spaces with other human beings.

It was March of 2020, and still cold, but the earth was visibly warming up. The cold came in from the wind, now; it didn't emanate from the ground. Rivulets of water ran between the continents of snow and ice that were the streets and the sidewalks and the tops of all the buildings. The sidewalks were full of people, talking, laughing, yelling — their hands in each others' hands, their breath mixing in the air. We were all warm and breathy and close to each other and alive in our anticipation of the spring. All winter we had been waiting, for the summer that is always worth it. It was coming. We could all feel it.

At work, people were nervous. An errant virus, some kind of flu, or whatever, had killed a few too many people in China's Wuhan district, had made a few too many people nervous, had lead to lockdowns and worry and whispers of more intense measures to stop the spread. I was not convinced. It didn't seem that bad. My faith told me something better was happening — why else would I feel so full, so charged? Why would I be striking out here, my feet hitting the ground with a rhythmic determination, the guitar solo from "What I Am" blasting through my headphones and rattling around in my chest, heading out into the future with all the drive of the newly converted? I was *sober now* — I knew nothing of pessimism, or panic, or bad faith. I never would again. The darkness was all behind me. The worst thing had already happened. It was March 12, 2020, and I was young and alive in the last great bohemian city. Everything was different now. Everything had changed.

Acknowledgements

Concepts and themes in this book are (of course) from my own life, in which I encountered the work of Esther Perel (*Mating in Captivity*, *The State of Affairs*), Kai Cheng Thom (*I Hope We Choose Love*), and Indigenous intellectual traditions. I've also been influenced by the podcasts *The Poetry Gods* and *Food for Thot*, which have profoundly influenced me, the comedy of Eddie Izzard, George Carlin, and Monty Python's Flying Circus, and the philosophy of Nietzsche, de Beauvoir, Sartre, Camus, Kant, Hegel, and Levinas — all of which I will be reading forever. Echoes of these works reverberate through the text.

Thanks simply must go to Clementine Morrigan, Jay Marquis-Manicom, Dorian Fraser, and Noah Hermes, who are not in this book. Also, my father, Don Ross, my stepmother, Brooke Miller, Julie Mannell (who was a teacher as much as an editor), the staff at Dundurn Press (especially managing editor Elena Radic for making it make sense), Coast Range Contracting, and several terrible jobs for making me angry enough to quit and work something else out. Thank you to everyone I wrote about, and all the party girls and the good-time boys, and all the crazy ones around the table. Have another one for me. Stay safe, but not too safe. I'll see you soon.

About the Author

Photo credit: Camellia Jahanshahi

Tara McGowan-Ross is an urban Mi'kmaq multidisciplinary artist. She was born in Toronto and grew up in rural Ontario and Halifax. She graduated with a bachelor's degree in philosophy and creative writing from Concordia University in 2016. She was the first runner up for the Pacific Spirit Poetry Prize in 2018, and she has been anthologized in *Best Canadian Poetry 2020* and *Anthologie de la poésie actuelles des femmes au Québec.* In 2021, one of her poems was chosen to represent Québécois literature in a public art installation in Montreal's *Place des festivals* for the city's *Fête nationale* celebration.

Tara lives in Montreal, where she writes, is a critic of independent and experimental theatre, hosts the Indigenous Literatures Book Club at Drawn & Quarterly, is very cool and attractive, and has fun all the time. *Nothing Will Be Different* is her debut work of non-fiction.

Visit her at girthgirl.ca